Crosby Records

BLUNDELL'S DIARY

COMPRISING SELECTIONS FROM THE DIARY OF

NICHOLAS BLUNDELL, ESQ.,

FROM 1702 TO 1728.

EDITED BY THE

REV. T. ELLISON GIBSON,

Author of "Lydiate Hall and its Associations," "A Cavalier's Note Book,"
&c., &c.

LIVERPOOL:
GILBERT G. WALMSLEY, 50, LORD STREET.
—
1895.

INTRODUCTION.

THE late Archbishop Whately is credited with the saying, that if he had to write a daily record of his life, he would soon wish his life at an end. Many a person begins a Diary, but few persevere with it for any length of time. The fidelity of Mr. Nicholas Blundell* to this self-imposed task is very remarkable. His Diary extends over a quarter of a century and no single day has been left unnoticed. It is very legibly written, entirely by his own hand, and is contained in three long narrow Volumes numbering altogether nearly nine hundred pages. The spelling is eccentric but no attempt has been made to correct even very obvious blunders. In so lengthy a record, there is, as may be imagined, much that would be of no interest to the general reader. On the other hand, many entries are of value, more especially in the absence of other local records of which that particular period is singularly barren.

The Diarist had neither the ability nor the learning of his grandfather, the "Cavalier," but he filled very worthily his position as a resident landlord. A lover of country life,

*For a full account of the ancient family of Blundell of Crosby, see the Introduction to "*A Cavalier's Note Book*." Also, "*Crosby Records*," Chetham Society No. 12 new series.

his interests were centred in the pursuits and pleasures of his neighbours and tenants. It is manifest that much more social enjoyment was got out of life in those days than is the case at present. Railways and the spread of education, have made a striking change in the condition of the rural population—a change not altogether to its advantage. Material comforts have been brought within its reach, but the close bond of companionship which formerly held society together has been rent asunder. Certainly the numerous festivities and amusements which he records as shared by friends and neighbours have totally disappeared.

In religion, Mr. Blundell adhered to the faith of his Ancestors. For this privilege he paid double taxes and felt in various ways the pressure of the severe penal laws then in force. Still, the great heat of persecution which some of his race endured* had, in his time, sensibly abated. Happily, he was not drawn into the rebellion of 1715, which wrecked the fortunes of so many of his co-religionists but his house was frequently visited and searched at that eventful period. On one occasion, he says "I set in a streat place for a fat man" which shows that he must have had recourse to the family hiding-place, contrived, no doubt, on a scale

*Richard Blundell, of Crosby, died in Lancaster Castle, 1591-2, a prisoner for the faith, having been committed there for harbouring a priest. William Blundell, his son, suffered many imprisonments and much loss of goods. Two-thirds of his lands were seized upon for recusancy and given to Court favourites, two of the number being Queen Elizabeth's cooks. He was fined £2000 for making a burial ground for his Catholic tenants and neighbours, who were denied burial at Sefton Church. His wife, though in a delicate state of health, was dragged to prison by the Bishop of Chester when her husband could not be found. She suckled her infant in Chester Castle and was only set free after a long imprisonment, through the friendly remonstrance of two powerful Protestant neighbours.

more befitting the dimensions of a lean curate. As soon as he could get away, he withdrew to the Continent till the trouble blew over.

Such a record as the one before us comes like a revelation from the tomb. It brings to light events hitherto shrouded in oblivion. It repeoples the land with its old inhabitants and introduces us to their homes, their occupations, their amusements and social life. We follow them in their daily path until the final summons, when the squire's Coach-carriage which was at the service of rich and poor alike, conveys them to their last resting-place.

Mr. Blundell's Diary covers the period when the Commerce of Liverpool was beginning to expand and its borders to need enlargement. He witnessed the opening of the first dock, and in his frequent neighbourly visits meets those who were then in a modest way laying the foundation of its future greatness. The Houghtons, Tyrers, Claytons, Clevelands, Johnsons, Pooles, Earles, Gildarts, Williamsons, and many others—names long associated with its fortunes—occasionally cross his path.

The last few pages of the Diary show indications of a failure of eyesight and this growing infirmity no doubt, led Mr. Blundell to abandon his task nine years previous to his death, which occurred on the 21st April, 1737, at the age of 68*.

*There are two inscriptions to the Diarist in the Blundell Chapel, Sefton Church. In one, he is said to have died "on 21st April, 1736, aged 66;" in the other "on 21st April, 1737, aged 68." His daughter Mary Coppinger is also twice commemorated and, in one place, her age is incorrectly given. The uncertainty of monumental inscriptions has been frequently remarked upon.

For whatever pleasure or information he may derive from a perusal of these pages, the reader is indebted to Colonel Nicholas Blundell, of Crosby Hall, who has kindly permitted the publication of these transcripts of the Diary of his Ancestor.

T. E. GIBSON.

BIRKDALE.

THE above introduction was written by the Rev. T. E. Gibson, shortly before his death, which occurred on January 26, 1891. Some time afterwards, I was asked to see the Diary through the Press, and I have done so. Colonel Blundell died on July 12, 1894, and was thus deprived of the pleasure of seeing in print a diary in which he was much interested.

AUGUSTINE WATTS.

LIVERPOOL, *August*, 1895.

EXTRACTS

FROM THE

DIARY OF NICHOLAS BLUNDELL,

OF CROSBY, LANCASHIRE, ESQUIRE.

1702—1728.

1702.

My Father went after diner to wate of my Lord Molineux July 27th. at yᵉ New Stand, where he was sodanly taken so very ill, that he sent for me to wate of him home and bring yᵉ Coach for him.

I sent for Dr. Farington to come to my Father, but he July 28th. was not to be found.

I went to Wigan and brought Doctor Frances Worthing- July 29th. ton along with me to Crosby.

Coll: Edm: Butler came to Crosby from Durham in his Aug. 1st. Way to Ireland, he sent to Wigan for Doctor Tho: Wor: who came late that night. I sent Tho: Howard to Whit-Church for Doctor Bostock but he came not.

Valentine Farrington, M.D., a younger brother of Wm. Farrington, of Worden, Esq., resided at Preston. Dr. Thos. Worthington is mentioned in *A Cavalier's Note Book*, p. 247. He died November 27, 1702. He was still practising at Wigan in conjunction with his son Francis. Dr. Bostock of Whitchurch had a considerable local reputation.

1702.

Aug. 2nd.   I sent to Dungen-hall to acquaint Coz: John Gelibrond of my Fathers danger. About half an Hour after Tenn in yᵉ morning being Sunday, many People in the Roome hearing Mass, and Mass just almost finished, My Dearest Father departed this life being much lamented by all; as his Life was virtuous and edifying so was his Death. Sweet Jesus Receive his Sole.

Aug. 5th.   My Father Wm. Blu: Esq. was layed in his Mothers Grave at Sephton it being her Weding Day. Wm. Arnold who had been a Faithfull good Servant and brought up from a Child at this hous departed this Life, he was Groome Coachman and Butcher.

Aug. 12th.   Mʳˢ Blundell of Ince came to see my Mother, so did Mrs. Walmesley of Moss-halk and her Son.

Aug. 13th.   Coz: Rich: Butler went towards Mr. Fleetwoods of yᵉ Bank.

Aug. 15th.   I went to Leverp: with Coz: Edm: Butler, we halled yᵉ Mary with a Hand-Karchaf but she answered not, he went on Bord yᵉ Harington for Dublin.

Aug. 18th.   Mr. Mullins came in yᵉ Morning to pray and stayed till next day, Mr. Tasburgh and Little Man came hither in yᵉ Afternoone.

Mr. Mullins was priest at Mossock Hall, in Bickerstaffe, a secluded spot a few hundred yards behind St. Mary's Chapel, Aughton. It had fallen to the Walmsley's by the marriage of the heiress, Elizabeth Mossock, with Thomas, third son of Richd. Walmsley, of Showley, Esq. The estate has since been sold by that family, and the old Hall having disappeared, a farm-house now occupies the site.

The Rev. Henry Tasburgh, S.J., lived at the New House, at Ince Blundell, built shortly before with the view of its being used as a school. It was never so used, but became the home of aged and infirm priests of the Society. It was given up after the death of Rev. W. Clifton, S.J., 1749.

1702.

By "Little Man" is meant his cousin, Rev. Wm. Gelibrond or Gillibrand, S.J., who was throughout his life a confidential friend and adviser. He was then doing duty as Chaplain at Crosby, but soon after went to Liverpool, and seems to have been the first priest settled there since the Reformation. He was of the family of Gillibrands, of Chorley, and died April 1, 1722, aged 60.

I delt Almes at 3d. p̄. Person myself to yᵉ Poore of this Parish.   Aug. 24th.

I sold my Fathers pad to Mr. Tasb: for £10.   Aug. 25th.

I writ to Coz: Standley at Preston to get my Brother Rich: made a Freeman at yᵉ Gild.   Aug. 28th.

Held every 10 years.

I hired Hen: Bilsbury for my Groome, am to give him 50ˢ. p. annum and one Livery Sute.   Sept. 1st.

Cap: Rob: Faz: had been at yᵉ Gild and came hither to-day.   Sept. 6th.

I went to Leverp: to yᵉ Buriall of Mr. Hewston.   Sept. 8th.

"1695, Oct. 18. — Levinus Heustoun Gentleman is elected Towns Baylive for the Year Ensueing."—*City Records*, iv., 706.

Wat Thelwall sayes he found Caterer of Formby on yᵉ Sands and carryed him to Bank-hall.   Sept. 12th.

Coz: Scarisbrick yᵉ Widow came to lodg here, her Coach was brocken here by yᵉ Horses running away when yᵉ Coachman had left them.   Sept. 17th.

I sold Codlings at 6ᵈ. p. cent and other Apples at 2ˢ. p. Buss.   Sept. 22nd.

I came to Prescot where I bought Fine Muggs of Mr. Cubben, thence I came to Leverpoole where I discoursed Mr. Houghton Merchant and so came home.   Sept. 24th.

1702.
Sept. 30th.

I went to Mosburgh to wish Coz: Molineux Joy and to welcom her into yᵉ Country. I met Sʳ James Poole &c as they were going to yᵉ Wood.

William Molineux of Mosborough Hall, near St. Helens, born September 4, 1669, had just married Anne, daughter of Sir James Poole, of Poole, Co. Chester. He was buried at Melling, 24th January, 1727-8, but his wife survived till 1751. Their son William married Frances, daughter of James Gorsuch, of Gorsuch, Esq., and died March 11, 1744, leaving an only daughter and heiress, Frances, wife of Sir Edward Blount, of Sodington, Co. Worcester, Bart. The estate was afterwards purchased by the Earl of Derby. A modern house occupies the site of the ancient Hall, but the moat may still be traced.

The Wood, in Melling, was then the property of this branch of the Molyneux family. They had left it for Mosborough, but a priest was kept there. Rev. Simon Bordley was the last Chaplain, and went to Moor Hall, August 28, 1746. The estate was sold about 1785. Thornton was originally the family seat, and the removal to Melling took place *tempore* Edward 3rd.

Oct. 12th.

Goos-Feast Munday.

A Club still flourishing at Great Crosby.

Oct. 15th.

I peesed again with John Lunt till Christmas upon my Mothers Request.

A servant-man whom he had discharged.

Oct. 17th.

I was at yᵉ Buriall of Doctor Tarltons Wife.

Oct. 25th.

Mr. Christopher Anderton dined here. I swaped with him for a Bay Hors I call Swap, and gave him Bay Butler and my watch &c in exchange.

Nov. 3rd.

Mr. Jamson Kept a Court for me at Margery Howerds.

Nov. 5th.

I sent Henry Bilsb: to Croxtath for a Pot of Venyson.

Nov. 7th.

I went after dinner to Leve: with Pat: Gelib: I found Coz: Harington at yᵉ Woolpack, I heard Lord Darby dyed sodenly at Chester.

I sent eight Beasts to Leverp: Fair and sold one for £3 . 5 . 0.

I went to Ormskirk and discoursed Mr. Howet concerning Mr. Risley his Hunter.

Mr. Rich: Molineux of yᵉ Grang and I set a Meer-Stone to be yᵉ bondery between his Cunny Warand and mine, it was set about half-way between a great Sandhill and Blansherds lain end upon a Hill called Tenn-penny Hill and linable with yᵉ two Meer-Stons at each end of Blansherds Lain, in presence of Pat: Gelibrond and Walter Thelwall and my two Waranders Thom: Kerfoot and Wm. Wignold. Sʳ James Pool and his son James came to lodg here. I sent my Grewhound Hector to be kept at Lidiat by Mr. Draper.

The Grange, a well-known farm near the Altcar Shooting Ranges, was long the residence of a branch of the Molyneux family. It had been originally given by the Blundells of Ince to the monks of Stanlawe (afterwards Whalley), and was purchased at the dissolution by an ancestor of Lord Sefton. A priest resided here during the last century and in the early part of the present. Mass was occasionally said in the house. Rev. Joseph Draper, S.J., was priest at Lydiate Hall, and his tombstone may be seen in the ruined Chapel of St. Katharine.

Coz: James Poole went in yᵉ Morning to yᵉ New Stand to meet Mr. Molineux of Croxtath a Shooting. Sʳ James Poole and I went to yᵉ Stand towards Noone. Mr. Molineux treated us there with Wine and Aile.

I went after Dinner to Leverp: I saw Mrs. Bootle and her Doughter Lidiat at Mr. Houghtons. I condoled with them yᵉ Death of Mr. Ja: Lidiat.

Mr. Jamson Kept a Court for me at Margery Howerds wᶜʰ was Aiourned to this day. The Joyner and Painter came hither to Look at my Brothers clock Kace. Collo:

1702. Butler came hither from Ireland after his great Escape at Sea. Eliz: Sumner Dary-Maid left my Service and was suckseeded by Mary Formby.

Nov. 29th.   I went after diner with Collo: Butler to Croxtath and suped there, we found Mr. Perce Moston and his Family there.

Dec. 4th.   I sent Rich: Ainsworth to Leverp: with a Load of Barly to be Malted it was toled by order of yᵉ Maior.

Dec. 7th.   I went after diner to Leverp: Walt: Thelwall discoursed yᵉ Maior concerning yᵉ Toling of my Barly. Coming home I met Mr. Peeters on yᵉ Sands he told me that yᵉ Great Crosby Men refused to Appear or Answer to yᵉ Court called then by him.

Dec. 10th.   I payed Mrs. Pluckington for Frute Trees.

Mr. Ralph Peters was Town Clerk to the Corporation of Liverpool, 20 August, 1707-1742. From the *City Records* we find rated

Mr. Wm. Pluckington, house, bowling green, and 2 fields in the Comon	3s. 4d.
Wm. Pl: more 2 acres 24 Perch	2s. 1d.
„ more 6 acres and L. of Comon	6s. 6d.

Dec. 19th.   I went to Dungen-Hall by Chorley where I found Coz: Jo: Gelibrond at his own house.

Dec. 21st.   His son and I went by Mr. Ashtons of Curedale to Lower Hall we dined there.

Dec. 22nd.   Coz: John Gelibrond and I went to Town-ley to welcom young Mr. Townley home at his return from Gant.

Dec. 23rd.   There was Very Much Snow. Mr. Lovell came from Stony-Hurst, he a Carrier and two Horses were lost for some time on yᵉ Moore.

Rev. George Lovell, S.J., was Chaplain at Dunkeahalgh [Dun-gen-hall], where Mr. John Gelibrond then resided. He was skilful in mathematics, but losing his memory became a child before his death. He retired to New House, and dying there December 12, 1720, was buried at the Harkirke December 14.

1702.

I went with Pat: Gelib: in yᵉ after Noone to Mr. Wairings. I ordered Walt: Thelw: to see Running Horses entered at He: Heskeths, Lord Molineux sent for me home from Mr. Wairings, he and his Son entered each of them a Running hors before me at my own hous by telling me their Names and describing them.

Dec. 30th.

Coz: Tho: Gelibrond and I went to great Crosby with an Intension to see Mr. Wairing, but we were sent for home to wate of Mr. Ralph Tildesley, Mr. Edmund Trafford &c. Coze: John Culcheth came to lodg here.

1703.
Jan. 3rd

I was at Great Crosby Race where Mr. Massys Gelding Limber hamm wone a Plate from Pedler, &c.

Jan. 4th.

Pedler belonged to Sir James Poole, Bart. Wm. Massey, of Puddington, Co. Chester, the owner of Limberhamm, died 1716, and left his estates to his Godson, Thomas Stanley, who died 1740, having taken the name of Massey. He bequeathed his property to his elder brother John, who, succeeding to the baronetcy 1792, retook the name of Stanley, and died 1794. From him Puddington descended to Sir John Stanley Massey Errington, who died 1893, and was the last male representative of the Stanleys of Hooton, and chief of the great house of Stanley.

I met Mr. Blund: acoursing, and saw two Hairs Runn that were found set, he went to Andertons, and Pat: Gelib: and I went home to writ a Letter to Mr. Philmot 'twas not well taken by Bl: Mr. Cataway a Missioner for Mary-Land and Mr. Draper came to lodg here.

Jan. 15th.

I went to Dine at Mosholk with Coz: Tho: Gelib:

Jan. 18th.

I Dined at yᵉ Grang wᵗʰ Lord Molineux &c. Sʳ Will: Gerard &c.

Jan. 20th.

1703.
Jan. 22nd.   Mr. Gower Pitched y⁰ Crow and threw y⁰ Hammer at James Farers.

Jan. 24th.   I writ to my Brother Richard into Virginia.

His brother, Richard Blundell, had gone out to Virginia to establish himself as a merchant. He had business connections with Mr. Houghton, a very prominent Liverpool merchant, whose factor he was to be. He married a widow and died shortly after, leaving a posthumous son, who did not long survive.

Jan. 26th.   I sent my Brothers Goods to Mr. Houghton at Leverp: in order to have them Shiped on Bord y⁰ Loyalty for Virginia.

Jan. 27th.   Pat: Rich: Lathom had his weding Dinner at this Hous.

Rev. Richard Lathom, *alias* Kirkham, S.J., was made a Spiritual Coadjutor February 2, 1703, which would be the occasion of his Wedding Dinner. He was about to sail for the Maryland Mission, then in the hands of the Jesuits. He died on the return voyage in 1708, aged 37.—See *Foley's Collectanea*, part I.

Jan. 29th.   I went to Leverp: with Pat: Rich: Lathom and helped him to buy goods, we discoursed Mr. Sharples at Swarb:

Feb. 3rd.   Mr. Smith, Mr. Ric: Lathom and I went to Carr-Hall we eat Eggs and Collops &c.

This would be Shrove or Collop Monday. Mr. Smith was the Jesuit Chaplain at Scarisbrick Hall.

Feb. 11th.   Mr. Worthington Junʳ of Blanscow desired to see me at my Mill, he would not come to Crosby Hall, he discoursed me concerning sending Joseph Wadsworth to Sea.

Feb. 12th.   I went to Leverp: to assist Mr. Worthington in Binding Jos: Wads: to Sea. I discoursed Mr. Houghton, Mr. Sharples &c., about it.

I discoursed Mr. Blackbourn at Moor Hall concerning Feb. 14th
Betty Blund :

The Rev. John Blackburne was a secular priest, then serving
Moor Hall, the residence of Mr. Wolfall. He died 1728, aged 74,
and is buried in the ruined Chapel of St. Katharine at Lydiate,
where the stone may still be seen, but the name has disappeared.

I went with Pat: Gelib: to Croxtath to wish my Lord Feb. 20th.
a good Journey to London, thence I went to Low-hill
where Mr. Harington, Mr. Hind &c. were come to meet
my Lord, they had a Feast of Sturgeon ; we drank
Fountineack &c.

Mr. Liborn fetched a Boat from hence wch I had taken Feb. 23rd.
up as a Wreck it was by Orders of my Lord Molin: but
not delivered to him by me or my Steward Walt: Thelw:

This and other entries shew that Lord Molyneux was very
tenacious of his right of wreck, ceded to his father by the Crown
in a previous reign. Mr. Blundell, of Ince, had in 1683 procured
from Caryll Viscount Molyneux a grant of title to wreck at
Formby, Ainsdale, and Birkdale, for the yearly consideration
of 12d.

I sealed a Bond of £60 to Coz: Wm. Houghton of Feb. 26th.
Park-hall.

William Houghton of Park Hall married Elizabeth, daughter
and heiress of Robert Dalton of Thurnham, in 1683. His son John
assumed in 1710 the name of Dalton, and joined the rebels in
1715. His estates were forfeited, but purchased for himself by
friends at a cost of £7,298 1s. 6½d. He himself was with Sir
Francis Anderton and others taken to London, tried, convicted,
and pardoned.

I went to Leverp: shewed two Horses to the Post to Mar. 5th.
sell him one of them. I Payed 7^s to Ri: Woods for
making a Duble brested coat.

I went to Chorley and discoursed James Nicolson con- Mar. 8th.
cerning a Mourning Saddle and houlters.

1703.
Mar. 15th.   I gave 2ˢ 6ᵈ to Brother Christopher towards yᵉ Repaire of yᵉ Cover over Holly-well. He came hither to begg for yᵉ Repare of it. Dr. Lathom came hither to shew yᵉ Petission wᶜʰ was presented to yᵉ Queen by Mr. Bannerd Howerd in behalf of yᵉ said Dr. Lathom, Mr. Haggerston &c.

St. Winifred's Well was then, as now, under the care of the Jesuit Fathers. Dr. Lathom had practised Surgery in Liverpool, and his wife Judith had kept a School, but the penal laws being against them as Catholics, they were persecuted by the Town Officials. In 1686 a Royal mandate was issued in their favor, which may be seen in *Picton's Memorials*, vol. 1, p. 132. It does not appear what was the nature of the present petition. Dr. Lathom retired to Aintree, and his death is noticed later.

Mar. 21st.   The Churchwarden Henry Williamson Acquainted me that Parson Richmond wished that he had pulled down more of the Parsonidg of Sephton.

Mar. 22nd.   I opened a Barrell of Apples wᶜʰ had layn in very dry Sea-Sand since they were gathered, they were very firm and sound, thô many had a little Speck of faided, and a very few were Rotten.

Mar. 26th.   I writ to Lord Langdale, inclosed it to Coz: Eyre yᵉ Lawyer and sent it to the Post by Pat: Gelib:

April 6th.   Aunt Frances had Account from Mrs. Bloore by orders of Lady Webb that I might wate of Mrs. Fr: Langdall as soone as I pleased.

April 7th.   Pat: Gelib: went to Lev: to buy Cloth for a Black Coat.

April 8th.   Tho: Howerd brought me Mr. Wingats Pistolls wᶜʰ he had borrowed of him for my Journey to Hathrop, they are Rather too Larg and so extraordinary fine I will not take them along with me.

Mr. Edw: Molineux came to wish me a good Journey to Hathrop. I sent Ri: Jump to Burdikin at Wigan for my Black Coat, but not being made he brought y° Cloth back.

I went to Leverp: to have a Black Coat made by Edw: Porter for my Journey to Hath:

I began my Journey towards Hathrop, dined at Warington, and lodged at Hoomes Chapell.

I went from Hoomes Chapell dined at Stone and Lodged at Aldridg.

I went from Aldridg bated at Birmidgham and Witch and Lodged at Wooster.

I went from Woster dined at Winshcomb and lodged at North Leech.

I came from North Leech to Hathrop found y° Family all there, and also my Lord Langdale.

Heythrop Park, near Chipping Norton, Oxfordshire, then the residence of Sir John Webb, belonged to the Earl of Shrewsbury, who in 1695 had entertained there King William the Third. Charles, 15th Earl, built a Catholic Church, completed in 1826, but the estate having fallen into Protestant hands, it was closed after the death, on February 8, 1858, of the first and only priest, Rev. Patrick Hefferman. It has since been pulled down by the present owner, Albert Brassey, Esq., and the materials used in the construction of a Protestant Church. The altar was purchased from the builder by Rev. S. Sole of Chipping Norton, who in 1882 transferred to that Church the bodies of Charles, Earl of Shrewsbury, and of the above priest, previously interred at Heythrop.

I went in y° Coach with Lord Langdale and Sʳ John Webb to wate of Collo: Ireton but he was not at home.

I discoursed Lord Langdale in his Chamber and Lady Webb in y° Dining Roome. I made my first adress to Mrs. Fr: Langdale.

1703.

April 20th. Coll Ireton came to Hathrop in yᵉ afternoone.

April 21st. Lady Webb discoursed me in yᵉ Garden. I discoursed Mrs. Langdale in yᵉ Kitchen Garden.

April 22nd. Lady Dowager Webb Read yᵉ Heds of Agreement of Marriage to be between Mrs. Fr: Langdale and me N. Bl: in Presence of Lord Langdale and Sʳ John Webb.

April 23rd. Mr. Trynder yᵉ Lawyer came to Hathrop for Instrucsions to draw Artickleys of Marriage.

April 28th. I presented my Dimond Ring to Mrs. Fr: Langdale.

April 29th. Sʳ John Waters and his Lady, Mr. Sheldon of Weston and his Son &c dined at Hathrop.

May 4th. I sent George Howerd, Sʳ John Cursons Servant to Oxford to take a place in yᵉ Coach for me to London.

May 5th. I writ at Water-Perry to Mrs. Fr: Langd: and sent it by Oxford Post.

Sir John Curzon, of Waterperry, Co. Oxon, registered his estate in 1718 as a non-juror for £203 10s. 2d. He died 1727, and his son Francis died without issue 1750, when the title became extinct.

May 7th. I dined wᵗʰ Coz: Henry Eyre, Mr. Lewson &c in Fullers Rant. I saw the Silent Woman acted.

May 8th. I met Mr. Rich: Norris in yᵉ Mall.

May 9th. I made my first visit to Mrs. Norris my Cozen, she is I think Sister to Coz H. Eyre.

May 11th. I walked to Westminster and saw yᵉ Tombs. Went at Night to Wills Coffy-Hous where I heard Mr. Lawson talk of Calculating Nativitys.

May 12th. I dined at yᵉ Blew posts in Deverax Court.

I came from London towards Water-Perry with a dis- May 13th.
puting Parson.

I came to Hathrop from Water-perry with Pat: Gelib: May 15th.

I walked with Mrs. Fr: Langdale to Fairford. Morris May 17th.
dansers came to Hathrop.

I rid out with Lord Gerard and Sr John Webb. I saw May 18th.
Sink Foyle grow. I saw three of Lord Whartons Horses,
I suppose they were Runners.

I went in ye Coach with Lord Gerard and Sr John May 19th.
Webb to see Mr. Green-wood at Bryes-Norton.

The Lords and Ladys of May came to dance at Hath- May 20th.
rop. I presented my Guilt Coffy Spoones.

We dansed after ye Taber and Pipe. May 28th.

I writ to Biss: Gifford by Request of F.L. May 29th.

Right Reverend Bonaventure Giffard, of the family of Giffard of
Chillington, was Bishop of Madaura, and became V.A. of the London District, March 14, 1703. He died March 12, 1733-4, aged 92.

I went a second time to London, lodged at Oxford with May 31st.
Mr. Trinder. I wated of Doctor Bayly President of
Maudlen.

I payed Mr. Person for a Weding Ring. June 3rd.

I rid out of my own Horses with Coz: Jo: Eyre behind June 4th.
Hampton to see Mrs. Hubbard, she was Doughter to Cap:
Brock.

I viseted Biss: Gifford. June 9th.

I dined with Lady Curson, tryed on my Weding Sute June 11th.
there and in other Places.

1703.

June 15th.   Lord Langdale Lady Webb S^r Jo: Webb &c heard ye Marriage Deeds read, all we at Hathrop concerned therein subscribed them before Four Witnesses.

June 16th.   Lady Dowager Webb acquainted me ye Marriage was to be ye day following.

June 17th.   I was Married to Lord Langdales Doughter by Mr. Sloughter a Clergy-man.

June 21st.   I went with Sr John Webb to Parson Burcher's and gave him half a Guiny as Marriage Dues.

June 25th.   My Charriot came to Hathrop to carry my Wife home to Crosby.

June 28th.   I began my Journey from Hathrop towards Crosby with my Wife, we lodged at Oster.

July 2nd.   I came from Colebrook bated at Warington, was met by Dr. Lathom and treated by him in ye Road. I brought my Wife home to Crosby.

July 8th.   S^r Wm. Gerard Merchant Houghton and Dr. Tarlton dined here.

July 9th.   Mr. Peter Mourton came to wish me Joy.

July 20th.   Coz: Eyre of Hasop and his Son and my Uncle Laurence Eyre came to Lodg here.

July 27th.   I wated of my Lord Darby at Lathom I found his Brother and Mr. Scaresbrick there, we played at Bowles.

July 29th.   I went to Whitlidg green to see the Match bowled between Mr. Molineux of Croxtath, Mr. Jo: Gerard and Mr. Massy Mr. Hugh Diconson, I joyned for a bottle with Mr. Bold and Mr. Atherton. I lodged at Mosburgh.

I went with Coz: James Poole to hunt with Lord Molin: in yᵉ New Park we killed a Buck.

I went with my Wife to meet Coz: Scaresb: Mrs. Hesketh of Rufford &c at Lathom Spaw, we dansed with Young Mr. Hesket of Oughton Mrs. Entwistley, Mrs. Ann Bold &c.

Lathom Spaw, which was destroyed by the sinking of coal shafts early in the present century, was situate opposite the entrance of what is now called Spaw Farm in Lathom. This the Editor ventures to say on the authority of one of the Wilbraham family. It was in good repute during the last two centuries, but the accommodation seems always to have been deficient. Dr. Borlase of Chester wrote two treatises in its praise, which are now scarce books. He sent copies of both to Mr. Blundell the "Cavalier," who in acknowledging the later one, published 1672, remarks—" To these waters next under God I do certainly owe my life. 'Tis now above four or five weeks since I gave them another visit by reason of our old acquaintance. I was pretty well when I went; I drank them eleven or twelve days and returned perfectly well home. Yet I find them somewhat costly, for my stomach is so good that I eat all before me."

I went with my Wife &c towards Holy-well we dined at Leverp: and Lodged at Chester.

I went to Preston, yᵉ Staff Quarrell with Mr. J. Ander- ton &c: from Preston I went by Curdeley to Lodg at Showley.

I carted over yᵉ Ford with Mrs. Walmes: &c we went to Rib-Chester.

I came from Showley by Mrs. Blackburns of yᵉ Hill to Lankaster.

I heard yᵉ Tryall between John Heys Atturney at Ormsk: and Mr. Ashton.

Coz: Culcheth and his Mother &c dined here. Two of Sʳ Rowland Standleys Doughters came.

1703.
Sept. 1st.

I went with my Wife to Garswood dined there and thence went to Burchley, we found not yᵉ Laydis at home.

Sept. 4th.

I dined at Croxtath found there Sʳ Roger Bradshaw and his Brother, Mr. Standlay of Preston, &c.

Sept. 7th.

I went by Croxtath and Ditton to Dutton-Lodg where I lodged.

Dutton Lodge, the seat of Charles, 6th Baron Gerard, of Bromley. He was son of Richard Gerard, Esq., of Wilderstone, Co. Stafford, who came up to London to give evidence at the time of the Titus Oates plot, but being himself accused was committed to Newgate and died in a few days of gaol fever. The last and 7th Baron Gerard was Rev. Philip Gerard, S.J., who succeeded his brother Charles in 1707, and died March 4, 1733, aged 68. Sir Harris Nicolas makes no reference to these two Lords in his *Synopsis of the British Peerage.*

Sept. 8th.

Lord Gerard I &c went to yᵉ Bowling Green we found Fox hunters there viz Sʳ George Warberton Mr. Ashton &c.

Sept. 10th.

Lord Gerard, Pat: Gelib: and I went to see yᵉ great Tree in yᵉ Park.

Sept. 11th.

There was a Whit Buck Killed in Dutton Park.

Sept. 18th.

Mr. Wairing came hither and made his Complaint to me that he might not keep Pigeons.

Sept. 21st.

I went to Ormsk: with Coz: Scaresb: where he met Mr. Sudall, Mr. Jamson, Mr. Thornton &c at yᵉ Wheat Sheaf and I think Mr. Scaresb: swore to yᵉ Bill and Answer relating to yᵉ Parsonage of Oughton.

Sept. 23rd.

Mr. Houghton and Mr. Ashurst dined at Scaresb: we had Musick at Night.

Oct. 13th.

I went to Ormsk: Race, five horses run and Mr. Edm: Traffords woone.

1703.

I came in y⁰ Coach with my Wife from Ormsk: betimes Oct. 16th. in y⁰ Morning, we got home before seaven of y⁰ Clock.

I went in y⁰ Coach with my Wife Mother &c to Wm: Oct. 18th. Thelw: and Mr. Wairings it being y⁰ Goosfeast.

Mr. Alban Butler came to me with a Letter from Lord Oct. 20th. Molineux.

I went to Leverp: discoursed y⁰ Gunner of y⁰ Elizab: Oct. 23rd. Viseted Mr. Pool's Wife of Leve:

I went to Leverp: with Coz: Th: Geli: I bought Solvers Nov. 5th. of Mr. Sheelds.

I met my Lord Molin: at y⁰ Breck a Hunting. Nov. 6th.

I met Lord Molin: a Hunting we found no Hair, we Nov. 8th. dined at y⁰ Sun at Low-hill, a larg Shot, ill drunk.

I met Lord Molin: &c Mr. Trafford and Mr. Blund: a Nov. 15th. Hunting at Low hill.

I sent Wal: Thelw: to More hall to enquire after Lord Nov. 17th. Biss:

I met Lord Molin: &c a hunting at y⁰ Breck we run Nov. 22nd. a Hair to Litherland.

Lord Biss: Smith of Callipolis in Asia and Mr. Martin, Nov. 26th. came to Lodg here.

Right Rev. James Smith, Bishop of Callipolis, V.A. of Northern District May 13, 1688. Died May 13, 1711, aged 66. He confirmed 110 at Crosby.

Lord Biss: went to y⁰ Grang dined there, and confermed Nov. 30th. above 100 as tis believed. My Wife walked towards y⁰ Grange in disgise.

1703.

Dec. 1st.   The case heard by Lord Biss: between Mr. Edw: Molineux, Rich: Tickley &c.

Dec. 2nd.   I wated of yᵉ Biss: part of yᵉ way towards Aigburth. Mr. Skarboroug from Townley came to lodg here.

Dec. 10th.   I received yᵉ Glasses from Chester for yᵉ Great Charriot.

Dec. 11th.   I met Lord Molin: and his Son a hunting at Litherland.

Dec. 12th.   I hunted for Sope and fond a great dele.

Dec. 14th.   I dined at Aigburth, Mr. Harington and his Son were gon a Hunting. I Found Mr. Rigmaden, Simpkins, Tho: Howerd &c in yᵉ North-Chamber Carding and Drinking.

Dec. 15th.   A Bedlumber was here and had nothing I think, he was rude.

Dec. 19th.   My Wife and I heard Mr. Edw: Molineux hold forth at Marg: Howerds.

Dec. 28th.   I went to Ince after dinner to solemnise Mr. Blund: Birth-day he being now 40 years of Age.   Mr. Ralf, Thomas, and John Tildesléy were there.

Dec. 29th.   I went with my Wife and Aunt to dine at Moor-Hall, we found there Mrs. Hesketh of Rufford, Mrs. Scaresb: Mr. Ireland &c.

Dec. 30th.   We came with Mrs. Scaresb: Mrs. Harington, &c to Ormsk: to see Mrs. Bold, and so home.

1704.

Jan. 4th.   I went to see Parson Richmond, found with him Mr. Marsden, Mr. Danvers and Mr. Poole of Leverp: I think Parson Rich: had nuly been cut for yᵉ Stone.

Jan. 9th.   I skated on Land-Lake.

I walked to Leverp: and dined with Captn Edw: Jan. 11th. Tarleton.

Captain Edward Tarleton had been commander of the Dublin man of war, and was Mayor of Liverpool in 1682. He had a numerous family, long connected with the fortunes of the city. Lived at Church Stile House, a quaint black and white timber building near the Church gate, Chapel Street, taken down about 1850.—*Picton's Memorials.*

My Wife went to be God-Mother to Mr. Fazakerleys Jan. 14th. Doughter Mary.

My Lady Molineux sent Mr. Butler hither of a How- Jan. 16th. do-you.

My Wife sent for Dr. Fabius, he said she was with Jan. 23rd. child.

I hunted about Litherland and Walton wth Leverp: Feb. 5th. Doggs in Company of Mr. Silvester Richmond and Mr. Molineux of Leverp: we had a long Chace.

I hired John Banister to be my cowman, am to give Feb. 7th. him 50^s till Christmas and half a crown more is referd to me, I gave him one shilling in ernest.

I went to Ormski: Cocking it being the second days Feb. 8th. fighting for a Plate, Mr. Blundell of Ince won it.

I went by Ormsk: thence Mr. Howet and Pat Gelib: Feb. 14th. went with me to lodg at Dungenhall.

I walked with Coz Tho: Gelibrond to Antley, Mr. Feb. 15th. Rushton was ill of ye Gout.

I went to ye Aile-hous in Rushton with my three Coz: Feb. 16th. Gelibronds, Mr. Howet &c we were very merry.

I saw Ri: Jump married to Cath: Fisher. Feb. 19th.

1704.

Feb. 20th. She quarrelled with me about her not tacking Phisick and my not coming to see and pitty her.

Feb. 24th. I went after dinner to Leverp: I saw Mrs. Travis who was Sick, and went to wish Dr Tarlton Joy.

Feb. 27th. My wife and Aunt went in ye Coach to Karr-hall.

Feb. 29th. Some good Wives came to turn Pan-kakes.

Mar. 8th. The Huxter women mesured Apples in ye Hall.

Mar. 12th. My Wife and I went to Margery Howerds to hear Mr. Edw: Molineux hold forth.

Mar. 13th. My Lord Molineux and his Son, Mr. Eastcot, Dr. Thos: Tildesley, Cap: Rob: Fazakerley came hither whilst I was Mesuring and Maping Land in ye Town Field.

Mar. 16th. I sent Henry Bilsbu: to my Lord Molineux and Mr. Babthrop after their Preservasion from Fier.

Mar. 20th. I went to Leverp: with my Instruments to Mr. Moss, I dined at Mr. Lancasters and drunk at Secombs with Mr. Hind, Mr. Harrington &c.

Mar. 28th. I sent Walt: Thelw: to order my Tennants in ye More-houses to sett Starr upon Fryday next.

April 3rd. I was at ye Race on Crosby Marsh between Mr. Har: Mair and a Hors of Mr. Molineux his of Leverp:

April 7th. I went with Pat Gelib: and his Nephew to Leverp: we dined at ye Angell, thence we went to Aigbourth and so back to Leverp: I found Sr James Poole at Mr. Molineuxes where I drunk some time. I heard the Cookow and saw one Swallow.

April 13th. Pat: Gelibrond found a Crosior Growing.

Richa: Ainswo: brought my new bed home from Mr. Aldredg, Uphoulsterer at Lev:

I went to Leverp: and heard upon yᵉ Sands that Mr. Edw·: Molin: was found ded on yᵉ Sands. Coz Butler went on Bord the Debora for Dublin Sanders Drury Commander.

I went to yᵉ Grange where I found yᵉ Corps of Mr. Edw: Molin: layed upon my Carriage in order to be buried.

Rev. Edward Molyneux resided with his brother, Richard Molyneux, Esq., at the Grange, and was an admirable missionary priest. A village tradition, given in the preface to *Crosby Records* (*Chetham Society*, No. 12) makes his death the result of foul play, but Mr. Blundell's entries give no countenance to this story. In the Harkirke register (*Crosby Records*, p. 81), the following entry is in the Diarist's handwriting—"Mr. Edw: Molineux bourn at Alt-Grang was unfortunately killed by a faule off his horse April yᵉ 28th, 1704, being in yᵉ 65th year of his age. He was a Clergy Priest of Doua and had for 38 yeares been a painfull Missioner in Formby, Crosby and many other places having under his charg at his death more than eight hundred penitents besides Children that depended upon him, he was buryed yᵉ 29th of Apr. A.D. 1704 in yᵉ Harkirk about tenn of yᵉ Clock at night."

I saw Th Gerard married at yᵉ Grang to Ailes Sumner.

Dr. Shaw and Mr. Edw: Molineux of Formby, shot Rooks with Stonbows at Ince.

I was at yᵉ Marriage of Edw: Tatlock to Ann Bootle.

I went with my Wife and Aunt to dine at Ageburth, there was Mr. Holford, Mr. Bretter, Mr. Smallwood &c.

I went to Ormsk: to yᵉ Buriall of Dr. Barton.

The Miller fidled in yᵉ Mill-Kill to yᵉ Neighbours.

I went to Wigan and there discoursed with Sʳ Roger Bradshaw concerning £100 owing by him to Mr. Christo:

1704.

Bradshaw I drunk with Sir Roger, his brother &c I saw yᵉ German Artist. I lodged at Doctor Worthingtons.

May 30th.   I went with my Wife to dine at Mr. Aldridges in Leverp: We were at the Buriall of our Landlord Rob: Secomb.

June 5th.   Pat: Tho: Wofold held forth the first time at Winny Marrowes, most of my servants went to hear him.

Rev. T. Wolfall had come to succeed Rev. E. Molyneux at the Grange. He was brother to Richard Wolfall, Esq., of Moor Hall, and had a brother John a Jesuit.

June 11th.   I went to Croxtath to welcome Mr. Carrall Molineux into yᵉ Country, the discourse of yᵉ Gold Watch.

June 13th.   I went to Low Hill to yᵉ Doctors and to Leverp: I drunk wᵗʰ Mr. Gleast and Dr. Tarlton, it was a wet night.

June 14th.   I dined at yᵉ Grange was present at yᵉ Valewing of Books I bought some, Great Gilbert Norris was there.

June 15th.   I discoursed Rich: Tickle of yˢ Town concerning his Sons Idleness.

June 19th.   I ploughed with a Culter and no Suck in yᵉ Mossheigh to find Stocks.

Stocks or roots of large trees are still found in ploughing the low lands, which show the former abundance of forests.

June 23rd.   I went by Ditton to Chester wᵗʰ Coz: Tho: Gelib: we lodged at yᵉ Golden Lion.

June 24th.   I went with Coz: Tho: Gelib: from Chester to Holiwell we lodged at yᵉ Cross-Ceyes.

June 25th.   I went into yᵉ Well with severall of yᵉ Pilgrime Sisters &c Smiths by Name in Sropshire.

1704.

Cap: Rob: Faz: came to borrow a horse to goe to June 26th. Leaton Rase on.

I went to Leverp: brought home a Cradle &c wch was July 1st. bought at Chester Fair.

I was at Great Crosby Race between Mr. Silv: Rich- July 3rd. monds Bay Mair and Mr. Ather: Gray.

Wal: Thelw: went to Lord Molin: Rase at Leaton July 5th. Heyes.

I opened a Box of Babby Clothes wch was sent to my July 7th. Wife by my Lady Webb.

I went to advise with Dr. Fabius, I dined there, thence July 14th. went to Leverpoole.

I rode to Adams Spaw to drink the waters. July 20th.

I gave one Shilling to Coz: Jo: Gelib: for wch he is to July 31st. give me Five Pound when his Brother is a Biss:

This was owing to the finding of a Crosier by Rev. W. Gilli-brand a short time back. He made a similar bet with the latter.

Lady Gerard of Bromley came to Lodg here. Aug. 7th.

I went with Coz: William Gellibrond and Mr. Richard- Aug. 8th. son to Mr. Fosters we Shot there with Bow and Arrows.

I went to Leverp: with Lady Gerard, my Wife &c we Aug. 9th. saw ye New Church and went to Mr. Richmonds.

I saw Rich: Tickley deliver at the Grange a Challice Aug. 11th. to Mr. Clark it was left by Mr. Martine to ye Parish of St. Patricks Kilkenney.

Mr. Howett dined here, he brought ye News of a great Aug. 13th. Victory got by Lord Marl: and of three Generalls taken.

1704.

Aug. 14th. I went to Preston Fair, I dined wth Mr. Waran Mr. Osbadelston at Rich: Jacksons.

Aug. 19th. I went to Croxtath with Coz: Rich: Butler and dined there with old Mr. Trafford of Trafford Mr. Wm. Escot &c.

Aug. 21st. I went to Adams Spaw with Coz: Rich: Butler thence we went to Mr. Fosters.

Aug. 29th. I went wth Sister Midleton to Mr. Howets where we found Sr Tho: Tankerd &c Mr. Scaresb: &c Dr. Traps and Mr. Entwistley.

Sept. 1st. Sr Tho: Tankerd &c Mr. Scaresb: &c dined here. Marsh and Anderton played.

William Anderton, the piper, had this year fallen into the hands of a press-gang, and Mr. Blundell wrote to Captain Bradshaw on his behalf. He says that he had hitherto supported a wife and seven children by his industry, and chiefly by playing on the pipes.

Sept. 13th. I Bound John Blund: Apprentice for Virginia before Mr. Mair of Leverpoole.

Sept. 15th. I went to Leverp: and put John Blund: on Bord ye Lorrell for Virginia, I paid £5 to Cap: Tarlton for his Passage.

Sept. 16th. I went on Bord ye Lorrell with Cap: Edw: Tarlton to see Jo: Blund: whom I was sending to Virginia to my Brother Rich: Blu:

Sept. 22nd. My Wife was delivered of her first Child called Mary.

Sept. 24th. We prayed on ye Stayers.

Sept. 25th. My Eldest Child was Christoned Mary, Coz: Scaresb: Godfather, Sister Midleton God-Mother.

I went to Leverp: and Drunk with Ben. Branker and Sept. 16th.
Mr. Pryer.

Coz: Rich: Butler and I took 3 Bottles of Wine and Sept. 17th.
cold Py to Litherland, where we met Lord Molin: and his
two Sons, they had been hunting.

Many Crosby Wives came to see my Wife. I showed Oct. 1st.
my Black Kattle to my Brother Langd:

Went to Morehall and found there Mr. Harington his Oct. 3rd.
Wife &c Coll: John Ashton came after dinner.

I met Lord Molin: a Coursing behind Crosby Schoole Oct. 16th.
he and his Son dined wth me.

Lord Langd: and I met Mr. Blund: in ye Mossess a Oct. 17th.
Coursing thence we went to the Goosfeast Anderton played
here at Night.

I went to Leverp: with my Wife and Mrs. Ann Aspinwall Oct. 23rd.
we went to see Mrs. Hurst ye Maires.

Collon Butler, his Doughter and Lady went hence to Oct. 26th.
Ormsk: I lent them a Pair of my Horses to help their
Wresty Grays to draw.

Mr. Char: Harington and his Sister and Mrs. Holdford Oct. 26th.
dined here.

Mr. Guildus came to draw out a Tooth for my Wife. Nov. 3rd.

I visited the Sick in Little Crosby. Nov. 27th.

I dined at Collo: Butlers thence went towards Dungenhall Dec. 6th.
but got no further than Park-hall where I Lodged.

I went to wish good Suckcess to Mr. Molineux of Dec. 14th.
Croxtath ere he went a Courting I dined there Mr. Blund:
of Prescot came to Croxtath.

1704.
Dec. 18th.   I went to Lodg at Dungenhall.

Dec. 19th.   Mr. Charles Townley Junior dined at Dungen : I helped to Bar out yᵉ Childrens Master Mr. Norcross. I went wᵗʰ Coz: Tho: Gelib: and Tom Walmesley to Antley Mr. Rushton was at home but the Doughters were not in the house, It snewed.

Dec. 21st.   I came with Mr. Wingate from Dungenhall.

Dec. 28th.   Collon: Butler, Mrs. Hesketh of yᵉ Meales Mrs. Ann Entwistley &c dined at Scaresb: and Dansed till next Morning.

Dec. 31st.   Mrs. Scaresb: my Wife &c went in the Coach to Gorsuch. Mr. Rob: Fazakerley of Ormsk: and I walked to Gorsuch, we Men were extreaimly Merry.

1705.
Jan. 6th.   I went after Diner to Ince wᵗʰ Coz: Rich: Butler he Ran and Cap: Rob: Fazak: hoped for a wager of 5ᴸ

Jan. 10th.   I went with Coz: Rich: Butler to see Parson Richmond, but he being gon to Leverp: we went to see Parson Marsden who we found ill of yᵉ Gout, coming home we called at Parson Wairings and eat an Oat Kake and Butter with him.

Jan. 16th.   I was at yᵉ Buryall of Mrs. Bootle at Melling there was Mr. Poole Merchant, Mr. Houghton Mr. Nich: Fazak: Swarbrick &c. From Melling I went to Sefton Church Ail-Hous to drink Coz: Rich: Butlers Fairwell there was Collo: Butler Mr. Howet &c.

Jan. 31st.   I went to Ormsk: to yᵉ Funerall of Mrs. Ann Bold there was Collon Ashton, Parson Sudall, Mr. Jamson &c: I dined at Collonell Butlers thence he and I went to yᵉ Wheat Sheaf where we found yᵉ Trustees of Peter Lathom viz Mr.

Scaresb: Mr. Rigby of Harrock, Mr. John Heyes &c. There was also Mr. Holland Lord Darbys Servant.

I went to Leverp: and bought a Hat of Mr. Chorley and discoursed Mr. Aldridge concerning a Bed for my Mother. I looked at young Mr. Emerys Clock. Feb. 3rd.

My Wife and I went to Lidiat, she fell of the Hors just after her mounting, we took a Fat Goose with us for Bess Fazak: Feb. 5th.

Collon: Butler dined here, he brought News of taking Horses in Cheshire. Feb. 6th.

I went to Mr. Wairings he spoke much against J 2^d Feb. 7th.

My Wife rode behind me to Ormsk: Feb. 19th.

Pat: Wofold gave Ashes here and spoke to us. Feb. 21st.

My House was slightly sirched for Armes by Mr. Leigh Capt: in Lord Darbys Regeament and by — Dutton the High Cunstable. Feb. 22nd.

Mr. Plumb and I discoursed Mr. Gleast at his Hous in Leverp: concerning his Morgage to us. I drunk at ye Angell with Mr. Morphoy, Mr. Gunter &c. Feb. 24th.

I sold my Rabet Skins viz 4 Doz: and 7 to John Stewerd for 14^s Feb. 27th.

I saw 3 Beggars whiped out of Leverp: Mar. 5th.

My Wife rid behind me to Leverp: she saw ye Elephant. Mar. 6th.

I dined at Garswood, there was Coz: Jo: Gelib: Mr. Will: Houghton &c: the Children not being at home I went after them to Burchley, thence to the Grank and so home. Mar. 9th.

I went to Croxtath to pay my first visit to Mr. Moli-
neux his Lady, I dined there as did also Mr. Chorley,
Mr. Wofold &c, Mr. Bowers my Lord Gerards Gentle-
Man was there.

Richard, afterward 5th Viscount, Molyneux had just married
Mary, daughter of Francis, Lord Brudenell. She brought him a
portion of £11,000, and there was a settlement made in her favour
of £1,200 per annum. She was 25 years of age at the time of her
marriage, and lived till 1766. They had no surviving male issue,
and he was succeeded at his death in 1738 by his brother Caryll,
of whom the diarist frequently makes mention.

I went with my Wife in y⁰ Coach to Ormsk: to welcome my Lord Mountg: and his Grand-Son Richard into
this Countrey.

This was Richard, 5th Viscount Mountgarret, who had married
for his first wife Emilia, eldest daughter of the "Cavalier," grandfather to the Diarist. Edmund, the "Colonel," was their eldest son,
and he was then living with his wife at Ormskirk, where now his
son Richard, afterwards 7th Viscount, joined them. Lord Mountgarret had been outlawed and his estates forfeited for his adherence
to James II., but his successor was restored in blood and honors
1721. The latter had three sons who successively held the title,
and the youngest, Edmund, conformed to the Established Church
November 7, 1736. In 1749 he took his seat in the House of Peers,
and was ancestor to the present Henry Edmund, 13th Viscount
Mountgarret. This house stands next in rank to the Ormond
family as head of the Butlers.

I sent Rich: Cartwrit to see Mrs. Scaresb: who was
Lying in of a Doughter.

Mr. Plumb and I met at Mr. Jamsons and discoursed
him concerning Gleasts Hous and his Morgage thence we
went to Mr. Peter Ashtons and he showed us Gleasts
Hous and Garden.

I Stated Accounts wᵗʰ Mr. Jos: Hawley for Mesuring
and Maping of y⁰ Township of Little Crosby, I gave him
one Guiney and am to give him two more if he be living

this day two years, he received Something formally in part of payment.

My Wife and I went to eat a Tansy at Char: Howerds, April 8th. Mr. Molineux of y⁰ Grange &c came to us.

I went with my Wife to Dr. Fabius. April 11th.

Dr. Daniel Fabius was a Baptist, and gave to that body a Cemetery at Everton, where he was buried in 1718.—*Picton's Memorials.* His name is perpetuated in Fabius Chapel, Everton Road.

Pat: Hesketh of Mosbourgh suped here. April 16th.

I appeared in y⁰ Bishops Court at Chester upon Account April 19th. of a Sitation procured against me by John Hurst, I dined at y⁰ Golden Lyon wᵗʰ Mr. Egerton, Mr. Wm. Massy &c thence I went to Poole to wish Joy to Sʳ James, when I came Sʳ James Poole, his Lady &c were just gone to Standlow.

Sir James Poole had just married his third wife, Frances, daughter and co-heir of Major-General Randolph Egerton of Bettey, Co. Stafford, and widow of Sir John Corbet, Bart. Stanlaw was the spot which the monks had formerly exchanged for the more pleasant abode of Whalley.

I dansed and Played at Bragg with y⁰ Ladys &c at April 20th. Poole. Mrs. Mary and An Standley came to Poole. I saw the three Women that were said to be Bewitched.

I came from Poole by y⁰ Rock Boat so to Leverpoole April 21st. and then home.

I sent Henr: Bilsb: to Croston wᵗʰ Bess and got her May 5th. covered with Dogg-Lad.

An inscription at Myerscough Lodge, "Old Dog Lad 1714," has puzzled antiquaries. It is supposed to have been a nick-name of Thomas Tyldesley who lived there, and who in his curious diary calls Mr. Winder "my brother Dog-Lad." Here we find it to be the name of a stallion which belonged to old Isaac Lightbourne of Formby.

1705.

May 11th. Walter Thel: left yᵉ hous in a fret upon Account of a falst Story told him by his Wife relaiting to my Wife.

May 12th. My Wife and I discoursed Ann Thel: she owned her fault, in raising a lye of my Wife.

May 14th. Rich: Falshaw Postilion to my Lord Gerard came hither, he sayed Mr. Jo: Gerard was dead.

May 26th. My Wife and I went in yᵉ Coach to Wigan, we were at Mrs. Aspinw: Dr. Worth: Mr. Langtons and Mrs. Heskeths we light at Diconsons, coming home Rowbothem yᵉ Taylor stayed us at Hollond to take mesure of my Wife.

June 2nd. I went after dinner to Leverp: I drunk with Parson Wairing, Edw: Tarlton and Thomas Brownbill. I also drunk with Major Broadknax.

June 6th. Rougbotham brought a Silk Mantue and Peticoat he had made for my Wife, yᵉ Silk was bought at Leverp: of Mr. Shaw.

June 8th. Severall Carts fetched Brick from my Brick Kill for Mr. Tasburgh but without my leave.

June 19th. I went to Leverp: and Received Harkerk Prints of Mr. Aldridg which he got printed for me at London of yᵉ Money found in yᵉ Harkerk. I drunk wᵗʰ Mr. Becket a Parson, Hunter the Tanner.

For a full account of the Harkirke see *Crosby Records,* which contains an engraving from this copper plate, still preserved at Crosby Hall.

June 22nd. I tryed an experiment wᵗʰ eleven living Miss in a Hot Pot.

Mice.

I went to Leverp: with my Wife she Rode single on Button, I bought a Livery of Mr. Maior for Watty, we were treated by Mr. Leadbeter with Anchovys and by Mrs. Secomb with Botled Punch.

Uncle and Aunt Gerard &c Lodged here.

Dr. Gerard had settled as a physician in Durham, and married Bridget, youngest daughter of the "Cavalier." He was of the Garswood family. Mrs. Gerard died June 27, 1707,

Lady Molineux was God-Mother to Mr. Blundells Dough- ter Ann, I Stood as God-Father for Coz: Francis Anderton, I dined at Ince with Lady Molin: Lady Gormonstown and my Wife.

I went to Speak to wish Joy to Mr. Norris, I dined there and called at Aigbourth.

This was on occasion of the marriage of Dr. Norris, July 12, to Anne, sole daughter and heir of Peter Gerard, of Crewood, Co. Chester. Of Dr. Norris, so long connected with the fortunes of Liverpool, something will be found in the Norris Papers.

Mr. Hen: and Rob: Witherington Presb: Lodged here. I gave 6^d in presence of ye two Mr. Witheringtons to Mrs. Aspinwall ye Midwife for wch she is to give me six Guineys whensoever she is Married to any one.

My Songoars in ye Flat Sung to me and I gave them Billets and Apples.

Songoars.—A songle is a handful of gleaned corn after it has been tied up.—*Wright's Prov. Glos.*

I went after dinner to Leverp: and bought something for a Coat for Mally. A Souldier and his Wife was set in ye Stocks at Leverp:

1705.

Aug. 26th. The News of a Battle twixt Vandosmey and Prince Eugeane was read in yᵉ Buttery by Pat: Gelibrond.

Sept. 6th. I was at Childoll Rase where two Mr. Molineuxes his Horses and two Mr. Haringtons Horses Ran, Mr. Char: Haringtons wan.

Sept. 10th. I Woun Pat Gelib: hat of him at Tables and lost it again.

Sept. 11th. I had a great Breaking, they were found with Meat and had a Fidler and Anderton at Night and four Garlands were brought to some Great Crosby Women after Supper into yᵉ Halle.

The breaking of flax was done by passing the stalks between ground rollers, and the broken shives were beaten out by revolving blades. The fibre being thus freed from its wooden core, was rendered fit for the market. As this process corresponded with the harvesting of corn, it was always an occasion of a festive gathering.

Sept. 20th. I heard yᵉ first time of yᵉ death of my Brot: Rich: Bl: he dyed in Mary-Land Nov. 30, 1704.

Sept. 25th. Mr. Hurst Maior of Liverp: his Wife and Doughter came hither.

Sept. 26th. Going to Leverp: Ri: Cartw: was stopt upon my Mare Harper with a Rope that Came cross yᵉ way from yᵉ Ship the Hope-well.

Sept. 30th. Mr. Wairing told me whot Gests he was to have at the Goos-feast and invited me thither.

Oct. 2nd. I went to Leverp: to Enquire after the death of my Brother I discoursed Mr. Worthington Mr. Houghtons Factor about him and his Widow. I drunk wᵗʰ Mr. Morecroft.

1705.

I went to Leverp: to enquire after the death of my Broth: Rich: from Mr. Lancaster and Mr. Cattaway, I gave Mr. Cataw: my Swourd. Oct. 7th.

Mr. Cattaway had been a Missionary Priest in Maryland. Probably the gift would be in recognition of some service rendered to his late brother. The Rev. Henry Cattaway, S.J., died March 13, 1718, aged 43.

I went to yᵉ Rase on Oughton Moss where Mr. Darey's Kricket beat yᵉ famous London Dimple and two others. Oct. 9th.

I went to Leverp: to discourse Mr. Houghton about my Broth: Rich: but he had not time, so I discoursed Cap: Edw: Tarlton and Captain Brown. Oct. 13th.

Mr. Worthington and I drunk at Tho: Heskeths wᵗʰ Parson Richmond, Sudall, Brookbanks Parson Wairing &c. Oct. 15th.

I went a Coursing to Holsold, I dined there at Seath Bibbys wᵗʰ Parson Brownhill Cap: Hambleton, Mr. Pet: Ashton, Mr. Scarisbrick Mr. Howet &c. Oct. 30th.

I went to Leverp: and drunk at yᵉ Talbot with Collo: White, Collo: Butler, Mr. Sheelds &c. Nov. 1st.

I was at Charls Howerds where Mr. Plumb kept my Court this day, he Lodged here as also did Mr. Clayton of Adlington. Nov. 13th.

My Wife rode behind me towards the Meales to see a Ship that was cast away but finding the way farther than we expected and hearing the Ship was broack to peeces we turned back homwards Re infectâ. My Servants Joyned and had a Snap-Dragon. Nov. 25th.

Marga: Oughton dined here she told us of Sʳ James Pooles goods being seased. Dec. 2nd.

1705.
Dec. 6th.   Wal: Thelwall bought me 10 Beas at Ormsk: very cheap viz for £11 . 15ˢ . 0.

Dec. 8th.   Pat: Gelib: went to Ormsk: my Wife and I went along with him to see him safe over Sefton Water.

Dec. 15th.   I went to Leverp: and made a viset to Mr. Houghton. I drunk at Mr. Smiths with him Coll: Butler, Sandiford, Mr. Sheelds, Mr. Howet, Mr. Wofold and Mr. Ince, some talk about Taxing Merchants.

Dec. 16th.   Pat: Gelib: came not to Calves Feet.

Dec. 18th.   I sent Ri: Cartw: to Scaresb: with Oring Coullerd Ribbans, I sent Watty to Leverp: for some fine Edging.

Dec. 22nd.   I payed Mr. Morecroft for Aurora Riban.

Dec. 30th.   I went with my Wife in yᵉ Coach to Ormskirk I dined at Collon: Butlers wᵗʰ Mr. Pet: Ashton Dr. Lancaster &c. Mr. H. Tyarer Caligula, Mr. Howet &c were there.

1706.
Jan. 3rd.   Mrs. Standley and Mrs. Trafford came wᵗʰ Mrs. Blund: of Ince to make a Viset to my Wife, Anderton played here at Night there was little dansing but great Carding.

Jan. 4th.   I went in yᵉ Coach to Leverp:, we were at Mrs. Sweetings, I drunk with Mr. Sheelds and Swarberick at Lathoms.

Jan. 6th.   I lent my Carriage to carry the Corps of Ellen Speakman to Alker.

Jan. 12th.   I came from Preston Fair to Bank where I dined at Mr. Fleetwoods wᵗʰ him, his Lady, the Parson, Mr. Hesketh Junior of the Meales &c.

Jan. 14th.   Mrs. Molineux of Croxtath was brought to Bed of her first Child tis to be called Mary.

1706.

I dined at Croxtath wth Coll: Butler, S^r Wm. Gerard Jan. 15th.
Mr. Wm. Molineux &c. Anderton was here at Night.

I Received at Leverp: £20 from Wm. Clough the Elder Jan. 19th.
for Rent. Leadbeter ye Groser gave me a Pint of Claret
in ye Talbot.

I went to Lever: to take leave of Coll: Butl: ere he Jan. 29th.
went towards Ireland, I Suped at ye Talbot with him Capt:
Pywell, Mr. Peter Ashton &c: we set up drinking till Morning,
we had ye Drum beat whilst we drank healths.

My Wife and I went to the Race at Childol, Mr. Feb. 4th.
Charles Haringtons Mare wone all the three Heats we came
home through Lev: and Mr. Plumb treated us with wine
and Sweetmeats.

I went to Ormsk: to fetch my Lord Mountg: hither Feb. 6th.
to Lodg for some time but he was not able to ride on
Hors-back.

Coz: Scaresb: dined here there came alog with him Feb. 8th.
Coz: Mary Bradshaw of Midlom, one Mrs. Ingleby and
Mr. Peketh Presb:

**Mary Bradshaw belonged to a branch of the Bradshaighs of
Haigh, settled at Middleham, Co. York.**

Mr. Tho: Gorsuch dined here. Mr. Charls Harington Feb. 10th.
came hither from Ince after dinner we played at Tick-tack.

**A kind of backgammon, played both with men and pegs.—
*Webster's Dictionary.***

Lord Mountg: had a Letter from my Ant Fr: Bl: to Mar. 4th.
advise him to keep in private.

**Francis Blundell, sister of the "Cavalier," a woman of rare
courage and ability, had devoted herself to the fortunes of Lord**

Mountgarret and his family from the day of his marriage with her niece, and had rendered them invaluable service. Now, in her extreme old age, we find her still watchful for his security. In the time of the Civil Wars, when her brother had to seek refuge elsewhere, she kept his house at Crosby, and had to endure the frequent visits of rude troopers, whose plundering propensities obliged her to bury her bread from meal to meal.

Mar. 8th.   Cap: Rob: Faz: brought us good News about the Bill against Papists.

Mar. 12th.   Collo: Butlers Servant Thomas came from Dublin and told us of the Death of yᵉ Collonells Lady.

Mar. 20th.   I was wᵗʰ Mr. Molin: of yᵉ Grange and Ralph Low my Lord Molineux his Steward in yᵉ Sand-hills, we order'd Stakes to be set to divide yᵉ Grange Warand from some of my Tenants Land.

Mar. 23rd.   Mr. Wairing introduced me to see Mr. Coopers Flower Garden at Leverpoole.

April 1st.   Mr. Babthrop dined here. I discoursed him concerning an Exchange for Mr. E. S.

Rev. Albert Babthorpe, S.J., fifth son of Sir Ralph Babthorpe, of Babthorpe, Co. York, was the last survivor of an eminent knightly family that had existed for twenty generations. Its staunch adherence to the ancient faith had exposed its members to the severest persecutions, in which all its once ample possessions melted away. (See *Foley's Records*, vol. 3, p. 192). Father Babthorpe was then Chaplain at Croxteth and Provincial S.J. He died April 13, 1720, aged 74. He is frequently mentioned in the diary of Bishop Cartwright, with whom he was on intimate terms while Chaplain to Sir James Poole, of Poole, near Chester. The priest designated by the initials E.S. was probably Rev. Edward Scaresbrick, S.J., uncle to the Squire of Scaresbrick, who had been Chaplain and Preacher to James II. His prominent position at Court rendered him obnoxious to the new Government, and he was now in his old age living very quietly at Crosby. He died February 19, 1709. Some of his Court sermons were published, notably one, *Catholic Loyalty,* which was printed by order of King James. He wrote also the *Life of Lady Warner*, printed 1692, and several unpublished letters of the "Cavalier" are addressed to him. He probably retired to Scarisbrick Hall, as we find him later on bringing Father Aldred to Crosby.

My Wife I &c dined at yᵉ Wool-pack. I bought some things at a Sale at Mr. Brooksbys. I bought some new Puter of Mr. Halsold. *April 3rd.*

Ellen Nelson had her Wages payed with orders to be gon, on account of some words that past, but she went not. *April 7th.*

I went to yᵉ Hall of Kerkby to see Edw: Webster, I found there Mr. Sharples, Mrs. Webster the Maiores of Leverp: Mrs. Hartley, &c. *April 12th.*

My Mother bid adue to Crosby, most of the neighbours came to take leave of her. I went in my Coach to Waring: wᵗʰ my Mother and Wife. We Lodged at Mat: Pages in Warington. *April 21st.*

My Mother and her Maid Mar: Wins: &c. took Coach at Waring: for London. My Wife and I Dined and Lodged at Southward. *April 22nd.*

Mrs. Blundell went to the Benedictine Convent at Ghent, where she had two daughters nuns. Here she ended her days piously on December 2, 1707, having made the vows of religion on her death-bed.

Southward is Southworth Hall, then tenanted by Mr. Golding, a Catholic lawyer. It was long owned by the Jesuit Fathers, who sold it in 1828. Some years ago the writer saw within it the room formerly used as a Chapel, with decorated panels, &c. The Hall itself has been re-fronted and modernised. All tradition of "Dobs Font" seems to have died out in the neighbourhood.

I bought a Little very fine Muslin for Ruffles at Mr. Morecrofts, he drank wᵗʰ me at yᵉ Wool-Pack. *April 30th.*

Collonell Butler and his Son James came hither out of Ireland after yᵉ death of his Lady. *May 3rd.*

1706.

May 8th. I subscribed to contribute to Leverp: Plate for a Hors Rase.

May 13th. My Wife and I went to Leverp: and saw Acted the Earl of Essex. Mr. Plumb and his Wife, Mr. R. Norris &c was there, we came home about two of ye Clock in ye Morning.

May 15th. I was at ye Great Plate at Lev: where Lord Molineux his Hors beat Mr. Sil: Richmonds Maor, I drunk a hors back with Alderman Tyarer &c.

May 16th. I was at ye little Plate at Leverp: where five Horses run for it, a Chesnut Horse belonging to one Robinson in Wales wan it. Col: Butler, Mr. Tute, Mr. Shields my Wife and I saw ye Gaimster acted at Leverp:

May 21st. Mr. Babthorp sent to Pat: Gelibrond not to leave us till farther orders.

May 28th. Coz: Dick Butler and I went to Leverp: we drunk wth Mr. Leadbeter at ye Golden Fleece. I bought stuff &c of Mr. Hurst for a Coat for Mally. Coming home we saw a great many Purposes between Bank hall and Leverp: rouling in ye Sea.

May 29th. Coz: Dick Butler and I went to Bank-hall to see Mr. Rob: Moore.

June 6th. I sent Mally to stay at More-hall. My Wife and I began our Journey in our Coach for York Shire, we called at Collo: Butlers in Ormsk: we made a small Stay at ye Ancker in Eckleston. I left ye Coach and Rid to Rushton More where I found Coz: Tho: Gelibrond. We Lodged at ye Blew Bell in Whaley.

From Whaley we went to Gisbourn thence to yᵉ Lamb at Skipton where we Lodged.

From Skipton we went towards Bluver-houses and were overturned a Little Short of Hasle-wood where we were assisted as I take it by one Mr. Knip, thence we came to Harragate and so to Stockhild.

My Brother Midl: shewed me his Fishponds and my Sister Shewed me outhousing.

My Wife and I went wᵗʰ my Sister in her Coach to Ribston Sʳ Henry Goodricks Fine Hous. Mr. Witham formerly of yᵉ Bass suped at Stockhild.

My Brother and Sister took my Wife and me in their Coach to Haslewood Sʳ Walt: Vavasors where we dined wᵗʰ Sir Wal: and his Lady.

Coz: Michaill Ann, his Wife, Mr. Marmaduke Ann and Mrs. Carlton dined at Stockh:

My Sister Midl: took my Wife and me in her Coach to Brammam Coz: Mick: Anns where we dined wᵗʰ Sʳ Walter Vavasor, his Lady, two Mr. Charltons &c.

My Brother Midleton took Coz: Mick: Ann and me in his Coach to see the Droping Well at Knesbrough, thence we wet to Harrogate where I taisted both yᵉ Sweet and Stinking Spaw Water, I saw there Morrison yᵉ Riming Musition, he played very well.

Morrison had played there 70 years at the time of his death, in 1732. He lived 102 years, and was succeeded by Metcalf, who died in 1810, aged 93. For an account of this extraordinary character, "Blind Jack of Knaresborough," see *Yorkshire Oddities*, by Baring Gould.

My Wife and I came from Stockhild, my Sister Midl: brought us in her Coach to York, we dined at yᵉ Falcon,

1706.

my Sister went home and my Brother Midl: went with us in our Coach to Holme where we Lodged.

June 20th.

I went with my Lord Langd: and my Brother Midl: to y⁰ Bowling-Green at Lansburrough my Lord Burlingtons, we found their Sʳ Tho: Rudston of Heaton and his Son, Mr. Rob: Doleman of Pocklington, Mr. Edw: Fenwick &c.

June 21st.

My Lord Langdale my Brother Midlet: and I went to Cliff Mr. Philip Langdales, he not being at home we staid till he came and then drunk and afterwards we took Bumpers on Horsback.

June 22nd.

My Lord Langd: hunted a Buck wᵗʰ Sʳ Marmaduke Constable they killed him. My Lord Langd: went to y⁰ Buriall of Mrs. Metham.

June 23rd.

Mr. Peter Vavisor of Willitoft, Mr. Langdale of Haughton, Mr. Doleman &c dined at Holme.

June 24th.

We dined at Evringham Sʳ Marmaduke Constables, there was Mr. Edw: Hales of Byland Abbey, Mr. Charlton Junʳ of York &c.

June 25th.

My Lord Langd: my Brother Midl: and I went to Pocklington and dined at Mr. Dolemans wᵗʰ Mr. George Palmer of Neybourn and his Broth: Will: Mr. Lauson of Moorby, Mr. Medcalf Sʳ Marmad: Constable, &c.

June 27th.

Parson Savage came to my Lord Langdales, we went together to Launsbr: Green where we bouled wᵗʰ Sʳ Marm: Constable, Mr. Edw Fenwick, Mr. Best of South Dalton, &c.

June 28th

Went to Reswick Castle where we saw the Widdow Lawder and a Son and Doughter of hers.

June 29th.

Mrs. Lawder &c came to Holme, Sʳ Marm: Constable, Mr. Fenwick and Mr. Charlton came we drunk hard in y⁰ Summerhous.

My Wife and I came from Holme to York in order to June 30th.
goe towards Durham, we dined and Lodged at ye Black
Swan. I went wth Coz: Tho: Gelib: to Mrs. Pastons.

We came in ye Stage Coach from Darlington to Durham July 2nd.
where we Lodged at my Uncle Gerards, we had in y^e
Coach with us one who passed for a great Fortune,
but we suppose she is not, we think her name is Wright.

Mr. Kennet of Coxoe, Mr. Bradshaw of Midleholme July 4th.
and his Doughter Mary dined wth us.

We dansed at Mr. Wood his School and afterwards we July 5th.
drank together and went with our Musick about the Streets.

My Wife &c went in Mr. Fosers Coach to Coxoe. July 6th.

Mr. Foser, Mr. Pudsye &c dined with us at Dr. Gerards. July 8th.
My Wife and I began our Journey in ye Stage Coach from
Durham to York.

My Lord Lang: Mr. Savage and I went to Launsburroug July 11th.
Green where we bouled with Sr Marma: Const: Mr. Jourden
Langdale, Mr. Faux, Mr. Best &c.

We Stired not from Holme I gather'd Goosberrys in July 12th.
y^e Garden wth Mrs. Errington.

My Wife and I came from Holme, we Passed over Booth July 13th.
Ferry y^e River Vese, we came to my Uncle Anns of
Burgwallis.

Vese == Ouse.

Mr. Tho: Percy of Stubs Walden and his Uncle suped July 18th.
at Burgwallis.

We went to Stubs Walden. July 19th.

My Aunt Ann took my Wife and me in her Coach to July 21st.
old Mr. Anns of Frickley, we suped there, there was old

1706.

Mr. Ann, Mr. George Ann and his Wife, Mr. More of Bamburrow and his Doughter.

July 24th.

Went to see Robbin-Hud Well and to Tho: Horncastles.

July 25th.

Went to Bamborrow Mr. Mores.

Many of the names above enumerated are to be found in *Cosin's List*, amongst the Yorkshire Catholics who registered their estates 1719. Lord Langdale of Holme, £599 8s. 8d.; Robt. Dolman of Pocklington, £582 1s. 9d.; Mr. Peter Vavasour of Willitofts, £135 10s.; Mr. Philip Langdale of Houghton, £697 4s. 4d.; Sir Marmaduke Constable of Everingham, £778 10s. 6d.; Mr. Geo. Palmer of Nabourne, £301 13s. 7d.; Hon. Ann Ann of Burghwallis, widow, £139 9s. 8d.; Marmaduke Ann of Frickley, £191 5s.; Mr. Geo. Ann of Doncaster, £183 3s.; Mr. Thos. Percy of Stubs Walden, £265 16s. 6d.; Cris. Cresacre More of Barnburrow, £351 15s. 5½d.; Marmaduke Langdale, estate at Holme, £118 12s. 4d.; William Palmer of Nabourne, gent, £40; John Forcer of Old Elvet, Durham, £325 9s. 0¼d.

July 28th.

Mr. Savill of Norton Priory and his Brother Came.

July 29th.

Came over Blackstone Edge to Rachdale where we lodged at the George.

July 30th.

At Wiggane I discoursed Mr. Graddall concerning yᵉ Commissioners who were siting upon yᵉ Estate of Mr. Diconson of Rightington.

Aug. 3rd.

My Brother Langdale was Marryed.

Marmaduke, who became in 1718 4th Baron Langdale, married Elizabeth, youngest daughter of William, Lord Widdrington.

Aug. 12th.

I Dined at yᵉ Wheat Sheafe in Ormsk: with my Lord Molin: and his two Sons, Sʳ Wᵐ Gerard Mr. Chorley and his Son &c. I was at yᵉ Rase on Oughton Moss where Lord Molin: his Gray Mare beat Mr. Haringtons Bay Mare three Heats.

Aug. 13th.

My Wife and I went to Croxtath to wate of my Lord and Lady Gerard of Brombley.

I went to Parson Wairings he Entertained me with ye discourse of his Sons being taken by the French.

Mrs. Walmesley of Showley and Mr. Gerard her Presb: dined here.

I went with my Wife &c to Dutton Lodg.

Sr Tho: Aston of Aston, his Lady and Brother came to Dutton Lodg.

We Hunted and killed a very Fat Whit Buck in my Lord Gerards Park, after diner we went to Bartington Bowling Green, we found there Mr. Bromfield &c.

We Discoursed of Learning and Salved Enigmas.

Pat Gelib: went with Coz: Dick Butler towards Mr. Woods his Schoole near Winchester. My Lady Gerard and my Wife went to Rock-Savage to wate of my Lady Eliz: Savage.

I went to Dutton Lodg to fetch my Wife home, I tooke ye Coachhorses along with me, ye Waters at Warington were so high out that tho it was Sunday I saw them leading of Corn.

My Lady Gerard took me and my Wife in her Coach to ye Out-side where we dined at Mr. Billingtons.

My Lady Eliza: Savage came to Dutton Lodg.

I Played at Tables with my Lord Gerard. John my Lords Brewer played on his Pips in ye Kitchen and some of ye Servance dansed.

My Lord Gerard and I went to Sr Tho: Astons we bouled there with Sr Tho: Ast: Doctor Norris &c.

My Lord and Lady Gerard took my Wife and me in their Coach to see ye Park and the great Tree.

1706.

Sept. 25th.   My Doughter Frances was born.

Sept. 29th.   My Doughter Frances was Christoned, Collo: Butler stood Godfather for my Brother Lang: and Mrs. Mills stood for my Lady Gerard.

Oct. 2nd.   I walked with Mrs. Mills and Mrs. Woods to see Tho: Marrows Breaking.

Oct. 5th.   Mr. Brownbill tought me to Cercle three Poynts.

Oct. 9th.   I went to Croxtath to wate of my Lord Cardigan and his Brother Brugenald, there was Parson Copley and his Brother, Mr. Rowly, Mr. Wm. Tunstall, Mr. Webber, &c.

Oct. 10th.   The Scoulding bout between Ails Davy and Darby's Wife about carrying away some wood.

Oct. 28th.   I sold my Wives Silver triming to Ben: Branker and saw it burned.

Nov. 3rd.   I discoursed wth Mr. Poynes he held fourth to his Auditory ye first time.

Father Poyntz, S.J., had come the day before as Mr. Blundell's Chaplain. This was his first Sunday.

Nov. 5th.   Tis said Leverp: Hounds hunted a Fox this day from Bank-hall to Knowsley Park.

Nov. 7th.   My Wife and I dined at Collo: Butlers, Coz: Ann Tildesley, Mrs. Ellen Entwistley &c.

Nov. 14th.   I sent Rich: Cartw: to Farnworth to pull ye Doars off my Formes which he tells me the Clark and he did doe.

Nov. 25th.   The Dispute in my Chamber between Pat: Gelib: and Mr. Poyns about ye hight of King David.

Dec. 11th.   We Dined in ye Parlor it being the first time it was uesed as a Parlor. We had two Fidlers at Night and dansed Country Danses in ye Halle.

Mr. Charls Harington and Mr. Jo: Chantrell dined here. They dansed Country Danses with us and Lodged here, we had two Fidlers Gerard Holsold and Marsh we dansed till towards two in the Morning.

I Lent Horses to Nancy Gorsuch and Jane Harrison to goe to Leverp: It was a day of Thanks giving and great reioysing for a Victory obtained by yᵉ Duke of Marlbourgh.

Mr. Poynes and I went to Mr. Wairings we had some Disputations, we stayed there pritty late.

This being yᵉ Twentith day of Christmas we had Anderton at Night.

My Wife went to Mrs. Bootle of the Peele to shew her her Finger that was Burned.

My Wife Mr. Mills and I went to see yᵉ Seller at Sefton.

I sold my Hors Buck to Wm. Anderton for one dayes playing of yᵉ Pips p̱ Ann: as long as he lives in Lancashire and for 25ˢ to be payed by Parcells as he can get it, if the Horse prove ill I promiss to bate him 5ˢ·

I writ a fowl drought of a Letter to the Provinci:

This letter, a copy of which has been preserved, was to request the Provincial S.J. to send him another priest in the place of Father Poyntz, who did not suit him. "We desire a Man of Wit and Conversation, one that can Preach well and is willing to take Pains among yᵉ Poore Catholicks of wᶜʰ we have a great many, and one that is of a good Humour and will be easy and contented with Tollerable good Fair &c &c." He does not name the salary, but the account books shew that £8 was given yearly to the Chaplain as long as he lived in the house.

Mr. Poynes went quite away from hence.

My Wife and I dined at Mrs. Plumbs in Leverp: I Payed yᵉ Scotch Shopkeeper for Cloth, I bought a Hat of

1707.

Mr. Chorley.   I exchanged some Silver Spoones with Mr. Sheelds.

Feb. 13th.   My Wife and I went to Lidiat to see Bess Fazak:

Feb. 17th.   When the Maids got up to wash they heard Knocking and Laughing at the Gates and Windowes.

Feb. 20th.   I went to see Lord Mount: who was Sick. I dined at Collo: Butlers it being my Aunt Frances' Birth day she is now 76 years of Age.

Feb. 22nd.   I went to Leverp: and drunk Punch at Mr. Tarltons.

Feb. 23rd.   Mr. Moston held forth here. My Wife and I went to Wm Thelwalls to eat Pankakes.

Feb. 24th.   Severall of yᵉ Tenants Wives came hither to eat Pankakes and be merry I was amongst them.

Feb. 25th.   My Wife Mrs. Mills and I went to Ni: Johnsons and eat Pankakes. Thence we went to Parson Wairings and took a Fidler with us.

Feb. 27th.   Collo: Butler sent his Servant hither to let me know his Father dyed this Morning.

Feb. 28th.   I went to Ormsk: to Condole with Coll: Butler for yᵉ Death of my Lord his Father Mr. Peter Ashton was there, I saw Mr. Wofold, Mr. Howet, Mrs. Ann Tildesley &c there at Prayers. Mr. La Grote showed me some Pictures of his Painting at Mr. Fazakerleys.

Mar. 1st.   Mr. Blund: lent me his Net to draw for some Fish for my Lord Mountg: Funerall.

Mar. 3rd.   I was at yᵉ Funerall of my Lord Mountg:

The funeral seems to have been as private as possible, and the burial took place at Sefton, no doubt in the Blundell Chapel. The Sefton Register records: " 1706. The Honᵇˡᵉ Richard Lord

Mungarrett, papist from Ormskirke, March 3." The late worthy Rector, Rev. E. Horley, told the writer that in no other year (or almost so) had he found the addition of the opprobrious term here employed.

I went to Leverp: Mr. Plumb shewed me his Tackley Mar. 4th. for Fishing, he came with me to y⁰ Woolpack where I shewed him some tricks on y⁰ Dise &c.

Mr. Brown formerly the Master of y⁰ Loyalty dyned here. Mar. 6th.

I made Coz: W. Ge: Salve alias Captain Midletons Mar. 10th. for a Bruse or Cut.

I dined at Croxtath, we drunk in the Cupula and saw Mar. 21st. y⁰ Servants Airing y⁰ Horses.

I bought some Flower sets at Leverp: I drunk with Mar. 22nd. Ben: Brank: he talked as if he would be good.

I took Ellen Riding sworne concerning stealing of Mar. 27th. Turves before Mr. Mayor of Leverp: he was on horsback going to Lancaster Assizes. Mr. William Tarlton went with me to Mr. Gibbones, he shewed me his Garden.

Mr. Wm Tarleton and Tho: Carter dined here. I April 1st. gave Mr. Wm Tarleton some Flower sets. They went to Cha: Howerds and there I found them with Rich: Tickley Mr. Darcy Chantrells wife, Mrs. Betty Baumber &c James Brown came to us with his Fiddle and we were very merry.

Dr. Fabius came to see Tho: Gower he let him Blood. April 3rd.

My Wife, Mrs. Mills and I heard Mass at Mr. Fosters. April 6th.

Pat: Wofold brought Mrs. Mills her snuff Box that April 7th. she had lost.

I put up some Escutcheons in y⁰ Hall, Lord Mount- April 8th. garrets was one of them.

1707.

April 10th. I went to Mr. Moston to shew him Mr. Babthrops orders to come hither on Monday or Tuesday in Easter Week.

April 14th. I went to Catherin Sargants in Farnworth where there was a meeting upon Account of choosing ye Chapell Wardens, I shewed there my Order from ye Bishops Court for my Seat in ye Chapell of Farnw: to Mr. Ainscow ye Parson, to Mr. John Corleys ye Schoolmaster &c, thence I went to Mr. Hardings and so to Wm. Cloughs ye Bank hous in Ditton where I Lodged.

April 15th. I was at prayers at Mr. Hardings, thence I went to Mr. Rights to a Sale of goods and thence to Wm. Cloughs to dinner. After diner I was at ye Townes meeting where there was Wm. Kennion, Jos. Bolton, H. Hey, &c. We chose a Maior and Drunk Anall Seed Water.

This was Mr. Hawarden's in Widnes, where Rev. Wm. Maire Vere Hawarden was then priest. The latter was educated at Douay, which he left in 1693, and died 1728. The Diarist had property at Ditton, Bankhall, &c., still held by the family. Hence his claim for a seat in Farnworth Chapel, which occasioned him much trouble and litigation.

April 16th. I called at Eckleston to see Mrs. Eckleston who had brock her Arme thence I went to Leverp: and Received a Hollow Cross Reliquary from Ben: Brankhurst.

April 17th. Pat: Gelib: went with me to Coz: Tho: Gelib: this being ye first time I had seen eather of them since they were Married, we met on ye Road Coz: Jo: Gelib: and Mr. Gradell.

April 18th. Coz: Jo: Gelib: came to lodg at his Sons.

April 19th. Coz: Jo: Gelib: his Son Tho:, Mr. Wm. Holywell and I went to Chorley to meet Mr. Brooks of Astley, we drunk at Ned Luckases there was with us Mr. Brooks, his Son-in-Law, Wm. Low, &c.

I came home from Coz: Th: Geli: I called to see Dol: April 20th.
Fisher and looked where they had been sinking for a Brine
Spring near He: Fishers.   I called at my Lord Mount:
Mr. Rob: Fazakerley was there.

Mr. Plumb dined here, he and I played at Cross and Pile. April 22nd.

I went to Eckleshall to meet y⁰ Corps of my Lord Gerard April 25th.
there was Sʳ John Crew, Sʳ Fraˢ Lester, Mr. Berrington,
Mr. King the undertaker, Mr. Fowler, &c.   I attended y⁰
Corps to Ashley where it was layed in a Vault.

I went from Bromley to Dutton where I Lodged two April 26th.
Nights.

I was admitted to see my Lady Gera: I walked in y⁰ April 27th.
Gardens and read most of y⁰ day.

Charles, 6th Baron Gerard, of Gerard, Bromley, married Mary,
daughter of Sir John Webb, of Odstock, Co. Wilts. The widowed
Lady Gerard was residing in Bruges in 1716, when the Diarist
met her at Lord Waldegrave's.   Her chaplain, Rev. Richard
Richardson, S.J., was with her.

Mr. Foster was buried.   May 10th.

Rev. Richard Foster, S.J. born March 11, 1672, ordained priest
at Prague, 1701, is thus noticed in the *Harkirke Register:* "Mr.
Rich: Foster was born in Sutton, came from Prage to be a
Missioner in these Parts, chiefly at Formby, he lived at y⁰ New-
house in y⁰ Car houses in Ince and dyed y⁰ 9th of May An. 1707,
and was buried y⁰ day following in y⁰ Harkerk next to Mr.
Ed: M."

I paid Easterdews and Clarks wages &c. to Wm. May 12th.
Harrison.

I went to Leverp: I was in y⁰ Town Hall or Chamber May 17th.
when a debate was argued before Mr. Morecroft y⁰ Maior,
Mr. Clayton &c. relating to Henry Wainwright who was
bound Prentice to James Harrison a Weaver.   I drunk wᵗʰ
Mr. Clayton and his Uncle Mr. Tho Clayton at Mr. Tuts.

1707.

May 21st.

Sʳ James Poole and his Son Frances lodged here.

In a letter to his mother of July 12, 1707, the Diarist says: "Sir James Poole goes from one good house to another, among the rest has been to mine, but his headquarters is at Mosburgh and Burchley and I hear that his son has proferd very Kind things, yet the Father cannot be prevaled with to do any thing for his own good, neither do I know that he has one penny but what his son Fran: gives him."

Sir James Poole was thrice married, his first wife being Anne, daughter of Thos. Eyre, Esq., of Hassop, Co. Derby, which brought him into connection with the squire. His eldest son, James, married, but died s.p. October 8, 1706. Sir James was a Catholic, as his family had always been, but his son and successor, Francis, conformed, and was M.P. for Lewes in 1743. The Baronetcy expired in 1821.

May 26th.

Madam Molineux of Croxtath and her Sisters-in-Law Mrs. Mary Molin: and Mrs. Betty made a Viset here.

May 27th.

Coming from Leverp: we called at Bank-hall and yᵉ old Woman shewed the House.

June 2nd.

My Wife and I went to prayers to Lidiat we dined there with Mr. Moston.

June 3rd.

I dined at Ince wᵗʰ Mr. Harington, his Wife Son and Doughter.

June 5th.

I dined at Mr. Plumb's wᵗʰ Mr. Chars Harington, I Looked at some of Mr. Eatons Books that he designs for his Aucktion. I drunk with him Ralph Tyrer &c.

June 6th.

My Wife came home, she had seen Blanscow, Parkhall, Rightington &c.

June 8th.

Mr. Moston went hence away in hast being called by Mr. Wilson yᵉ Atturney to Marry him. Mrs. Blund: of Ince and one Mrs. Osboldeston made a Viset here.

June 9th.

My Wife went wᵗʰ an Intention to goe by Ruck-horn to yᵉ Outside, I went wᵗʰ her as far as Leverp: and there I

stayed Mr. Eatons Aucktion of Books till towards nine of
yᵉ Clock, there was Parson Marsden Mr. Allanson, Browbill,
Mr. Brankhurst, &c.

1695. Mr. Josh. Eaton, Bookseller, admitted free.—*City Records.*

I was at yᵉ second dayes Auxion of Mr. Eatons Books June 10th.
at yᵉ Woolpack in Leverpoole. There was Parson Alanson,
Mr. Brankhurst, Brownbill &c.

I went to welcome home my Lord Mount: after dinner June 11th.
we went to wish Mr. Wilson Joy, thence we went to yᵉ
Black Bull, I lay at my Lord Mountgarrets.

Alderman Clayton, Mr. Tyrer Junior, Mr. Tute and June 19th.
their Wives made a Viset here.

At Leverp: I drank at Mr. Brankhursts with Mr. Hurst, June 21st.
and at yᵉ Post Office with Mr. Molin: of yᵉ Grang.

My Wife and I began our joyrney towards Holly-well June 23rd.
we went over in Eastom Boat. Lodged at Mr. Taylors
yᵉ signe of yᵉ Golden Lyon in Chester.

Went from Chester to Holly Well. Lodged at yᵉ Starr. June 24th.

My Wife, Mr. Plumb and I came from Hollywell over June 26th.
Shotwigg Ford, it was very deep, thence we came to yᵉ
Wood-side where we got over.

Wm Clough Junior payed me some Money, we counted June 28th.
part of it upon yᵉ hors-stone when it was duskish.

Mr. Wm. Clough was tenant at Bankhall, Ditton.

I went to Dungen-hall to advise with Coz: John Gelib: June 30th.
I called at Coz: Tho: Gelibronds where I dined. I found
there his Mother-in-Law, Mrs. Wesby. Mrs. Hesk: of yᵉ
Maines came as did also Dr Fran: Worto:

July 1st.   Mr. Livesley and one of his Doughters came to Dungen-hall. Mr. Clifton of Lithom and his Lady and 4 or 5 of their Children came to Lodg there as did also Mr. Walmesley of the Lower-hall and his Lady.

July 2nd.   We Dined in the Great Dining Roome at Dungen: I walked in yᵉ Stone Gallery with Pat Tho: Geràrd &c.

July 3rd.   Coming home I stayed at Whitley Hills where I saw them rase up a Millstone.

July 5th.   Mr. Blundell of Ince and Mr. Thomas Standley of Preston made a Viset here. I Received a Letter from Doctor Gerard with advice of my Aunts Death.

July 10th.   My Wife rid single to Mosburg.

July 14th.   Mrs. Bootle of yᵉ Peel came to Blood me for my fall.

He had fallen from his horse on his return from Liverpool on the twelfth.

July 23rd.   My Wife rid behind me to yᵉ Grange but Mrs. Molin: not being at home we went to yᵉ North end but neather Richard nor his Wife were at home.

July 24th.   I went to Ince with an Intention to goe to yᵉ Flowering of Ince Cross with Mr. Blund: if he went, but he not being at home I came back, Some of yᵉ Servants went.

This pleasing village custom, held on the Feast of the Nativity of St. John the Baptist, has long since fallen into desuetude.

July 25th.   My Wife, Mally and I went to Leverp: Fair. We eat some Cold Salmon &c at Mr. Plumbs.

July 28th.   I dined at my Lord Mountg: wᵗʰ Coz: Selbys two Sons.

July 31st.   I went to Leverp: to take leave of my Lord Mountg: when he went over yᵉ Water in order to goe for Ireland, he gave me his Will to keep.

When Mr. Moston was to goe hence his Mare was wanting so I sent him home on my horses, but his Mare being found soon after, I sent Charles Howerd with her to Lidiat, also to Scarisbrick Ormskerk and More hall.

It was the custom of Mr. Blundell to celebrate his father's anniversary in a religious manner. With this object he procured the services of as many priests as possible. On this occasion he had six, viz.:—Rev. Tho. Scarisbrick, S.J., brother of the squire; Tho. Wolfall of the Grange; John Mostyn, S.J., of Lydiate; Gerard Barton of the Granke; John Blackburne of More Hall, and another.

Coz: Edw: Scarisb: Senior came hither and brought Mr. Aldred along with him to live here.

Mr. Aldreds Portmantle was brought hither from Ormskirk.

My Wife, Coz: Edw: Scarisb: Mr. Aldred and I went to ye Grange we found there one Mr. Brockalds Pat: Tho: Wofold treated us wth Punch.

I walked with Mr. Aldred into ye Fields and showed him some Pits he might fish in.

Mary Molineux went away in a Passion and Stayed away all night.

My Wife stood Godmother for Mrs. Eckleston to Mrs. Blundells fifth Doughter.

I heard Rob: Blund: swear very much in the Town Medow as he was Shearing Beans. Jo: Banister got ye Clanaboyes and Batchler Apples.

Mary Brown would needs have gon away in a fret at Night tho ye Doars were Lock'd Nan Skinner was scouring Puter then.

Mary Brown left her Service.

1707.

Sept. 1st.   I sent W. Thel: to Hooton to congratulate yᵉ Birth of Mr. Standleys first Child it being a Son.

Sept. 6th.   I sent a Present of Apples &c to Mr. Clayton and Mr. Houghton.

Sept. 7th.   A Servant of Wm Cloughs yᵉ Younger came to Acquaint me that his Master was dead.

Sept. 20th.   At Leverp: I drunk with Dr Tarlton, James Houghton and Wm Atherton. I payed 20ˢ at yᵉ Exchange Coffyhous for a Periwig.

Sept. 29th.   Mr. Aldred dined at Lidiat with Mr. Andrew Moston &c.

Sept. 30th.   Wᵐ Fisher went along yᵉ Laines with me to seek for Run Sand.

Oct. 6th.   I Lead some Run-Sand from yᵉ Ford for my Flower Knot. The Jury met in the Townfield about seting out some wayes, we discoursed about ye Doostone thats set in Ri: Harrisons But.

Oct. 7th.   Mr. Ald: and I dined at Mr. Plumbs in Lever: thence we went to lodg at Hooton.

Oct. 8th.   Sⁱʳ Rowland Standley, his Son and I went to Poole town and drunk Claret at Sams.

Oct. 9th.   Mr. Standley, Mr. Aldred and I went to Poole Hall to see yᵉ Widdow.

Oct. 10th.   Mr. Aldred and I came from Hooton, Dr. Tarlton treated us with Wine at his own house, Mr. Plumb tryed his Lamp with two Weaks.

Oct. 12th.   Mr. Aldred and I went to Wm Thelwalls it being Crosby Goosfeast.

Oct. 13th.   Mr. Plumb and Dr Tarlton came to Cource with me. Mr. Bixter and Mr. Syer of yᵉ Ford came to us. Mr.

Hurst and his Wife dined here. Jo: Banister got a Pumpion that grew here 32 lbs weight (4ft. 2in. by 3ft. 5½in.).

Mr. Plumb kept my Court at Charles Howerds. Oct. 14th.

I went to Bold to wate of Mr. Molin: but he was gon a Oct. 15th. hunting, I dined there, Mrs. Molin: of Mosburgh was there.

I sent my Cart to Leverp: with Apples wch I sold for Oct. 17th. 2ˢ 6ᵈ per Buss:

Mr. Aldred and I went a Coursing thence to Mr. Wairings Oct. 20th. and eat some of his Goosfeast Cheer.

I sent Thelwall to Garswood to Congratulate the Bearth Oct. 21st. of their third Son.

My Wife and I went to Querks to see a Stage-Play Oct. 28th. acted, we called at yᵉ Hall of Ince and Mr. Blund: went along with us, we onely stayed part of it; there was Rich: Tickley, Mr. Molin: of yᵉ Grange, Mr. Rob: Chantrell and their Wives &c.

My Wife, Mr. Richardson and I went to Leverp: I Nov. 8th. bought some Brandy at Mr. Earls for Coz: Scarisb: and myself, a Woman demanded tole for it, I brought her before Mr. Maior who said I was not to pay any thing.

We had 217 at Prayers. Nov. 9th.

My Wife, Mr. Aldred and I went to Leve: Fair, I tasted Nov. 11th. some Wine and Brandy at Swarbericks, he gave us a treat of Sturgeon.

I went to Ormsk: to see my Aunt, I dined there with Nov. 13th. Mr. Wofold, Mrs. Hesketh of Rufford &c. Mr. Fazak: and his Wife gave me an Account of Cha: Howerd. I payed for a pair of Spit-Boots, Rich: Robinson was present at the Eagle and Child.

1707.
Nov. 18th.
Mr. Thom. Wofold told Mr. Aldr: that Mr. Babthrop was comne to yᵉ New-house.

Nov. 24th.
Mr. Darcy Chantrell and his Brother Rob: came hither Mr. Aldred and I went to the Chappell where Jo: Jackson was teaching to writ.

John Jackson of Little Crosby A Teacher of the Mathematics and Writeing Master . . . has a Wife and 4 Children . . . Peticons to be free.—*City Records.*

Nov. 25th.
My Wife and I went to Scarisb: to Christon Frances their third Doughter, my Wife was God-Mother and I stood for my Lord Mountg: My Wife fell of her Hors Coming home and hurt her Arme.

Nov. 29th.
I went to Leverp: and gave to Mr. Morecroft and Mr. Alanson each of them a Hare, I paid Mr. Alanson for Nailes, Tooles &c I paid Swarberick for Brandy and Vinegar. I drunk with Mr. Morecroft, Mr. Sandiford Parson Wairing &c. I think it was at Smiths near yᵉ Exchange.

Thos. Alanson was an ironmonger in Liverpool in 1686. John Sandiford, Town Clerk, was suspended on July 11, 1708, "for high Omissions and irregular transactions." He was subsequently discharged and £40 per annum allowed him for life. Sylvester Morecroft had been Mayor in 1706.

Dec. 2nd.
Pat: Gelibrond went hence, I could not prevale with him to hear yᵉ discourse about Leige.

Dec. 3rd.
Mr. Aldr: and I got yᵉ Schoolboys at Great Crosby leave to play. We took Parson Wair: to Nich: Johnsons and treated him, some little discours about Priests not Marrying.

Dec. 9th.
I went to the Moorehouses and ordered most of yᵉ Tenants to Bring some Boone Hens.

1707.
Dec. 15th.

Mr. Plumb, Mr. Ald: and I took down the Bed and Most of the Hangings in yᵉ Parlor Cham: we looked about then for Rats and Kill'd two.

Dec. 18th.

Doctor Tarlton came to Great-Crosby and sent to borrow my Grewhounds.

Dec. 19th.

I received an account of my Mothers death.

Dec. 20th.

My Wife and I went to Leverp: to buy Mourning for my Mother, we bought it at Mr. Hursts and some Musline &c at Mr. Morecrofts.

Dec. 30th.

Coz: Tho: Gelib: I and our Wives went in yᵉ Coach to Leverp: Mr. Ald: went along with us, we shewed our Wives the Sugar house. Mr. Plumb and Cap: Rob: Fazak: came to us at yᵉ Woolpack.

Dec. 31st.

Wm Anderton and Rich: Tatlock played here we had a Merry-Night, severall of Ince Servants were here.

1708.
Jan. 1st.

Most of my Servants if not all went to Ince to yᵉ Merry-Night.

Jan. 4th.

My Wife went to prayers to Leverp: to Pat: Gelib: at Mr. Lancasters.

Jan. 14th.

I had prayers for my Mother with five Sacerd: Mr. Hunter from Stony-hurst dined here. Richard Jackson yᵉ Innkeeper in Preston came along with him.

Rev. Thomas Hunter, S.J., born in Northumberland June 6, 1666, died February 21, 1725. While Chaplain to the Sherburn's, of Stonyhurst, he wrote in reply to Dodd, *A Modest Defence of the Clergy and Religions, &c.*

Jan. 17th.

I made a Viset to Widdow Blundell and Mrs. Standley at Preston.

Jan. 18th.

I went to Rich: Molin: and acquainted him that I had bought Mrs. Blackburns Estate, he told me that he would

1708.

not goe off it till Candlemas come twelve Months. Jo: Kerpy and Eliz: Py came to be Married but Mr. Aldred being gon to Lidiat to see Sr Pierce Mostons Son, they stay'd till he came after Super and then they were Marryed.

Jan. 27th.   Mr. Ald: shot a Bittern &c.

Jan. 31st.   I drunk wth Mr. Chorley ye Haberdasher at ye Woolpack, we discoursed about Shearing &c.

Feb. 3rd.   Mr. Ald: and I made up a Shod-Sledg or Tronow, my Wife, Bradley &c went with us to Formos-poole and rid in it. Mr. Aldred and I decided the difference between Henry Bridg and Wm. Davy ye Skinner.

Feb. 6th.   Mr. Ald: fixed a back to ye Sledg or Trenow.

Feb. 7th.   My Wife and three Servants walked to Lev: I walked after them and shot at ye Sea side. I called to look at ye Oyl mill. We all dined at ye Woolpack. Ere we came out of Town Mr. Plumb came to us and profered us a horse but we did not accept of it.

Feb. 8th.   Mr. Plumb lodged here he tryed to goe on Skates on the Carthous Pit.

Feb. 9th.   My Wife played at Whisk with us after Supper.

Feb. 17th.   My Wife and I saw them throw at ye Cock in ye Town-Field.

Feb. 23rd.   Leversage the Haberdasher brought a Hat hither for Mr. Ald:

Feb. 24th.   We went with Pat: Gelib: to Ned Howerds and shewed him the Chappell.

Mar. 2nd.   Mr. Wairing told us his Son was in danger to lose his Passage for Ireland, ye Ship being gon and he was fourced to ride after her on Shore and so get on Borde if he could.

1708.

We called to see Parson Wairing, he was trobled with Mar. 8th. yᵉ Stone and Gravell.

Mr. Aldred red to me yᵉ Prognostications of Esqʳ Mar. 9th. Bigerstaff.

In the following year, 1709, Swift was amusing himself and the readers of the *Tatler* with an account of the death and funeral of Patridge, one of these pretended astrologers.

We went to see Lord Molineux his Captain yᵉ Runner. Mar. 15th.

I went to yᵉ Funerall of old Widdow Culche: there was Mar. 17th. Mr. Blackbourn of Orford, Cap: Will: Bradshaw &c she was buried at Winwick.

My Hous was Serched for myself Horses and Armes Mar. 19th. &c by Ed: Willoby Esqʳ, Lievetennant Tomp: — Orme yᵉ High Cunstable &c: they seazed upon two of my Coach Horses viz: Jack and Robin and they are to be sent to them tomorrow.

I sent my two Horses according to Promis they were Mar. 20th. returned to be forth coming when called for.

I took a Wheel down out of the Fals Roof and mended Mar. 22nd. it to Spin Gersy with.

The false roof would be a hiding place. He had probably seen the wheel when occupying it during the search.

Most of my Servants went to see a Play at Mr. Smiths April 5th. in Sefton.

Mr. Ald: shaved my head. April 10th.

Mr. Rich: Molineux of the Grange and his Wife dined April 11th. here.

I Dined at Mr. Plumbs he and Doctor Tarlton drunk April 17th. with me at yᵉ Woolpack. I stated accounts with Halsold

1708.

yᵉ Brasier. I went to Mr. Coopers and saw his Flower Garden and also saw Mr. Danvers his Garden. I sent 4 or 500 Eggs to be sold in yᵉ Market at Leverp: I think they were all sold by two of my Maids.

April 20th.
I sent Henry Sum: to Fetch home my two Horses Hob and Buck and sent Rob Tompson for Bess and her Fole, I had sent them abroad to be secured.

April 24th.
I went to Leverp: and drunk at Dr Tarlt: wᵗʰ him Parson Stith and Mr. Walsh. I drunk at a Little Hous wᵗʰ Merchant Poole and Mr. Plumbe.

Rev. Robert Stythe, one of the two Rectors of Liverpool 1699. He died 1719. Rev. Henry Richmond was the other (1700), and died 1721. Mr. Welsh was the Curate.

April 28th.
Mr. Jo: Sherbourn and I went to Showley we Lodg'd there as did also Mr. Houghton of Thurnhom.

May 3rd.
I invited Parson Wairing to Dinner it was chiefly on account of a Dispute formerly between him and Mr. Ald: but he could not come.

May 16th.
Mr. Plumb sent an Express to give me Notice concerning an Information made against Mr. Blundell of Ince by Parson Ellison. I went to Ince to acquaint M. Blund: therewith and writ from thence to Mr. Plumb.

The Rev. Timothy Ellison was of Formby, and seems to have been the only parson in the neighbourhood disposed to invoke the Penal Law against the Catholics. His name occurs very rarely in the Diary.

May 18th.
My Wife dined at Bold she went on horsback and came yᵉ same day back, it was very wet and windy.

May 22nd.
I brought yᵉ Bowles down and showed them to Mr. Aldred he and I bowled a little in the Great-Courts.

My Wife, Mrs. Plumb, I &c went to Great Crosby and saw the Recruting Officer Acted, we drunk at Margarit Athertons with Parson Wairing, Mr. Bixter &c Mr. Syer of the Ford and his Wife, Mr. Lathom the Landlord of the Wool-pack and his Wife Suped here and after Super we went to Great Crosby and heard part of the Gigg.

My Wife and I went to Ormskirk Fair. My Lord Mountg: was come home out of Ireland after his Confinement in the Castle. My Lord Mountg: Coz: Scaresb: and his Lady, Mr. Wofold &c Rafled for a Tay-Table at Mr. Howets, all we that Rafled suped there.

I sent 30 Pair of Pigeons or more to Bold of a Present to Mr. Molineux.

They were sent on horseback in a pair of panniers covered with netting.

My Wife and I walked to Lidiat, coming back we called to see James Lidiats Wife, we lost our way in ye Medowes coming home and was directed right by John Lunt.

I went to Leverp: and had Rich: Ainsw: examined (for Robing me) before Mr. Rich: Norris ye Maior, Sr Tho: Johnson, Mr. Maydit, Mr. Morecroft &c.

Lord Mountg: came hither to heare Mr. Ald:

I went after dinner to Ormsk: to wate of my Lord Mountg: I found Mr. Syer of ye Ford at my Lords he was about swaping his Running Hors with my Lord Mountg: but they did not bargan, I Bowled wth my Lord Moutgarret, Mr. Leigh, Mr. Peter Ashton, Caligula &c from ye Bowing Green we went to the Black-bull to drink.

Lord Mountg: Coz: Scaresb: and his Wife I and my Wife went to Leverp: we made several Visets there viz: to Sr Tho: Johnson, to Mr. Clayton, &c.

1708.

June 17th. My Lord Mountg: Coz: Scarisb: and his Lady, I and my Wife dined at Agebourth. Mrs. Ann Harring: came hither with my Wife in the Coach.

June 19th. Lady Anderton, Mr. Blund and his Wife and Mr. Charls Harington dined here with yᵉ Rest of my Guests. One and twenty Adders were taken on my Midings.

June 21st. I sent Mrs. Ann Rothwell with a Present of 22 Adders to yᵉ Doctors of yᵉ Low.

This would be Dr. Fabius.

June 23rd. Mrs. Bootle blodyed my Wife. I gathered some Flowers for Flowering Great-Crosby Cross to-morrow.

June 24th. My Wife and I were at the Flowering of Great Crosby Cross. I Steeped my Feet in hot Whey for about two Hours to make my Cornes come out by yᵉ Roots but I think 'twill doe no good.

June 26th. My Wife and I went to Lodg at Coz: Tho: Gelib:

June 27th. Mr. Anderton of Euxton and his Wife, Mrs. Traps yᵉ Widdow and Mr. John Farnworth came after dinner.

June 28th. Mr. Brooks of Astley came to us. Pat: Gelib:, Coz: Tho: Gelib: Mr. Howet and I shot with Bow and Arrows and when we had done we went to Ned Luckases to pay our loosings in Aile.

June 30th. Coz: Tho Gelib: and I went to Yarrow Bridg, we bowled there with Sʳ Tho: Standish, Mr. Rob: Leigh, Parson Shaw, Mr. Allison, James Nicholson, &c.

July 2nd. My Wife and I came from Chorley, I called at Blanscow, thence to Wigan and dined at Dr Worthi:

July 7th. My Wife and I were at yᵉ Funerall of Mr. Bootle of yᵉ Peele, there were there Parson Dain, Parson

1708.

Fleetwood, Mr. Nich: Fazaker: Mr. Carroll Bootle, Mr. July 10th.
Bixter &c.

Darby Wife brought a Picture for Mr. Aldr: Alter-peece July 12th.
from Dr Lathoms which he had lent me.

I went to y⁰ Bowling-Green (at Liverpool) wᵗʰ Mr. July 16th.
Morcroft there was on y⁰ Green Mr. Rich: Norris, Dr
Tarlton Mr. Sheelds &c: Mr. Sheelds kicked y⁰ Bowl.

I dined at my Lord Mountgarrets, I was at y⁰ Funerall July 17th.
of old Mrs. Welsh, there was Coz: Rob: Scaresb: Mr.
Hesketh of Oughton and his Son &c.

Coz: Mun: Butler went with me to Lev: I bought July 19th.
some Wine in Lanslets Hey.

I went to Ormsk: Sessions where Mr. Molin: of Bold, July 26th.
Mr. Trafford, Mr. Harington I &c compounded to prevent
conviction, we Appeared in Court before Sʳ Tho: Standley
Dr Norris and Mr. Case all Justises of y⁰ Peace, We
Catholicks that got of our Convictions dined alltogether at
Rich: Woodses, after dinner we went to y⁰ New-Club-hous
and thence came back to Rich: Woodses and drunk Punch
with Sʳ Tho: Standley.

Mr. Blundell of Ince was one of the party, and this step was
perhaps the result of the information laid against him by Parson
Ellison, and which might at any moment have been lodged against
the rest. A composition at sessions freed them from the higher
penalties which would have followed a conviction in the Superior
Courts.

I saw y⁰ Souldiers Fortune Acted in Ri: Harris: Barn. July 29th.

Mr. Aldred went hence to live in y⁰ Town.

I served Mr. Aldr: y⁰ first time he Sayed in his New July 30th.
Chappell.

My Wife came home from Burchley, she had been July 31st.
some time at Wigan drinking Hilton Spaw water.

1708.

Aug. 4th.

I Bowled at Ince Green with old Rob: Bootle, Edw: Trustrom &c. Gill yᵉ Excise-man and yᵉ Inquisitor over him came to yᵉ Aile-hous whilst we were drinking.

Aug. 6th.

Cap: Rob: Faz: and I went to Mr. Aldreds, we found him in yᵉ Cross-field, he had been taking young Bitterns.

Aug. 7th.

The Souldiers Fortune was Acted in my Hall, Wm Marser did not Act.

Aug. 12th.

Mrs. Ann Rothw: and some Children of yᵉ Town Songoed Wheat for me in yᵉ Cross Field.

Aug. 13th.

The Actors of yᵉ Souldiers Fortune came hither and sung the Gigg.

Aug. 14th.

I saw my Lord Darby the Maior of Leverp: make his Entry into the Town.

Aug. 18th.

I went to Lancaster to prosecute Rich: Ainsw: for Robery. Mr. Plumb overtook me in Maile. We dined together at Coolings yᵉ Miter in Preston, thence I went to Marshalls the Queens Arms in Lancaster where I lodged.

Aug. 20th.

Rich: Ainsworth was found guilty of Robery before Judge Trecy.

Aug. 21st.

Rich: Ainsw: and two others were burned in yᵉ hand. I dined at my Inn with Mr. Parker of Brusam.

Brusam—Browsholme.

Aug. 22nd.

I made a Viset to Coz: Blundells from thence I went to Coz: Standleys, Coz: Tho: Culcheth went with me, we found there his brother John Cul: Mr. Blund: of Ince, Dr Farington &c.

Aug. 24th.

Most of my Servants went to Charls Howers to see yᵉ Souldiers Fortune Acted.

1708.

I made a Viset to Mr. Hollands of Sutton, thence I Aug. 25th. went to y⁰ Hall of Wofold.

I gave Mr. Norris y⁰ Maior of Leverp: a Bottle of Wine Aug. 27th at Proctors. Mr. Plumb was with us.

I went to Croxtath to welcome my Lord Molin: home Aug. 29th. from Bardsey.

Bardsea, three miles from Ulverston, had been then recently purchased from the Andertons, of Clayton, by Lord Molyneux for a hunting seat.

I began y⁰ first time to make Milk Punch. Aug. 30th.

I stood Godfather with Coz: Bridg: Blund: to Mr. Sept. 12th. Blundells sixth Doughter viz Eliz:

I went to Ormsk: to see Dr Gerard. Sept. 13th.

I went to wish Sʳ Fracis Anderton and his Lady Joy, Sept. 16th. they were gone to Culcheth but they came home to Lostock where I Lodged.

Sir Francis Anderton had at that period no right to the title of baronet, his elder brother, Lawrence, being a monk abroad. He had just married Frances, daughter of Sir Henry Bedingfield, of Oxburgh, Co. Norfolk, Bart., but his wife did not live long, nor had they any issue.

Sʳ Nicho: Sherbourn, Sʳ Wᵐ Gerard, Mr. Thomas Sept. 17th. Culsheth &c dined at Lostock.

Sʳ Fran: Ander: and his Lady went to Shaw-place to Sept. 18th. wate of Lord Willoby, I went with them and Carryed Mrs. Ann Harington behind me.

Coz: Bacon and I saw y⁰ Souldiers Fortune Acted or Sept. 21st. at least most of it at Mrs. Ann Rothwells. My Wife walked to Ince but came back to see part of y⁰ Play and all y⁰ Gigg.

1708.
Sept. 22nd. I helped John Farer and others to find out whether Mrs. Ann was cozened in her Shot at yᵉ Play.

Sept. 30th. I sent Coz: Bacon back to Standish. I made Wax of yᵉ Combes I had, it was extreamly Bad.

Oct. 13th. My Wife and I went to Aigbourth to wish Mr. Charls Harington Joy he had then brought his Wife thither. We dined there with Sʳ James Poole, Mr. Molineux of Mosbourgh his Wife, Brother William, one Jolly a Scotch Taylor &c.

Mr. Charles Harrington, eldest son of John Harrington, Esq., of Aigburth (buried at Huyton Church, April 14, 1714), had just married Anne, daughter of Sir Rowland Stanley, of Hooton, Co. Cheshire, Bart. They took up their abode at Scholes Hall, where he died, and was buried at Huyton, March 12, 1719. She was buried at Huyton, October 14, 1722. Mr. John Harrington had acquired Aigburth by marriage with the heiress, Dorothy Tarleton. In 1713 John Harrington, of Aigburth, petitions the Lords for a Bill to sell his wife's property in Liverpool—43 tenements, Harrington Street.

Oct. 15th. My Wife and I was at yᵉ Buriall of Bryan Bryanson Rich: Tickley, Mr. Molineux of the Grange and their Wives were at yᵉ house.

Oct. 16th. I drunk at yᵉ Woolpack in Leverp: with Mr. Plumb and Ben Brankhurst I settled accounts with Holsold yᵉ Brasior. I and Rob: Sutton endeavoured to make John Aindow to goe home with his Wife.

Oct. 18th. It being Crosby Goosfeast I dined at Mr. Wairings with him, his two sons, one Williamson yᵉ Schoolmaster of Formby, Tho: Syer of yᵉ Ford &c. The Maids stayed late and were locked out.

Oct. 19th. It being Crosby Goosfeast my Wife and I went to Wm Tarltons, thence we went to Nich: Johnsons, Wm Tarlton and his Wife were with us, thence we went to Ned Hattons.

Peggy Thelw: and I songowed for Apples in my Orcherds.

I went to Leverpoole and made a Viset to Mr. Brownbill
in his New hous in John Street. I brought my Weding
Coat to Mr. Plumb for him to take with him into Ireland,
but he took it not.

I went to Leverp: and found Mr. Houghton at his
Bowling Green, I drunk wth Mr. More of Manchester at
my own Inn.

I made up some Doses of Powder for ye Falling Sickness for Mary Pilkingtons Sister.

Going to Dungen hall I called at Seath Woodcocks and
saw Mr. Barlows Water Engin.

I went from Dungen to Showley to wish young Mr.
Walmesley Joy of his London Wife.

Thomas Walmesley, son and heir of Richard Walmesley, of
Showley, Esq., and his wife, Jane, sister of William Houghton, Esq.,
of Park Hall, was born October 21, 1685. He had recently married
Mary, daughter of William Colgreave, Esq. In 1870, the Showley
estate was sold by Thos. George Walmesley, Esq., to the late Mr.
James Eden.—*Abram's History of Blackburn*, p. 459.

I dined at Preston with Coz: Jo: Gelibrond Mr.
Gradall &c.

I dined at Mr. Aldreds with Mr. Moston, Mr. Thornton
and Dr Worthington, it being ye Doctors birth day he gave
us a bole of Punsh, whilst we were at dinner Mr. Babthrop
and Mr. Manock Came to us and dined.

I Began to make a dose of Phisick for Wm. Tompson
for ye Dropsy.

My Wife was going towards Leverp: but Harper would
not carry her, so she was fourced to light and walk back,
I went with her single to Leverp:

1708.

Nov. 22nd.   I strained my Ink which I have ben long in making.

Nov. 25th.   I walked to see Parson Letus but he was gon to Walton, his Landlord Mr. Lucas was at home.

Nov. 26th.   My Wife went to lodge at · Neston at Mr. Darcy Chantrells.

Nov. 29th.   Mr. Aldred, Parson Wairing, and Parson Letus dined here.

Nov. 30th.   I was going to Ince to see Mr. Tasburg but hearing he was not at home I turn'd back and found Grace Pilkington endeavouring to open yᵉ Dining Roome dore with some Keys she had got to get Apples to give to Ince Servants.

Dec. 1st.   Mr. Aldred and I dined at Mr. Thorntons at yᵉ New-hous.

Dec. 7th.   Lord Mountgar: and Pat: Gelib: went to Leverp: to meet Sʳ Wᵐ Gerard and Sʳ Rowland Standley about Mr. Chantrells business of Noctorum.

Dec. 9th.   My Wife went to see Mrs. Scarisb: who was lying in of her son Joseph.

Dec. 10th.   Mr. Gilbert Sail of Hopkar gave consent (to a sale of land by Sʳ Roger Bradshaigh) he being one of Sir Rogers Creditors.

Dec. 16th.   I endeavourd to cast up part of yᵉ Slating and Flaging at Ditton but was so long blundering about it that I dozed my self.

Dec. 20th.   Mr. Aldr: gave my Wife a very fine Pair of Ivory tenns of his own making.

Dec. 21st.   I heard Mass at Lidiat thence I went to Lord Mount-garrets I dined there whilst I was there Mrs. Hesketh of

Rufford went past, she was going to Thurnom. I went
awhile to yᵉ Club to yᵉ Golden-Lyon there was there
Lord Mountga: Mr. Tho: Leigh, Mr. Peter Ashton, Mr.
Howet, &c.

Mr. Faza: Mr. Howet and I went to Ince to wate of
Sʳ Francis Anderton and Mr. Harington &c it being Mr.
Blundells Birthday we had a Bowl of Punch there. Our
Wives went in yᵉ Coach to Parson Richmonds of Walton.
We had Musick at Night.

My Wife Mrs. Faza: and Mrs. Howet went in our
Coach to Ince to wate of yᵉ Young Lady Anderton. Sʳ
Francis Anderton drove yᵐ home. He had been here
before with Mr. Ch: Harington and his Brother John we
drunk yᵉ Butlers health in my Seller. We had two Fidlers
Tatlock and Wassall.

Sʳ Fran: Anderton Mr. Blund: Mr. Charls Harington
and their Ladys Made a Viset here, old Mr. Haring: &c
was also here, the Gentlemen drunk in yᵉ Gallery. Mr.
Plumb lodged here, he I, &c dansed country danses after
Super.

My Wife, Mrs. Fazak: Mrs. Howet and Mr. Faza:
went in yᵉ Coach to see a Rase on yᵉ Sands between one
Hors of Sʳ Fran: Anderton one of old Mr. Haringtons
and two of Mr. Chs Har: it was cheefly for diversion and
for some few shillings which was layed out in a Treat at
Mr. Ald: Mr. Faz: his Wife and my Wife went to Ince
a Maskarading.

Mr. Fazak: and I went to the Grange, there was there
Sʳ Fra: Ander: Mr. Blund: Mr. Char: Haring: and their
Ladys &c Pat: Wofold treated us men with very good
Punch.

1709.

Jan. 4th. I cupled Hector and Speed together and led them thorough ye Town to teach them to goe quietly cupled.

Jan. 5th. Mr. Fazak: went hence Mr. Aldred and I went with him to Ormsk: we dined at his hous thence we went to Lord Mountgar: we were at ye Club ye Golden Lyon with Mr. Howet &c.

Jan. 8th. My Wife and I went to Leverp: Bradley went along with us in order to make an End one way or other with her Preston Spark. My Wife and I got a Snap of a dinner at Mrs. Lancasters we bought some lofe Sugar there.

Jan. 11th. Mr. Aldr: and I had a deal of discourse about Fatoning of Kattle and Sheep after ye Beyond-Sea manner.

Jan. 13th. Mr. Walmesley the Elder of Showley lodged here. Wassal ye Fidler played here at night. I played at Cut in ye Hall.

Jan. 14th. I went with Mr. Walmes: to Th: Syers of the Ford, Mr. Wal: sold some land to him I played some tricks there of Leger de Mesney.

Jan. 15th. Mr. Walm: went to Leverp: he Mr. Ald: and I drunk wine at Mr. Morphews I bought some Brandy of him Mr. Pryer drunk at ye Woolpack with me.

Jan. 22nd. My Wife went with me to Leverp: Mrs. Allison treated us with Jocolet.

Jan. 23rd. I went to Lidiat and heard Mr. Moston hold forth, I dined there. My Wife heard Mr. Burton hold forth at Formby.

Rev. Christopher Burton, S.J., had succeeded Rev. Richard Forster at Formby. He ended his days at Watten, July 23, 1744, aged 73. His sister Catherine, a Carmelite Nun at Antwerp, was eminent for piety, and her life by Rev. Thomas Hunter was edited in 1876 by Father Coleridge, S.J.—See *Foley's Records.*

In yᵉ Evening Mr. Plumb and I went to yᵉ flight at Formospoole but we Shot nothing.

Holme shaped a Pair of Breeches for me of Norway Leather.

I went to Leverp: I drunk in yᵉ Woolpack with Mr. Plumb, Mr. Secomb yᵉ Maior, Mr. Pryor &c I sold a Gold Ring and some Silver Lase to Mr. Branker. Mr. Ald: Ch: How: and Wm Anderton shot among them three Swans the largest of them weighed above 27 Pound 5ft. 4½in. long and 8ft. 5in. across. Ch: How: gave me one which I sent to Mr. Plumb.

I gave Jo: Blundell severall peeses of Parchment to be Taylors mesures. I mended a Smoothing Iron.

Mr. Trafford of Croston, Mr. Blund: of Ince and their Wives made a Viset here.

I went to yᵉ Aile-hous at Sefton Church to consult about scouring yᵉ River Alt. I met there Mr. Blund: of Ince, Mr. Maile, Mr. Tatlock, Mr. Fazakerley of Prescot, Yeomor of yᵉ Gore, Ro: Bootle, &c.

I went to Ormskerk to wate of my Lord Mountgarrets Eldest Son Coz: Richar: Butler who was come home from Schoole.

I fetched a load of Malt from Mr. Houghtons Kill at Leverp: it being yᵉ first I have had made there.

A Grand falling out with Bradley upon which she went out of yᵉ Hous with an intention to goe quite away but she came back againe.

I took yᵉ Coffy Mill in peeses to see what was yᵉ falt with it.

1709.

Mar. 7th.   Lord Mountg: and his Son, Coz: Scaresbrick and his Lady dined here.

Mar. 8th.   We eat Pankakes at Ri: Newhouses and Ra: Nel: thence we went to Ni: Johnsons and eat Pancakes we saw part of a Cock fight in Great Crosby.

Mar. 10th.   My Wife and I made a Viset to Parson Letus and his Wife it being ye first time we had ben there to see them since they were married.

> Rev. Wm. Latus, Curate of Sefton, had married Anne, daughter of John Crosse, of Crosse Hall, Chorley, and his wife Ann, daughter of Mr. Samuel Yate, of Middle Cheney, Co. Northampton. He died 1719.

Mar. 12th.   I drunk at ye Woolpack wth James Williamson and his Son Henry, with Rich: Plumpton, James Duxbury &c.

Mar. 14th.   I dined at Carr Hall with Mr. Burton and Mr. Moston. Mr. Tho: Gorsuch and Mr. Mainard came hither.

Mar. 18th.   I went to Mr. Ropers and discoursed him about ye Management of Clover Grass, thense I went to Leverp: and discoursed Mr. Secomb ye Maior about buying some Clover Seed for me.

Mar. 19th.   I went to ye Funerall of Mr. Howet of Ormsk. Lord Mountg: Mr. Molin: of Mosby: Mr. Scarisb: Parson Siddall, Mr. Jo: Heyes &c were there.

> From this array of names it is evident that Thos. Howet or Hawett, Esq., held a very respectable position in life. His daughter Mary married, 1709, John Westby, of White Hall, near Garstang, Esq.

Mar. 21st.   I payed Wm Harrison, Clark of Sefton, 2^d instead of Paist Eggs.

Mar. 25th.   Walter Thelwall left my Service he has been Servāt here about 35 years.

1709.
Mar. 26th.

I was at yᵉ Funerall of Edm: Trustroms Wife. This was yᵉ Fiveteenth Buriall that has ben out of Ince-Township since about a week before Christmas and yᵉ Sexton told me he thought there had not been above six more in that time out of all other parts of yᵉ Parish.

Mar. 28th.

I went after Mr. Blu: when he was going towards yᵉ Rase at Leton Heys.

April 1st.

I Counted yᵉ holes in yᵉ Dove Court there was 689. I went to Leverp: and sold my Rabet Skins to Leversage. Mr. Scofild yᵉ Apothecary gave me some Jue Jubs and Date Stones.

April 6th.

Lord Mountg: and his Son Rich: and Sʳ James Poole dine here, after dinner I went with them to Dukes we drūk a Bowl of Punch there and looked at yᵉ three Running Horses.

Marmaduke Maltus, of Great Crosby, Innkeeper, was at this time trainer for Lord Molyneux.

April 10th.

Sʳ Jam: Poo: went hence I went wᵗʰ him as far as yᵉ Hall of Magull where I became acquainted wᵗʰ Mr. Smith and his Wife.

April 11th.

Mr. Faz: of yᵉ Hill house dined here.

April 15th.

My Wife had yᵉ first certain Account of my Grand-Mother Webs death from my Brother Langdale.

April 18th.

Rich: Harrison dyed about 3 in yᵉ Morning he had been servant 18 years to my Grandfather he was a truly Honest Man and of very sound Judgment. Wᵐ Starkey dyed about eleven of yᵉ Clock at Noone he was my Cow-Man and had ben Servant to yᵉ Family about years and I think never a meniall Servant in mÿ Fathers time nor of a great will of mine but towards yᵉ latter end of his time I mantained him at my own hous with Apparell and all things necessary.

April 19th.

Ri: Harrison and Wm Starkey were buried, they (were) met at ye Cross by Watkinsons, my Wife, I and Mally were at their Funerall as were all my Men Servants.

April 24th.

I went to Ditton and lodged at ye Bank.

April 25th.

I heard Mr. Mair pray, James Hough: Hen: Roson &c were there. I was at Farnworth in ye Chappell when ye Chappell Wardens brought in their accounts, there was present Parson Ainscow, Mr. John Write, Mr. Nich: Bold of Marsh Hall, Samuell Williamson, John Holden, Peter Slinhead &c I did there declare I would not pay by way of a Church Ley towards mantaining ye Parson and tho Six Church Leys had ben gathered I got mine back againe, then I gave 6^s 6^d to Parson Ainscow as a free Giuft.

April 26th.

I Went to Southward and heard prayers at Ralph Keyes. I dined at Southward. Mr. Golding came home after dinner.

May 1st.

Duke Bluddyed my Wife, Nich: Johnson Wm Gray, I &c were present.

May 4th.

I was at ye Funerall of Mr. Magull of Magull there was at ye Hous Mr. Blund: Parsons Brownbill, Walker, and Letus, Mr. Carrold Bootle, Mr. Pe: Morton, &c.

May 7th.

I went to Leverp: I set a great while wth Mr. Sil: Richmond at his Hous, we discoursed about Planting, sowing Cole Seed and improving Groud.

May 11th.

My Wife went to Leverp: with an Intention to have gon to Hooton, but ye Sea being very rough she did not venture over. Parson Bruce Lodg'd here.

I sowed one Buss: of Barley in yᵉ Cowhey dresed May 13th. with Oyle and other Ingredients as Powder of Coleseed &c but it did not answer expectation.

I went to Leverp: I bought a new half Buss: and saw May 14th. it Cut and sealed in yᵉ Exchange. I drunk with Mr. Tute Captain Tarlton, Mr. Molin: of yᵉ Grange &c at yᵉ Kings Armes.

Mr. Silv: Richmond came hither, I went out with May 17th. him to look at some Ground to see if it was proper for Cole-Seed.

Wᵐ Ainsw: went to Burchley of a How-doe-you to May 21st. Mrs. Poole who was Lying in.

I was at yᵉ Sale of Timber at Mr. Bootles in Melling May 25th. it belongs to Thomas Hurst Ship Carpinder of Leverp:

My Wife went to Burchley to see Mrs. Poole who was May 26th. lying in.

The She-Gallats was Acted Imperfectly in yᵉ Hall. May 27th.

Bradley, Wᵐ Ainsw: Dorothy Blundell &c were con- May 29th. firmed at More Hall. My Wife and Mrs. Howet went to prayer to Lidiat they dined there.

I came home through Leverp: and went to yᵉ Castle May 31st. to see what alteration was made.

Most of my Servants were at Ince to heare the Bish: June 2nd. Lord Bish: and his Companion Mr. Riding made a Viset here.

This would be Bishop Smith, who did not give confirmations at Crosby on this occasion. His Chaplain, Mr. Royden, born 1662, ordained priest at Douay, 1692, was Vicar General.

My Wife went to Croxtath to welcome home my Lady June 11th. Molin: from Bardsy. I met her at Leverp: and came

1709.

June 12th.   home in y⁰ Coach, we made a Viset to Mrs. Clayton.   I was some time with Little Mr. Kelly.

June 14th.   Mr. Ald: and I made a Viset to Ince, we set some time with Mr. Tasb: in his Chamber.

June 17th.   I Acquainted Tho: Blansh: that Will Tompson and others complained he did not do Neighbourly things.

June 18th.   I dined at Garswood and signed some writings for selling Knoctorum to Mr. Chantrell, he came with me as far as Knowsley where we called and drunk at the Gates.

June 20th.   I drunk at y⁰ Wole-pack with Mr. Hurst, Mr. Plumb, Mr. Poole of Low-hill &c.

June 22nd.   I played some tricks of Legar demesne before some of my Marlers.

          I went to Leverpoole it being the first Market that was on a Wednesday. I druk at y⁰ Woolpack wᵗʰ Mr. Tandy Sʳ Cleave Mores Ingeneer for his Water, wᵗʰ Mr. Hurst, Mr. More-Croft, Mr. Alanson &c.

June 27th.   Tomkins a Hater of Leverp: Came to looke at my Wool he bought it not.

June 28th.   Coz: Scarisb: and I were at y⁰ Funerall of old Mrs. Blundell of Ince, oure Wives also met y⁰ Corps there was at y⁰ Funerall Lord Mountg: and his Son, Mr. Standley of Preston and his Son &c, as we were coming out of y⁰ Church Mr. Clayton of Leverpoole and Mr. Hurst just came.

    Mrs. Blundell was Bridget, daughter of the famous cavalier, Sir Thomas Tildesley, Knight, who fell at Wigan Lane in 1651. Henry Blundell, her husband, had died in 1687, and she died at Preston, where she had resided during the latter years of her widowhood.

Coz: Scarisb: and I were at Wigan Cocking, we dined
at Twotalls with S^r Fr: Anderton, Mr. Hesketh ye High
Sheriff, Mr. Dodd, Mr. Cheetom Mr. Brathord &c I Joyned
with ye Sheriff for a Bottle of Wine at Dinner, when y^e
Cocking was over I drunk above Stayres with S^r W^m
Gerard, Mr. Townley, Mr. Lancton, Mr. Hu: Anderton &c.

Lord Mountg: and his Son and Mr. Tho: Leigh dined
and Suped at Scarisbrick. I saw Mr. Smith of Croston
doing somthing at Coz: Scarisbricks great Diall.

The Rev. John Smith, S.J., had been Chaplain at Scarisbrick,
but was now with the Traffords, of Croston. He died 1754, aged
85. Rev. John Maynard, S.J., succeeded him at Scarisbrick.

Coz: Scarisb: I and oure Wives dined at my Lord
Mountgarrets, we dansed at Houghtons with my Lord
Mountg: and his Son and Doughter Emilia who was
lately come from York and with Mr. Thomas Legh.

Ince Gardiner helped Jo: Banister to Innoculate.

My Wife and I went to Leverp: I drunk a while at
Mr. Sil: Richmods with his Brother Henry and I think
Mr. Brooks of Norton, Mr. Waintworth &c.

Coz: Dick Butler went in ye Coach with my Wife and
me to Leverpoole, Coz Dick Butler and I drunk Wine
with Mr. Rolins at his Hous. Mrs. Sheelds Son played
to us of ye Violin at the Woole Pack.

Mary Winstanley told me the Business was quite of
with her Warick-Shire Spark.

My Wife, Mrs. Howet, and I went to Wigan, we
dined at ye Leggs of Man. I met the Duke of Norfolk
and his Dutches behind Ashton in their way towards
Stonyhurst. I drunk at Ashton with the Duke, his two

1709.

Brothers, Sir Nicholas Sherbourn, Sʳ Wᵐ Gerard &c. I Wated of yᵉ Duck and Dutches &c to Wigan and supped at Tootalls with the Duke of Norfolk and his two Brothers, Sʳ Nicholas Sherbourn, Sʳ Fran: Anderton, My Lady Dutches of Norfolk, Lady Savell, Lady Howerd &c.

July 29th.

I Wated of yᵉ Duke and Dutches of Norfolk &c out of Wigan part of their way towards Preston.

Thomas, 8th Duke of Norfolk, had just married Mary, only daughter and heiress of Sir Nicholas Sherburne, Bart., of Stonyhurst, Lancashire. The Duke died without issue, December 23, 1732, but the Duchess survived him till September 24, 1754. She spent her widowhood at Stonyhurst, but took a second husband in the person of the Hon. Peregrine Widdrington, belonging to a noble Northumbrian family, whose fortunes were shipwrecked in the disasters of 1715. The monument to him in Mitton Church is one of three erected by his lady, all sufficiently prolix, and yet the fact of their marriage is not recorded. Dr. Whittaker says that she had no mercy on the stonecutter.

July 31st.

I went to Ince to wish Mr. Blund: welcome home from York-Shire Spaws.

Aug. 2nd.

He (Mr. Aldred) began to gather Pins for one year.

Aug. 7th.

I went to Dr. Lathoms and asked him for a Receipt for one at York Schoole.

Aug. 13th.

Going to Leverp: I called at Bank-Hall, Mr. More shewed me part of a Sluce which Tandy had made for his Waterwork.

Aug. 15th.

Mr. Worthington of Blans: came to us, coming home (to Coz: Tho: Gellibronds) Coz: Tho: Gelibrond I &c Stormed Bark Stack Castle.

Aug. 16th.

I went to Preston Faire, I dined at Coz: Walm: Mr. Houghton yᵉ Elder came. I drunk at Dick Jacksons with Mr. Barlow of Barton Mr. Leomond &c.

1709.

My Wife and I began our Joûrney toward Whit-Chourch, Aug. 18th. we came too late for yᵉ Boats at Leverp: so we went over at Runkhorne after wᶜʰ we lost our way and went to Windy Weston where we got a Guide that brought us to Fradsom.

We went from John Websters the Signe of yᵉ Bears Aug. 19th. Paw at Fradsom to Whit-Church to Mr. Benbows yᵉ Signe of yᵉ Red Lyon where we dined and discoursed Dr. Bostock about my Wives Paine in her back, from Whit-Church we went to Chester where we lodged at Mr. Taylors yᵉ Signe of yᵉ Golden Lyon.

We saw several of yᵉ Paletines in the Wool-hall &c. Aug. 20th. We dined at Chester and thence went to yᵉ Rock hous, but the Boat was gon, so we got a Smoke made, but no Boat coming to us we went to yᵉ Wood-Side where Mr. Darcy Chantrell came to us and got a Boat for us, so we came home.

Jo: Banist: and I clensed some of the Windows with Aug. 23rd. Chalk but it did not do well.

There came an express from Croston to enquire for Aug. 25th. Wall Frute &c for Sʳ Nicho: Sherbourne.

Jo: Banister went to Leverp: and sold some Pigeons Aug. 26th. that yᵉ Croston Express would not take with her. I went to my Burners in the Winterheys and gave them a Sillibube.

Coz: Dick Butler dined here. Mr. Ald: and I went Aug. 30th. with him to yᵉ New-hous from thence Mr. Burton came with us to Ince Greene, we four Played at Bowles Mr. Molin: of yᵉ Grange was there.

1709.
Aug. 31st.

I Transcribed my Grandfathers Song to y° Tune of Roger o' Coverley, tis to be sent to Mr. Townley of York.

This lively song of the "Cavalier's" will be found in *A Cavalier's Note Book*, p. 233. Mr. Charles Townley, brother to Richard Townley, of Townley, Esq., was a literary as well as a very amiable man. A short account of him is given in the *Palatine Note Book*, vol. I, p. 125, and at p. 134 some correspondence between him and the "Cavalier" is inserted. Mr. Townley died at York in 1712, and was buried April 29, at All Saints' Church.

Sept. 3rd.

I wated of Dr. Clayton at his Brothers.

Sept. 7th.

I went to Grange Bowling Green, there was Mr. Fazak: of y° Hill hous, Mr. Formby, Parson Letus, Rob: Bootle y° Elder, Mr. Burton &c. Mrs. Poole of Burchley lodged here.

Sept. 9th.

I went in y° Coach to Leverp: wth my Wife and Mrs. Poole of Burchley, we went to Mr. Hursts then to Mrs. Letonbys, then to y° New Church thence to Mr. Scarisbricks, thence to Mr. Dones, next to Mr. Claytons and so home.

Sept. 10th.

My Wife, Mrs. Poole, Mr. Ald: and I went in y° Coach to Lidiat to see Mr. Moston.

Sept. 11th.

We dined at Ince; there dined there Mr. Wofold of Morehall his Wife, his Sister Wall and brother William. Mr. Scofield y° Appothecary from Leverp: came hither.

Sept. 22nd.

Pat: Wofold, Brother Formby and Mr. Ald: called here.

Sept. 26th.

I payed Mr. Tasb: 15^s for a Medall of King Charles.

Oct. 13th.

At Ince we found Dominick Sherbourn.

Oct. 14th.

Coz: Dick Butler and I Coursed a Hare that Jo: Blund: Write found set, they were breaking at his Hous and lifted me.

1709.

Lord Mountg: and his Son dined here I went with Oct. 18th. them to Great Crosby Goos-feast, we eat at Wm Tarltons, we went to a Rase on Crosby Marsh between a Black Mare of Jo: Gerards of Garswood, and a Bay Mare of Leverpoole.

Went to Ince to wate of Sr Wm Gerard and my Lady, Oct. 20th. we found there Lord Molineux, Mr. Scaresb: Mr. Harington, Young Mr. Gerard of Highfield, &c.

I set up a good new Dyall Post in the Bleaching yard. Oct. 21st.

Wassall played here, we had a Merry Night. Oct. 28th.

I sent Jo: Banister with a Brace of Hares to Alderman Nov. 2nd. Clayton.

I went to Bootle to see how Sr Clave Mors Waterwork Nov. 7th. went forward.

Mr. Aldred went with me to Mosb: we dined there Nov. 8th. with Sr James Poole, Mrs. Mary Standley of Hooton &c. Mr. Molin: of Mosburg gave me some Carp Fray &c which we took to day with drawing and draining part of his Fishpond.

Darby's Wife brought me from Mosbu: 138 Carp Fray, Nov. 9th. 8 Tensh Carp or Mungrills and 22 Loaches.

The old Man Tho: Kirklington who sells Picturs and Nov. 12th. Tenns was here.

I Hiered Cha: Howerd to be my Ploughman, Coachman Nov. 17th. &c and am to give him 50^s p Ann:

Mr. More of Bank-hall and one Mr. Fitz Gerald dined Nov. 23rd. here.

Leverpoole Hounds hunted near the hous. Nov. 25th.

1709.

Nov. 27th.   I sent Jos: Massy to Leverp: for a Pennance becaus he refused to fetch a Mugg of Butter out of yᵉ Town.

Nov. 29th.   I went to Leverp: and made a Viset to Mr. Plumb who was not very well. I drunk Mr. Chorley's farewell with Mr. Alanson, I saw Sʳ Clave More at yᵉ Post Office.

Nov. 30th.   I went to Warington Fair and sold my Mare Harper she is designed for one Mr. Bradshaw of Manchester for a Hunter; there was one Mare sold at five farthings p Pound. I dined at Dʳ Booths in Waring: with Mr. Maior alias Hard:

Dec. 5th.   We made some Math, a mistake both in yᵉ Quantity of Hunny and Water.

Dec. 6th.   I hung up my Paletine Church in the hall.

Dec. 14th.   I went to see Parson Letus who was ill of a brocken Legg, I found there Mr. Walker, Curat of Male. I found Darby and Skinner Blundell playing at Tables at Ailes Davys after eleven of yᵉ Clock at Noon they had been playing all yᵉ Night.

Dec. 27th.   Mr. Blund: and his two Sisters Bridget and Dorot: suped here. Wassell was here we had a Merri night we dansed Country Danses.

Dec. 28th.   Wassell was here we had a Merri night and Fyered yᵉ Gunns.

Dec. 29th.   Lord Mountg:, Mr. James Tildesley, and Cap: Rob: Faza: dined and lodged here. Coz: Doro: Blundell and Mrs. Holland from Leverp: Lodg'd here, we dansed Country Danses after Super.

1710.

Jan. 9th.   Dr Smithson came to see me and let me blood.

Jan. 22nd.   I sent Joh: Banist: to yᵉ Funerall of Lord Mountgarrets youngest Doughter, but it seems she was buryed last night.

Mr. Ri: Wairing came to take leave of me, he designs Jan. 31st. to goe to Bristold.

I Rosted my Steeped Wheat to make Coffy on but it Feb. 6th. did not doe well.

Mrs. Brid: Blund: and her Sister Dorothy came to take Feb. 7th. leave of my Wife being they were going away from Ince.

Jo: Banist: sowed some Tobacco Seed. Some of it Feb. 13th. came up but he brought it not to any perfection.

My Wife and I dined at my Lord Mountg: it being y^c Feb. 20th. first time we had eather of us ben there since his Son and Doughter had the small Pox. Young Mr. Tyrer sent hither for some Pigeons.

The Boys of this Town flung at a Mallard in a Tub Feb. 21st. of Water.

I called at Darbys and discoursed him and his Wife Mar. 2nd. about their Son Katching Rabets.

I payed Wm Harrison 2^d instead of Paist Eggs. Peter Mar. 13th. Whit read *Masinellows Revolution at Naples* to me.

My Wife and I went to see Peter Whits Ship that Mar. 30th. lyes in Farcloughs Lake, he dined with us at John Rimers in ye Meales and after dinner he went on bord his Ship the Betty with us.

Farcloughs Lake is set down on a chart in the Liverpool Library, published by Samuel Fearon and John Eyes (1738), entitled *A Chart of the Sea Coast from the Harbour of Wyer to Black Comb, &c.* It was a gut or fret in the bank opposite "The Sugar Houses" near North Meols, and was apparently two miles long by about half a mile broad, nearest the sea, narrowing landwards. (Communicated by Mr. P. Cowell, Librarian).

Peter Whit: was going in his Ship from Farcloughs April 5th. Lake towards Leverp: but he himself landed near y^e

Grange, he sent his Ship forwards and Walked hither on foot, I lent him a Hors to ride on to Leverpoole. I sent John Banister to Leverp: with a present of Apples to Mr. Houghton, Mr. Clayton &c.

April 10th.

Went to Farnworth, to the Cocking at Giligants ye Signe of the Naggs Head. I drunk with Mr. Hardig of ye Lougher house, Mr. Harding of the Hook Hous, Jam: Houghton, &c.

. April 13th.

Pat: Wofold gave me 10ˢ thô not to be known from whom it came.

This was a case of restitution through the confessional.

April 14th.

I went to Leverp: in Expectation to have seen a great meeting of Quaickers but most of them were gon. Mr. Plumb acquaîted me with a discovery how he had been robed and otherways abuesed by a Woman, he shewed me severall Letters from Oliver Lime.

April 15th.

I went to Leverp: with my Lord Mountg and his Son Richard and saw them take boat in order to goe over ye Water and so to goe to Holy Head.

April 16th.

Mr. Boyer of Aintry and his Wife dined here. I went to my Lord Mountgarrets to take leave of his Son James who was going for Blandick.

Blandyke is St. Omer's College, the famous Jesuit place of education.

April 20th.

I went to Scarisb: to take leave of Coz: Scarisb: two Elder Sons who were for going to Blandick. I dined with old Mr. Harington, he came homwards with me, we called at Mr. Irelands in Maile.

April 25th.

Parson Wairing and his Son Gerard Wairing made me a Viset.

1710.

I went to Leverp: and drunk at Mr. Silv: Richmonds April 29th.
with him and Parson Foxcroft who was formerly Curate
of Sefton.

I payed two Grats to Wm Crisp my Lord Molin: his May 3rd.
Bayly for two years Customary Rent. The Young People
of this Town had Musick at Night and a Bone Fire.

I sent a Present of Young Pigeons to Coz: Molin: of May 11th.
Mosbourgh for storing his Dove-Court.

I went to Leverp: James Halsold ye Braysior treated May 12th.
me with Pickled Oysters. I met Mrs. Allison and her
three Sons walking towards Litherland.

Went to Ince Green and bowled with Parson Letus, May 17th.
Mr. Burton and Rob: Bootle, Mr. Nich: Fazak: was
there and bowled.

My Wife and I saw ye Strange Starr it appeard about May 18th.
ye East and Shot downwards towards ye North the Streamer
of it seemed to be fully four yards long, it appeared about
half an hour after Nine at night and lasted about ye Space
of half an Ave Maria.

There were about 64 Young People playing in a Ring May 28th.
on my Green and about 20 Spectators.

The first Swarme of Bees I had ye year Knit upon Jo: May 30th.
Banisters hat when he had it on his head.

We met Mr. Blund: coming home from Dr. Bostock. June 8th.

My Wife took up Coz: Emelia Butler and my Aunt June 14th.
Frances in ye Coach, we all went to Oughton Moss and
saw a Plate Runn for by five Galawayes, a Hors of my
Lord Chulmundeleys wane it.

Went to Leverp: and saw ye Play acted called June 15th.
Sephonisba or Haniballs Overthrow. I discoursed Dr

1710.

Smithson about his Ordering too much Lodinum for Mr. Lancaster.

June 16th.   I began to still some Eye-bright.

June 24th.   Dr Cawood the Oculist from Dublin came to look at my Eyes, he Lodged here.

June 28th.   I went with Doctor Cawood to Leverpoole to assist him in geting Acquaintance and to procure a Chamber for him where his Pasients may Come to him, we drunk at the Post Office with Doctor Smithson, Doctor Person &c.

June 29th.   My Wife went to Ince to take Leave of Mr. Blundell and his Lady ere they went to Harragate Spawes.

July 5th.   Pat: Parker yᵉ Provins: Mr. Babthrop &c came hither. Pat: Smith of Croston lodged here.

July 14th.   I began to learne of Dr Cawood to play at Picket.

July 17th.   Dr Cawood and I went to Prescot, I went to Mr. Oliver Lime to know whether he would venture with Dr Cawood for his Eyes, we light at yᵉ Signe of yᵉ Ship and discoursed our Land-Lord, Tho: Moss.

July 20th.   I Began by Orders of Dr Cawood to take Drops, Eye Bright Tea and to put Clary Seeds into my Eyes.

July 22nd.   Dr Caw: and I went to Leverp: we Looked at yᵉ Dock that is in making, we went to see yᵐ make White-Mettle Muggs.

July 24th.   Dr Caw: went to yᵉ Flowering of Ince Cross.

Aug. 2nd.   I gathered 1163 since this day twelve Month.

This entry is explained by one made August 2 in the previous year, viz.: "He began to gather Pins for one year." There was probably a bet on this subject between the squire and his chaplain.

I Waired 24ˢ in Chinea in my Hale for my Wife. Mr. Aug. 10th.
Ald: Dr Cawo: and I went to the Grange Greene and
saw a Match Bowled there between two young Men of
Ince and two old Fellows of Formby, a Slave come from
Turkey was on the Green.

Mr. Ald: Dr. Cawood and I went to Ince Green to Aug. 15th.
see yᵉ Match Bowled between the same two Formby and
two Ince Men; Ince Green was so wet that the Spectators
would not goe on it, there was there Mr. Formby, Parson
Letus, Rob: Bootle and his Son &c.

My Wife, Aunt Frances, Coz: Emi: But: &c., dined Aug. 18th.
at Eckleston, there was there Mr. Molineux of Bold, his
Lady and abundance of Company.

The Stone Cross in yᵉ Town was set up unknown to Aug. 23rd.
me by yᵉ Order chiefly of Wᵐ Gray the Overseear of yᵉ
High Wayes.

I began to pull down yᵉ end of the Chappell in order Aug. 29th.
to build it up with Brick.

I went to Leverp: and drunk at yᵉ Mariners Armes Aug. 31st.
with Tho: Brownbill &c. I bought a fancifull Ring of
Mugg Mettle to drink out of and brock it ere I got it home.

Young Mr. Tyrer and Mr. James Tildesley called here, Sept. 1st.
they had ben a Parleamenteering.

My Ditchers found a Basket Hilted Sword and a Lock Sept. 9th.
of a Gun or Pistoll as they were ditching between yᵉ Long
Garden and yᵉ Bleaching Yard, tis probable they had laine
there since the time of yᵉ sivell Wars.

One from Leverp: I suppose yᵉ Huntsman was here Sept. 13th.
to enquire for some of Leverpo: Hounds as were strayed
here away.

1710.
Sept. 18th.   I went to Formoss-Poole Gutter expecting to have found 8 Men at work but tho it was past four of yᵉ Clock I onely found one man there yᵉ rest not as yet being comm from their Dinners or Rather from yᵉ Ailehouse.

Sept. 19th.   Coz: Richard Butler dined at the Stand with my Lord Molineux, Mr. Molineux of Mosburgh &c.

Sept. 20th.   Coz: Rich: Butler of Bristold went h̄ece. I went with him to Leverpoole but being they could not get his Horses into yᵉ Boat he Stayed at Leverpoole all Night. We drunk a Bowle of Punsh at Mr. Tates. Grays Brandy and Toste.

Sept. 26th.   I went in yᵉ evening to Ince Green there was there Mr. Formby, Lightbown of Formby &c.

Oct. 3rd.   I went to Grange Green with Mr. Ald: we bowled there before dinner with Parson Letus &c it was yᵉ finishing day of Ince Green for this Season.

Oct. 9th.   I sent Wᵐ Ainsw: to Culcheth to wish Mr. Culsh: Joy.

Mr. Thomas Culcheth was then newly married, but died s.p., and was buried at Winwick, October 8, 1747. His estates passed to his cousin, Thomas Stanley, Esq., of Eccleston-in-the-Fylde, whose daughter and heiress, Meliora, married William Dicconson. Esq., and died s.p., when the property went to the Traffords, who sold it early in this century.

Oct. 16th.   It being Crosby Goosefeast I dined at Parson Wairings with Mrs. Cross, Parson Letus' Sister in Law, Wm. Harrison yᵉ Clark and his Wife &c.

Oct. 17th.   My Wife went to see Coz: Scarisb: who was lying in of her son Henry.

Oct. 18th.   John Adulph Castalier a German shewed here a Coach and Four Horses with People in it made all of Ivory that did not weigh two Graines.

1710.

Widdow Bolton a Chirurganess came hither to dress a Oct. 20th. Cut that Fanny has got over her Eye.

I lent Darby my Lottery for two Dice being he was to Oct. 21st. have a Cake play to night.

Cap: Rob: Faza: went with my Wife and me in y⁰ Nov. 1st. Coach to Formby.

I Went to Chorley Town to meet Young Mr. Gerard of Nov. 30th. -Highfield and Pothecary Gerards Son.

1711.

My Brother Langdale Mr. Ald: and I went in y⁰ Coach Jan. 2nd. to Leverp: we drank at Swarbricks and at y⁰ Talbot.

We had a Merry-Night. Tatlock played of his Pipes Jan. 3rd. and Fiddle.

Brother Langdale my Wife and I dined at Ince, Mr. Jan. 7th. Wᵐ Gibson was there.

Mr. Ald: and I went a Skaiting to y⁰ Old Moss there Jan. 21st. was there Mr. Taylor of Orms: y⁰ Watchmaker.

I went to Leverpoole with my Wife &c. We saw y⁰ Jan. 27th. great Saxon Maxemilian Christofer Miller. I drunk at y⁰ Wool-pack, with Mr. Plumb Mr. Allison and Dr. Fabius and with Mr. Ford y⁰ Putear, Dr. Traps &c.

Mr. Ald: and I went to Mr. Ni: Fazakerley of y⁰ Jan. 31st. Hill hous.

Mr. Burton and Mr. Green of Hooton came hither. Feb. 7th.

Rev. Stanislaus Green, S.J., was chaplain to the Stanley family of Hooton, Cheshire. He died 1722.

The Push Ploughers began to Push in y⁰ Winter heys. Feb. 20th.

Ra: Peters pay'd me £5 from Mr. Wilding 'tis put out Mar. 3rd. to Interest for y⁰ Poore of Little Crosby.

1711.

Mar. 8th.   Mr. Aldred gave me a Paire of Ivory Tenns which he made on purpose for my own use.

Mar. 11th.   Mr. Blund: Mr. Ra: Tildesleys Widdow and Mrs. Ann Harington made a Viset here.

Mar. 12th.   I cut a good deale of Eye-bright for me to smoke.

Mar. 13th.   I Began to draw out some Pictures wth my Pensall for my Rugg work and to try to finish one of them with cut Woosted but it did not doe right.

Mar. 20th.   Cap: Rob: Fazak: brought us word that ye Family of St. Germans was privately gon away in ye Night.

Mar. 24th.   I went to Leverp: and gave directions to Norton ye Sadler to make me a Hammer-Cloath. I spoke to Mr. Low for some Glass-bottles.

Mar. 29th.   I went to Leverpo: I drunk at ye Woolpack wth Mr. Alanson and Samwell Edwards. I proposed a Swap with Samw: Edw: between my Button and his Gray Galloway.

Mar. 30th.   Rich: Cartwrit let my Wife blood in ye Foot.

April 3rd.   Coz: Scarisb: I and our Wives went to a Race on Oughton Moss, when the Race was past Mr. Scarisb: and I went to Lancets the Signe of Queens Head in Ormsk: where we drunk Wine with Sr Tho: Standley, his Son, Capt: Standish, Parson Hindley of Oughton, Mr. Ashurst of Ashurst &c.

April 4th.   Mr. Scaresb: and I dined at Burchley with Sr Wm Gerard and his Brother John, Mr. Banks of Winstanley and his Brother ye Parson, Mr. Leigh of Lime &c.

April 23rd.   I tought Jo: Sumner, Wm Marrow, Rob: Tompson &c to play at Penny prick wth ye Foot balle. I sent Wm Ains: to Hooton to see Coz: Standley, she is ill of ye Small Pox.

1711.
April 24th.

My Wife rid behind Mr. Ald: to Dr Lathoms to prayers, they dined there.

Dr. Lathom, being old and infirm, had a private chapel at his house in Aintree.

I went to Preston to wate of my Coze: Eyre and his April 30th. Lady. I suped with them at their New Lodging and with Mr. Standley and his Grand-Mother Patton, Parson Young &c. I Lodged at Rich: Jacksons ye Signe of ye whit Bull in Preston.

I Dined at Coz: Eyres with Mr. Standley of Bigarstaff May 1st. his two Aunts, Mrs. Whithead and one of her Sons, Parson Young &c. I made a Viset to Mrs. Ann and Bridget Blundell, to Mr. Walmesley Junior and Mrs. Walmesley Senior. I was at ye New Coffy hous with Coz: Eyre where he, young Mr. Standley, Mr. Walles &c played at Passage; Cap Sidall Dr Farrington &c played at Inn and inn.

"'Passage' is a game of dice to be played at but by two, and it is performed with three dice. The caster throws continually till he hath thrown doublets under ten, and then he is out and loseth; or doublets above ten, and then he passeth and wins."—*The Complete Gamester*, 1680.

"'In' signified that there was a doublet or two dice alike out of the four; 'In and in' that there were either two doublets or that all of the four dice were alike; which swept all the stake. 'He is a merchant still, adventurer at in and in.'"—*Ben Jonson, Webster's Dictionary.* (Communicated by J. W. Bone, Esq., F.S.A.)

Then to Chorley to ye Funerall of Mr. Walmesley of May 2nd. Dungen-hall there was there Sr Thom: Standleys Son, Mr. Rob: Leigh, Mr. Brooks of Astley, the four Trustees, viz S^r Ni: Sherb: Sr Wm Gerard &c I went with ye Corps as far as Rodbourn towards Blackbourn.

Francis, only son of Bartholomew Walmesley, of Dunkenhalgh, Esq., who died January 7, 1701-2, had followed his father to the

1711.

grave at the early age of 14. His sister Catherine was now sole heiress of the family estates, and married, when only 15, on March 1, 1712-3, Robert, 7th Lord Petre, who died of smallpox early the following year. She gave birth to a posthumous son, Robert James, the adventurous baron of Pope, in the *Rape of the Lock.* Lady Petre re-married, in 1733, Charles, Lord Stourton, and died in 1785, aged 88. Her descendant, Henry Petre, Esq., now holds the property.

May 3rd.
The young people of this Town had a Merry-night at yᵉ four Lain ends. Tatlock was their Musition.

May 16th.
Mr. Ald: went with me to Ince Green where I Bowled yᵉ Match wᵗʰ Mr. Rob: Blund: which we made yester night viz one Game hand to Fist and after that single ends for an hour.

May 19th.
I sent Cha: Howerd to yᵉ Buriall of Hen: Livesley.

May 30th.
Speed was severely whiped for taking a Shoulder of Mutton off yᵉ Spit.

June 3rd.
Mr. Ald: and I went to Ince to welcome home Mr. Blundell from Whit-Chourch.

He had been to consult Dr. Bostock, and must have died very shortly after this visit.

June 4th.
I went in yᵉ morning to my Burners in the North hey and gave those leave that had a Mind to goe to Ince to Prayers being Mr. Blund: was newly dead. I also went thither to prayers.

June 7th.
I was at yᵉ Funerall of Mr. Blundell of Ince, there was Mr. Tyrer yᵉ Maior of Leverp: Alderman Clayton, Mr. Tyrer the Atturney &c.

June 14th.
I went to Great Crosby Court, I drunk with Mr. Ford yᵉ Steward &c, I shewed there some tricks of Legerde-mesney to Parson Wairing, James Williamson, Mr. Thomas yᵉ Officer &c.

June 17th.
I Killed three of my Kats for eating yᵉ Cheeses.

My Wife went to Mrs. Bootles of yᵉ Peele to shew her a Soar place she has in her Legg.

My Wife and Pat Gelib: made a Viset to my Lady Anderton at Ince. Mr. Ald: and I Bowled at Great Crosby Green wᵗʰ Parson Letus, Mr. Gerard Wairing and Mr. Thomas.

My Children and the Maids went to Formby Fair.

Pat: Turbervile prayed here and preached, he dined here.

Rev. John Turberville, S.J., a relative of Lady Anderton, was her chaplain at Lostock, and had come to Ince with her. In *Lydiate Hall and its Associations* may be seen some letters of this father, relating to the curious complications that arose from her disposition of her Lydiate estate.

Coz: Dick Butler sent to invite me to his Ball at Ormsk: this Night but I went not.

Went to yᵉ New-house to make Mr. Tasburgh a Viset he being comn thither yester day to live there.

I went to Leverp: and drunk wᵗʰ Cap: Clayton at his own house.

Mrs. Scarisb: and Mrs. Ellin Entwisley dined here. Mrs. Moline: of yᵉ Grange and her Sister Betty Blund: Suped here.

Coz: Dick Butler and his Sister Emilia went hence towards Ireland, they went over yᵉ Water and designed to goe to Parke Gate.

I saw Peter Slinhead stand in yᵉ Pillery at Leverp: for writing against Dr. Secheverall and the Church of England. I discoursed Mr. Houghton Merchant about Husbandry but chiefly about improving of Land.

1711.
July 22nd.

I went to Croxtath to welcome home my Lord Molin: I found there old Mr. Harington and Will: Nelson.

July 27th.

Ned Hawkseye began to make a peece of a Wall in yᵉ Harkerk of some of yᵉ Chappel Chamber stones.

Aug. 5th.

Lady Anderton and Mr. Turvile came hither, t'was the first time he has ben here.

Rev. Charles Turville, S.J., had just come to be chaplain at Ince. He was born March 10, 1683; son of Wm. Turville, of Aston Flamville, Co. Leicester, Esq., and his second wife Isabella, daughter and co-heiress of Sir Aston Cokayne, Knight, of Pooley, Co. Warwick. In 1722, when Mrs. Blundell left Ince, he accompanied her abroad as her chaplain. He was with her till her death in 1753. He then retired to Watten, and died there 1757, aged 74.

Aug. 8th.

I went to Ince Bowling Green there was there Mr. Nich: Faza: Mr. Formby &c I went of yᵉ Green to help to pull a Mare of Rich: Whitheads out of yᵉ Ditch. I was sent for home of yᵉ Green because Cap: Clayton of Leverp: his Wife and Sister were come hither.

Aug. 31st.

I Began again to work at my Rug-work-Paint thô I once had an unsuckcesfull tryall at it before.

Sept. 2nd.

My Wife and I dined at Scarisb: we went to wate of Madam Walmes: of Dungen-hall, Dr Lancast: and Mrs. Fazake: dined with us there, we brought Mrs. Fazak: home to Ormsk: in our Coach.

Sept. 8th.

I went to Leverpoole to have met Mr. John Hurst of yᵉ Scouls but he came not.

Sept. 15th.

I met Mr. Hurst of yᵉ Scoules at yᵉ Wool-pack in Leverp: I drunk there with Cap: Rob: Fazak: &c., I saw at Leverp: a Shew of a Little Woman. Hen: Williamson told me he would not stand to yᵉ Arbitration between him and ye Waranders if old Rob: Bootle were an Arbitrator.

This dispute was concerning rabbits taken by Williamson.

I went to Ormsk: and drunk at ye Talbot with Mr. *Sept. 17th.* Walmesley ye Watch-maker, coming home I called of John Sedon and discoursed him about sowing Malt-dust upon Medowing.

I went to Garswood and dined there with Mrs. Walmes- *Sept. 20th.* ley, Mr. Scaresb:, Mr. Jo: Gelibrond &c. Mounsuer La Abbe tought Mrs. Walmesley &c to Dance at Garswood.

I went to Leverp: designing to have ben at ye Funerall *Sept. 22nd.* of Mr. Evans but he was not buried to day.

Mr. Evans, a dancing master, had taught his art to the Diarist's daughters.

I went to Leverp: to desire Mr. Tyarer the Maior of *Sept. 29th.* Leverp: or Mr. Clayton to meet Mr. Nicho: Faza: and Mr. Brooks upon Wednesday at Charls Howerds.

The business was to view Formospoole Gutter and other water courses, which were troubling the squire and his neighbours not a little. Mr. Tyrer met the party as desired. Mr. Molineux, of the Grange, Mr. Blundell, and others were present at the inspection.

I put some Peach Stones &c to Infuse in Brandy to *Oct. 12th.* make Ratefia on.

I drove a Pin at Jo: Tickley's Rearing. *Oct. 13th.*

My Children went to Great Crosby Goos-feast they *Oct. 14th.* Lodged in Great Crosby.

It being Great Crosby Goosfeast I dined at Parson *Oct. 15th.* Wairings with him, Parson Letus and his Wife and Sister-in-Law, Parson Marsden, Parson Mount, Mr. Williamson

1711.

and Mr. Whithead Shool - Masters of Formby, Dr Tarlton &c.

Oct. 17th.   We began to Hatchell and Spinn this years Flax.   My Wife sent Jo: Banis: to Scarisb: of a How-do-you to my Lady Tankerd.

Oct. 18th   I found Rob: To: and Hen: Kerf: playing of Reed Pips when they should have been geting Potatows.

Oct. 20th.   I fetched home 4 Piggs and one Speaning from Ormsk:

Oct 22nd.   I went to Ja: Brows in expectation to have seen a Match of Shooting wth Bowes and Arrows but ye Formby Archers came not.   I found at James Browns Pat: Wofold, Mr. Aldred, Mr. Burton, Mr. Edwd Molineux of Formby &c.

Oct. 28th.   I went to see Parson Wairing, he being very ill; his Brother ye School-Master of Prescot was there, I signed a Petission to ye Company of Merchant-Taylors of London in behalf of Mr. Gerard Wairing that he might Suckseed his Father.

This petition had the desired effect. The Grammar School at Great Crosby is still flourishing, and an elegant building has been recently erected to replace the old structure.

Oct. 31st.   I attended ye Corps of Parson Wairing to Sefton there was Parson Letus, Mr. Peter Morton, Alderman Webster, Alderman Hurst, Mr. Allanson &c there was also at Parson Wairings, Parson Becket, Parson Mount &c., ye Corps was carried on my Coach Carriage.

Nov. 1st.   My Wife went to condole Mrs. Ann Wairing for ye death of her Father.   My Children went in ye Coach to Formby Allotide.

Nov. 11th.   I stood God-father with Mrs. Howet to Coz: Tho: Gelibronds Son John.

My Wife and Children went to Leverpoo: Fair.

I sold my Mare Punsh to Rich: Westhead for £4 in Nov. 13th.
hand and eleven pound more to be paid upon ye Birth of
my first Son by my now Wife. I Lent my Coach Carriage
to carry the Corps of Elizab: Farclough to Sefton.

Ned Hatton came to me to Petission I wold be off Nov. 15th.
ye bargan I had made with Ri: Westhead but I would
not consent to it.

I sent Wm Ainsw: to Rich: Westhead with my Mare Nov. 21st.
Punsh being he had bought her of me some time agoe, but
he sent her back in hopes I would come upon a new
Bargan but we stuck to ye first bargain.

My Aunt Frances Blu: being dead I went to Ormsk: Dec. 2nd.
to see who was to be her Executors, Coz: Jo: Gelibrond
being one.

I went to Ormsk: and brought ye Corps of my Aunt Dec. 3rd.
Frances Blu: thence on my Coach Carriage and buried
her in ye Harkerk; Coz: Jo: Gelib: Pat: Geli: Doctor
Lancaster, Mrs. Ann Gorsuch &c came along with y^e
Corps.

Frances Blundell, sister of the "Cavalier," of whom some
account has already been given, was 80 years of age at the time
of her death.

I sent my Mare Punch to Rich: Westheads he was Dec. 4th.
not at home but after some time his Wife took charg
of her.

Mrs. Blundell and her Kinsman Mr. Steven Anderton Dec. 6th.
made a Viset here.

I found Sr Francis Anderton and Mrs. Blund: at Mr. Dec. 8th.
Aldreds but he was gone to help Ginnet Arnold to die.

1711.
Dec. 9th.

My Wife went to see Mrs. Poole of Burchley who was lying in of her son Richard.

Dec. 10th.

Sʳ Fran: Ande: I &c Rid down to yᵉ Sea Side and saw them take Flooks. I layed the Wager with Mr. Steven Anderton about the Number of Holes in a Flagelet.

Dec. 13th.

Rich: Webster came hither at Night and brought along with him yᵉ Foolish Fellow Will: Speakman that played upon an Eller Pipe.

Dec. 15th.

Gabriall Norris Wife sent a Present to my Children of a Pack of Frensh Cards.

Dec. 19th.

My Eyes being not very well I spent most of the after Noone in sourting the printed Sheets of yᵉ Book entickled *Quid me persæqueris* and in laying as many Sheets together as made up bookes a peece.

> This was a treatise on the Penal Laws, but there does not appear to be any printed copies now in existence. It was written by the "Cavalier," who says—" In the year 1661 I printed a small book on that subject, which I have shewed to few, and I think it was never exposed to sale."—*A Cavalier's Note Book,* p. 150.

Dec. 20th.

I began to make some Aqua Celestis a new way viz: to whicken it with East lick Aile but it did not answer expectation.

Dec. 28th.

We had a Merry Night, Tatlock played here of his Pips and Fiddle, there was pritty throng Carding, one Company played at 6ᵈ p̄ Cut till after Nine next Morning.

Dec. 31st.

My Wife &c went to Leverp: in the Coach, they brought Betty Secomb my Landladys Doughter of the Wool-pack back with them to lodg here.

1712.
Jan. 3rd.

Coz: Tho: Gelib: and I &c. dined at Lanslets yᵉ Queens Head in Ormsk: wᵗʰ Cap: Brown, our Wives dined at

Mrs. Howets. I saw Mrs. Walmesley going from Scarisb: to Garswood to solemnize her Birth-day to-morrow being then 14 years of Age. Sr Wm Ger: and his Doughter Mary, Coz: Scarisb: and his Lady, Coz: Jo: Gelib: &c were along with her. I was at Mr. Houghtons where ye privy Sestions were held by Sr Tho: Standley Mr. Brooks, and Mr. Nicho: Fazak: Little Crosby had a Tryall wth Ince Town there, concerning ye Settlement of Rich: Swift &c, we lost ye Sute.

Mr. Ald: and I went to Leverp: I went to see Mr. Houghton ye Merchant who was so ill I could not be admitted to speak to him. Jan. 15th.

I went to Aintry and looked at Doctor Lathoms Housing called Aintry Hous to see in what repair it was in. Jan. 16th.

I went to see Parson Richmond of Walton who was sick, I found there Parson Marsden and I think Parson Becket. Jan. 18th.

Mr. Ri: Molin: of ye Grange came hither and paid me his 10 Penny Rent. Jan. 21st.

My Wife and I went to Leverp: and heard Mr. Manock Preach. Mr. Tute and Mr. Morphew &c were there, we dined at Mrs. Brownbills with her and Mr. Manock. Jan. 27th.

A room in the house would then serve as a chapel—the first building of this character dating about 1736. This was destroyed by the mob after the defeat of the Jacobites in 1745. Rev. Francis Mannock, S.J., was second son of Sir Francis Mannock, Bart., by Mary Heneage, born October 18, 1670, died at York, December 21, 1748.—*Foley's Records*, vol. 5, p. 367.

I bought Lining Silk &c at Mr. Hursts to make up a Sute of Clothes for myself ye Outside was of our own spining. I went to ye Buriall Place to see Hu: Bullen Feb. 12th.

1712.

goe past as he was removing hous into Darby, he had fourteen carts and mine was one of them.

The burial place (Harkirke), though now enclosed within the walls of Crosby Park, formerly adjoined the public road; near it are the remains of a very ancient wayside cross.

Feb. 23rd.   I drunk at Mr. Hursts with him, Parson Richmond, Mr. Silvester Richmond, Mr. Brenan, &c.

Feb. 24th.   Mr. Taylor of Ormsk: Watchmaker dined here, he gave my Wife a pair of Silver Clasps for her Necklases.

Feb. 25th.   The Souldiers Fortune was Acted at Mrs. Ann Rothwells in this Town. My Wife went with me both to y⁰ Play and Gigg. The Actors of y⁰ Play were Thos Farer Sʳ Davyd Dunce, Wᵐ Marrow Captain Bewgard, Watty Thelw: Sʳ Jolly jumble &c. `

Mar. 3rd.   Mr. Gera: Wairing made a Viset here, Young James Williamson y⁰ Saylor came with him. I went with Sʳ Jas Poole to y⁰ Hall of Maile, thence we went to Parson Daines of Melling.

Mar. 4th.   Severall of y⁰ Neighbours turned the **Pan-Kakes** here after supper and dansed in y⁰ Hall, Hen: Kerfoot played to yem.

Mar. 11th.   Winny Scot was here to Consult about y⁰ misunderstanding as is between her and her Husband, I gave her my advice and let Wᵐ Weedow help to make them Friends.

Mar. 15th.   I went to see Mr. Hurst who was ill of y⁰ Gout and Gravell, I think old Mr. Poole was with him.

Mar. 18th.   Toping y⁰ Parriter was here a beging for Corn, I gave him some. As I was going to my Setters of Star to hinder y⁰ Sand from recking up my Grand Water-Course I met in yᵉ Town Wᵐ Harrison yᵉ Clark of Sefton I gave him 2ᵈ instead of 12 Paist Eggs.

Rich: Cartw: let me blood. Mar. 27th.

I gave my Coz: Tho: Gelibrond a Bowl made of Mar. 29th. Tobacco. I sent Jo: Banister to yᵉ Funeral of Nich: Shepheard.

Being extreamly ill of a continuall Fit of Hekoping Mar. 30th. which lasted for about 15 Hours without ever any Long intermission both Dr Will: Lancaster and Dr Andrews came to me.

Doctor Lanc: came to see me. I got up being on yᵉ April 1st. mending hand.

They sent from Mosb: Morehall and Ince to see me. April 2nd. Edw: Hatton, Tho: Blansh: and severall of my Neighbours came to see me.

Mr. Ald: prayed here and preached a Passion Sermon. April 18th.

This was Good Friday.

My Wife and I saw part of yᵉ Play called yᵉ Schoole April 21st. of Complements Acted at He: Bushels by a Company as came from towards Scarisb:

I went with Mally to yᵉ Whit-Mettle houses (Liverpool) April 23rd. and bought a Punsh Bowl.

I went to Leverp: and gave Mr. Clayton a Receipt for April 26th. £100 from Sʳ Roger Brad: owing by Bond from his Grandfather to Mr. Christopher Bradshaw.

Mr. Christopher Bradshaw died in 1678, and left the "Cavalier," who could never recover this sum in his own lifetime, one of his executors.

1712.
May 3rd.

I went to Leverp: and fetched Mally home behind me, we saw the Drummers Wife of Leverp: whipt for Stealing. I drunk at yᵉ Woolpack with Mr. Plumb and Whit yᵉ Barber, I payed Whit 25ˢ for a Perrywig. The young people of this Town had a Merry-night Tatlock played to them my Wife and I went to see them dance.

May 6th.

I went to Ormsk: Sessions in order to have got a Hunderd Bridge made over Formospoole Gutter but could not. I dined at Lancets with Mr. Faz: of yᵉ Hill-hous, Lawyer Blundell, Atturney Green &c there was at yᵉ other Table Mr. Clayton of Leverp: Merchant, Mr. Brooks of Ormsk: Lawyer Starkey &c I drunk at yᵉ Talbot with Mr. Rob: Fazakerley and Doctor Lancaster.

May 13th.

I went to Ormsk: Rase with my Wife and Mally in yᵉ Coach but I rid upon yᵉ Ground, there was my Lord Peters and his Lady, Lawyer Starkey, Parson Letus &c the Rase was won by an Iron Gray hors of one Mr. Batters he run against my Lord Molineux his Darcy &c. I bought a Hat of Quaker Holme.

May 16th.

Mr. Ald: shewed me how to take yᵉ Meridion.

May 20th.

They began to spin some of yˢ years woole to make me a Sute of Cloths on.

May 21st.

I dined at Garswood with Sʳ Will: Gerard, Lord Peters, Mr. Culcheth and their Ladys, Sʳ Francis Andrews &c. I went in yᵉ Evening with Sʳ Will: Gerard and Sʳ Fra: And: to Burchley and so home.

May 22nd.

Tho: Kerklington was here, I went out with him a Simpling to yᵉ Sand Hills.

May 23rd.

My Wife went to yᵉ Peele to shew her foot to Mrs. Bootle which was soar with being Bluddied.

I was at Ince Green but did not bowl, there was Parson Letus, Parson Wairing, Parson Darbyshire of Formby, Rob: Bootle &c.

My Wife, I and my children were at the Funerall of John Bryanson of the Morehouses, there was Mr. Molineux of the Grange, Rich: Tickley &c.

I took Tho: Hartley and Geo: Nailer of Leverp: hunting Wild Ducks in the Cowhey, they had one Gun but wood not deliver it.

I went to Ince Green, there was Parson Sherley of y⁰ Meales, Mr. Lancet of Ormsk: &c.

My Wife rid behind me to Leve: we saw y⁰ Play Acted called y⁰ Earle of Essex there was present Mr. Heskaine, Mr. Jams Gleast, Will: Rollins &c. My Wife and I came home in y⁰ Wet between 4 and 5 next Morning.

When I came home I found Parson Gerard Wairing and John Dugdale &c who were comne along with Geo: Nayler to petission for him he being one of them as I prosecuted for Shooting a Wild Duck in y⁰ Cowhey.

My Wife began her Journey towards Holywell she Rid to Leverp: and designes to walk the rest.

I went to Leverp: and saw Acted in y⁰ Castle the Play called y⁰ Yeoman of Kent, there was at y⁰ Play Mr. Sandeford Junior, Will: Rollins, James Gleast &c.

I made a Sword Dance against my Marlpit is flower'd.

I went to Leverp: and to the Printhous tis y⁰ first time I was to see it.

I was very busy most of y⁰ after-noone shaping Tinsall &c for the Garland for my New Marl-pit and after Supper yᵉ Women helped to Paste some things for it. I began to teach the 8 Sword Dancers their Dance wᶜʰ they are to Dance at yᵉ Flowering of my Marl-pit. Dr Cawood played to them.

July 8th.   I was very busy making Kaps &c for my Marlers and Dansers, severall of Great Crosby Lasses helped me. The Young Women of this Town, Morehouses and Great Crosby dressed yᵉ Garlands in my Barne. I tought my 8 Sword Dancers their Dance, they had Musick and Danced it in my Barn.

July 9th.   I was extreamly busy all Morning making some things to adorn my Marlers Heads. My Marl-pit was flowered very much to yᵉ Satisfaction of yᵉ Spectators, all the 14 Marlers had a Particular Dress upon their Heads and Carried each of them a Musket or Gun. The Six Garlands &c were carried by young Women in Prosestion, the 8 Sword Dancers went along with them to yᵉ Marlpit where they Dansed, the Musick was Gerald Holsold and his Son and Rich: Tatlock, at Night they Danced in yᵉ Barne. Tho: Lathord of Leverpoole brought me to yᵉ Marlpit a Dogg Coller against my Bull Bate as is to be in yᵉ Pit.

July 15th.   I Baited a Large Bull in yᵉ Bottom of my New Marl-pit, he was never baited before as I know of, yet played to admiration, there was 8 or 9 Doggs played yᵉ first Bait and onely two yᵉ 3ʳᵈ bait, I think there was not above two Doggs but what were very ill hurt, I gave a Coller to be played for but no Dogg could get it fairly, so I gave it to Rich: Spencer of Leve: being his Dogg best deserved it.

July 18th.   Mr. Ald: began to make some kaps for some of my Sword Dancers against yᵉ Finishing day.

I went to Ince Bowling Green where I found Parson _{July 21st.}
Sherley of Meyles, Parson Darbyshire, and Mr. Whithead
the School-Master of Formby &c.

I had my Finishing day for my Marling and abundance _{July 23rd.}
of my Neighbours and Tenants eat and drunk with me in
yᵉ after noone, severall of them had made presents to my
Wife of Sugar, Chickens, Butter &c. All my Marlers,
Spreaders, Water-Baylis and Carters din'd here, we fetched
home yᵉ Maypowl from the pit and had Sword Dansing
and a Merry-Night in yᵉ Hall and in yᵉ Barne, Richard
Tatlock played to them.

Jo: Tickley told me his Secret and his greatest Troble _{July 25th.}
and advised with me about it.

I went to Mr. Ald: where I found Mr. Tho: Ford yᵉ _{July 31st.}
Puterar, Jack Whit yᵉ Barber, Doctor Barret and Pothecary
Lathom.

In his *Anecdote Book* the Diarist says—"I knew one Thomas Ford
a Brazier at Leverpoole who could have writ his name upon a wall
at arms length with half a hundred weight hanging at his little finger."

I went to Leverp: Dr. Caw: and I made a Viset to _{Aug. 2nd.}
Mr. Hurst, he shewed us his new hous.

I walked into yᵉ Town with Pat: Jam: Gorsuch, after _{Aug. 7th.}
dinner he and his Sister Ann made a Viset to Will:
Williamsons of Litherland.

My Children buried one of their Babbys with a great _{Aug. 10th.}
deale of Formallity, they had a Garland of Flowers carried
before it, and at least twenty of their Playfellows and others
that they invited were at yᵉ Buriall.

Mr. Roby breackfasted here, I went with him to Vew _{Aug. 11th.}
Fermospoole Gutter where he considered about making a
Bridg over it.

1712.
Aug. 14th.

Mr. Standish, Mr. Rog: Diconson and their Ladys dined here.

Aug. 15th.

Dr. Cawood and I made a Viset to Mr. Moston of Lidiat, coming home I shewed him Sefton Seller. My Children saw part of a Stage Play at Melling.

Aug. 20th.

I was searved with yᵉ Sherriffs Writ upon yᵉ Sute of Mr. Molineux of yᵉ Grange, it was about yᵉ Water Courses. I went to Prescot and advised wᵗʰ Lawyer Blund: about this Business.

Aug. 21st.

I went to Ormsk: and gave Mr. Tyrer my Note that I would stand Sute against Ince. Mr. Hesketh of Ryfford spoke to me in behalf of Thomas Hartley about his Shooting Wild Ducks in my Demesney.

Aug. 24th.

Mr. John Jackson one of the Masters of Mathematicks at Leverpoole made me a Viset.

Aug. 25th.

Doctor Lancaster of Ormskirk and Coz: William Walmesley the Watchmaker dined here.

Aug. 30th.

I went to Lever: I drunk at W. Griffys wᵗʰ Mr. Plumb and Dʳ Caw: I saw yᵉ Little Woman Catherin —— she was a Hanaverian, she was as near one yard and Insh high as could be. I attended the Corps of my Landlady Secomb as far as into yᵉ Church Yord, there was at yᵉ Buriall Hous, Mr. Maior, Dʳ Tarlton, Parson Stith, Parson Walsh &c.

Sept. 1st.

I had a Cradle from Leverpoo: for Mowing Oats I shew'd it to Henry Ashcroft but he ues'd it not today.

Sept. 8th.

My Black-Bull was Baited at Mrs. Ann Rothwells there played but three right Doggs and two of yᵐ were ill hurt.

1712.

My Wife, Mrs. Scarisb: and Pat Edw: Scarisb: went Sept. 12th. in y⁰ Coach to Lever: they saw a Play Acted called y⁰ Queene of the Scots.

This Rev. E. Scarisbrick, S.J., was brother to the squire.

Dr Caw: helped me to examain my Simballing things. Sept. 18th.

Mr. Plumbe and I went on borde Mr. William Kellys Sept. 20th. Ship the John of Dublin.

I called at Dr Lathoms and chapterd Betty Lathom Sept. 21st. about her unkindness to her Uncle and Aunt. Y⁰ Bet between Mr. Ald: and Mall: But: about Mesuring an Eshen.

Mrs. Fleetwood Butler Lodged here. Sept. 22nd.

We went to Parson Wairings but he being gon to y⁰ Oct. 2nd. Funeral of Mrs. Moreton we went to James Davys.

My Wife and Mrs. Fleet: Butle: went to Leverp: Oct. 4th. Ch: How: overturn'd y⁰ Coach upon Lever: Rocks and dammadged it very much and hurt my Wife and Mrs. Butler, he brock it worse in Great Crosby Field.

I wore my second homs Made Sute. Oct. 5th.

Mr. Golding sent hither for some Young Pigeons to Oct. 11th. stock his Dove-Cort with, I gave him a dozine or more.

I went to Great Crosby Goosfeast with my Wife &c. Oct. 12th.

I and Mally went in our Coach and six to lodge at Oct. 13th. Mosburgh. The Water in Rainford was very high and came into y⁰ Coach and wet some of our things in the Male Trunk and Boxes.

Mr. Ro: Molin: Mr. Ald: and I dined at Garswood. Oct. 15th.

1712.

Oct. 16th. Sr Will: Gerard and his Brother John and Mr. Worthington of Blanscow dined at Mosbu:

Oct. 17th. Mr. Poole of Burchley and his Wife dined at Mosb: Mr. Fra: Escot came in the after noone.

Oct. 18th. Mr. Molineux of Mosb: and I met Mr. John Gerard of Garswood a hunting.

Oct. 19th. Coz: Molin: and I went on Hors Back to Burchley; our Wives Mrs. F. Butler and Mally went in ye Coach, we dined there with Mrs. Eckleston.

Oct. 21st. Mr. Knight prayed and dined here and then went towards Leverp:

Oct. 23rd. Will: Ainsw: bought me Seven Manks Bullocks at ye Hall of Maudsley.

Oct. 26th. I was at Margery Shepheards at ye Marriage of her Doughter Ailes to Roger Oneale.

Oct. 31st. I gave John Bannister a Quarters warning, but since we have peesed againe, so he dose not Leave my Service.

Nov. 4th. I came to Ja: Bryans: and mesured ye Eshen about wch Mr. Ald: had Layed a wager formerly, it held something above 19 Quarts.

Nov. 6th. I Coursed a Hare in Thornton, Parson Mallery, Mr. Eckleston ye Brewer, old Rob: Bootle &c was present.

Nov. 18th. Mr. Manock brought ye News that Duke Hammilton and Lord Mooe had killed each other in a Duell.

Nov. 20th. Went to Leverp: saw a Poppet Show in ye Lord Street.

Dec. 1st. I was at ye Funerall of Mr. Male of Male, there was at ye Hous Alderman Clayton and Mr. Shaw of Leverp: Mr.

Poole of Low Hill, Parson Becket, Parson Letus, Mrs. Bootle of yᵉ Peele &c.

My Wife, Mally and I lodged at Mr. Golding at Southward, Mally rode thither behind me, we found there Lawyer Johnsons Doughter of Warington and Mr. Booth. Dec. 27th.

Mr. Booth went with Mally and me to Dobs Font. Dec. 28th.

Mrs. Golding my Wife and I dined at Culsheth, Mr. John Culsheth was there, Mrs. Gold: Rode thither behind me. Dec. 29th.

Mrs. Golding my Wife and I dined at Mr. Langtons of yᵉ Low with young Mr. Gifford and Mr. Helme. Dec. 30th.

Mr. Golding I and our Wives and Mally &c heard Mass at Mr. Jo: Corleys and dined there. Dec. 31st.

Mr. John Corley and his Wife din'd at Southard. 1713. Jan. 1st.

My Wife I and Mally came home from South: we light at Winwick and went into yᵉ Chourch to look at Mr. Leighs Monumēt. Jan. 2nd.

We had a Merry Night, Rich: Tatlock play'd here we had a great many Dansers, they Dansed my Sword Dāce, I played at Cut in yᵉ Paintry with Jos: Blansheard of the Lady Green, Rob: Massom &c. Jan. 6th.

I got my Breakfast at Ell: Harrisons being I had not eat any Christmass Fair with her. Jan. 10th.

They began to spin Gersey. Jan. 20th.

Mr. Molin: of the Grange being dead this Morning my Wife and I went thither to pray but all yᵉ Masses were over ere we came. Jan. 27th.

I went to the Grange to pray for Mr. Rich: Molineux I heard 3 Masses and said yᵉ Office for the Dead with yᵉ 4 Priests. Jan. 28th.

1713.

Jan. 29th.   I went to yᵉ Funerall of Mr. Moline: of yᵉ Grange, there was Mr. Wofold of More-hall, Mr. Harington, Coz: Molin: of Mosburgh, Parson Letus, Mr. Nicho: Fazak: Mr. Formby &c.   I lent Cap: Rob: Faz: a Mare to ride on to yᵉ Buriall.

Jan. 31st.   I had a New Side-Saddle brought home as Mr. Norton made twas of Leather, it was hansoled to night by five Women.

Feb. 4th.   I went to Croxtath and dined there wᵗʰ my Lord his two Sons Carroll and Thomas, Mr. Harington &c.

Feb. 8th.   My Wife, Mally, and Coz: Nanny Gorsu: went to yᵉ Grange to condole Mrs. Molin: for yᵉ death of her husband.

Feb. 11th.   Mrs. Bridget Alanson and Mrs. Betty Chorley came to lodge here, they came hither on my Horses from Leverp: I made a Mixture of part of a Legg of rosted Mutton &c., to draw Rats togeather to one Place, I think it kill'd none of them.

Feb. 12th.   My Wife and I went in yᵉ Coach wᵗʰ our Gests to Mr. Smiths of Mail.

Feb. 13th.   Mr. John Simpson and Mr. Nathani: Brown-Sword dined here they came to fetch our Gests away.

Feb. 14th.   I sent Wᵐ Weedow to Club-More with some Geese &c. I helped Ned Farer and Nich: Davy to set out a Cock-Clod at the four Lane Ends.

Feb. 17th.   I was at yᵉ Cocking at Mrs. Ann Rothwells at yᵉ Four Lane Ends, there was four Battles, a Cock of mine play'd one; there was Mr. Ald: Mr. Burton, Lunt yᵉ Schoolmaster of Ince &c.   We concluded to have a Cocking there upon Eeaster Munday, to play eather Battle Victory or Battle Royall.

1713.

John Banister went to Ormsk: of a howdoe-you to Feb. 19th. Mrs. Fazak: who was Lying in.

My Wife tryed to make some Red Ginger-Bread after Feb. 23rd. y⁰ York Fassion. I went in y⁰ Morning to y⁰ Saile of goods at the Grange, I bought some small Casks and some Pewter.

I went to Wigan and discoursed Doctor Tho: Worthing- Feb. 24th. ton about seting his Hous ready Furnished, it was for my Brother Langdale.

Mr. Shepheard was here and Acquainted me that those Feb. 27th. of Ince were willing to have y⁰ Sute refer'd but will not own that they desire it.

Mr. Scarisb: and his Lady dined here, they brought Mar. 1st. their Son Robert, he is for going to Blandick.

I went to Leverp: and discoursed Mr. Plumb about y⁰ Mar. 2nd. Sute depending betweene Ince and me. Mr. Simpson treated me at his Hous. I drunk at y⁰ Woolpack with Mr. Alanson and Dr Tarlton.

I went to Prescot and light at Tho: Moss'es y⁰ Signe Mar. 3rd. of y⁰ Ship, I sent for Lawyer Blund: and discoursed him about y⁰ Water-Cours Sute, I made a Viset to Oliver Lime.

There were some Hunters in y⁰ North-Hey and Little Mar. 9th. Eases, I heard it was Mr. Molin: of Wooton hunting y⁰ Fox, my Wife I &c went up into y⁰ Leads to look at them.

I went to Leverp: and made Mrs. Holiwell a Viset Mar. 13th and wished her Joy. Parson Stith shewed me his Garden.

There were 186 People at Prayers at Mr. Aldreds this Mar. 15th. after noone.

1713.

Mar. 20th.   I weighed my Cock and some others as are up in my Pens.

Mar. 21st.   I spard four Cocks that are up in my Pens to feed.

Mar. 22nd.   Jo: Whitley brought me a Cock wch he lent me against my Cocking on Easter Munday.

Mar. 25th.   I made a Match with John Rose to play my Ditton Cock Clumsy agaīst one of his. I sent a Chess-bord and Men of a Present to Sr Will: Gerard.

Mar. 27th.   Four of ye Coks in my Pens were spar'd.

Mar. 28th.   Now ye Sute depending seems to be at an end between Ince and me about ye Water Courses.

Mar. 29th.   I began my Journey towards Lancas: in Order to try Tho: Hartley for destroying ye Game within ye Lord-ship, I dined at Mr. Ri: Walmesleys in Preston, I made a Viset to Mrs. Fleetw: Butler and then went towards Lanc: with Mr. Tarlton ye Maior of Leverpoole and Lodged at Marshalls the Signe of the Queens Arms, I suped there wth Mr. Darcy Chantrell.

Mar. 30th.   I dined at my Lodgings wth Mr. Parker of Broosom Mr. Lister, Mr. Darcy Chantrell &c.

Mar. 31st.   I dined at my Lodging in a by Roome with Mr. Winter Parson of Cockrom. I had my Tryall wth Tho: Hartley and cast him.

April 1st.   I dined at my Inn with Cap: Parker of Broosom. My Fighting Cocks were spared ye third and last time.

April 2nd.   I called at Parson Winters at Cockrom. I dined at Rich: Jacksons in Preston, I went with Mr. Rich: Walmesley to look at Mr. Husons Hous to see if it would be proper for my Brot: Langdale. I made a Viset to my Lady Eliz: Eyre and to Mrs. Fleetwood Butler.

Rowland Eyre, of Hassop, Derbyshire, Esq., had a house outside Preston, which was occupied by the King's troops in the siege of that town, 1715. His wife, Lady Elizabeth, was a daughter of Luke Plunket, Earl of Fingal. They were both buried at St. Wilfred's, now St. John's, Preston, Mr. Eyre dying on March 22, aged 72, and his wife on August 26 of the same year, 1729.

Mr. Ald: prayed and preched here a Passion Sermon.   April 3rd.

I broke Lent with Black-Pudings as were made before Christmas.   April 5th.

This was Easter Sunday.

We had a great Cocking at Mrs. Ann Rothwells they   April 6th. played Battle Victory I had two Cocks in ye Battles and one of y^m got two Battles, there were nine Battles played this afternoone. Mrs. Blund: and Mr. Turvill made a Viset here, but I came not to them from ye Cocking.

Toping the Pariter was here abeging Corne I gave   April 7th. him some.

I gave Ned Howerd £3 towards inlarging his Chappell.   April 15th.

This was the chapel in Little Crosby Village used by Mr. Aldred. " Mass was said in the roof or attic of the cottage, and the marks of the stone steps leading to it are still visible; the steps themselves were, I believe, removed by my father after the death of an old woman, Jane Fisher, who lived there upwards of 90 years." (Note by Col. N. Blundell.)

I bought six plate Buttons of Mr. Shields for my Frock.   April 18th.

Mr. Smith of Sefton was here, his Landlord Captain   April 24th. Croston came with him.

The Crossions went to Great Crosby and ye Antecros-   April 26th. sions played at ye Cross in the Townfield after Supper.

1713.
April 27th.

My Wife had two small Peeces of Searge brought home from Leverp: by one that dyed them for her, they were of our own spinning of Gersey.

May 5th.

I met yᵉ Corps of my Lady Molin: at Ormsk: and attended it to yᵉ Funerall at Sefton, there was Sʳ Wᵐ Gerard, Mr. Standish, Mr. Roger Diconson &c.

This Lady Molyneux was Bridget, daughter of Robert Lucy, of Charlecote, Co. Warwick, Esq., buried in linen and the forfeitures paid. William, 4th Viscount Molyneux, re-married at Warrington on July 22, 1716, Mary Skelton, and was buried at Sefton, March 12, 1717-8.—*Payne's English Catholic Nonjurors*, p. 113.

May 18th.

I was at Sefton Ailhous at a Parish Meeting concerning repairing the Steeple, there was Mr. Williamson of Litherland, Mr. Parr, Mr. Shepheard &c.

May 19th.

Catty Howerd and Nanny Blund: should have set up in yᵉ night with their Sweet-hearts but they were discover'd and prevented.

May 20th.

John Blund: came and chaptered his Doughter Nanny for her last nights Proiect.

May 22nd.

Parson Wairing and Mr. Peter Morton called here as they were going to Ince Green, I went along with them and bowl'd there with Parson Letus, Parson Darbyshire, young Mr. Butler of Radcliff &c.

May 25th.

I made a Viset to Parson Wairing, there was his Uncle Hen: Wairing, Parson Letus, Parson Walsh, Tho: Syer of yᵉ Ford &c.

May 27th.

Parson Wairing and his Wife made a Viset here, tis yᵉ first time she has ben here since she was Married.

Rev. Gerard Wareing had just married Julian Crosse, sister to the wife of Parson Letus. He died March 23, 1730, aged 42, as his stone in Sefton Church testifies. He left his young children ill provided for. Mrs. Letus writes to her brother-in-law, John France, begging clothes for John, "who was to go to Dr. Bromfield. She keeps the girl, though more than she can afford; the other boy is with brother Farnworth."—*Rawcliffe Papers*. The uncle Henry was schoolmaster at Prescot, and another uncle, Thomas, was vicar of Garstang, and died October 22, 1722. The inscription on his tombstone at Churchtown terminates with the Catholic formula, *Requiescat in pace.*

I sent Henry Kerfoot to Hooton to see my Cozen June 1st. Standley who was lying in of her Son Henry.

I paid Will: Harrison yᵉ Clark of Sefton my Easter June 5th. dues and Clarks wages. Will: Ainsworth took a bull of mine with him to the Hall of Eckleston as he had sold to yᵉ Steward, Mr. Waterworth.

Will: Ainsw: bought me some Timber at yᵉ Hall of June 9th. Martine.

I took a Drought of Sack and Oyle but found no great June 12th. good by it.

I went to Leverp: with my Wife, she showed her Legg June 13th. to Mrs. Maginis.

Mrs. Bootle of yᵉ Peele sent to invite my Wife to dine June 15th. with her at yᵉ Peele. Mr. Trafford of Croston and his Son John dined here they went with us to a Hors Rase as was on Great Crosby Marsh, there was Mr. Langley, Mr. Ford yᵉ Putarer, Mr. Simpson &c.: yᵉ Mistake of a Guiney given to my Servant.

I being one of Dʳ Lathom's Executors I went to his June 24th. Hous to order his Buriall, he was carried on my Coach Carriage to Walton Church there was at his Buriall Jo: Tyrer, Mr. Bower and his Wife, Mr. Crisp &c there was at the Hous Mr. Shaw of Ormsk: John Crew &c.

Pat Buno Anderton made a Viset here. June 25th.

Mrs. Molin: of Wooton, her Doughter Mary and her June 29th. Sister-in-law Mrs. Mary Molin: dined here.

1713.
June 30th.   Old Mr. Walmesley late of Showley came betimes in yᵉ Morning.

July 1st.   I went to Ormsk: to Doctor Lancasters, there was Mr. Scarisb: Mr. Peter Ashton, Mr. Woodrove, Mr. Harding of Sutton &c.

July 4th.   Rob: Bootle and Umphrey Coppold paid me for some Paving Stones, they Smoked their pips with me.

July 5th.   My Wife, Mrs. Molin: of yᵉ Grange, Fanny and I went in yᵉ Coach to Scarisb: we found Mr. Barlowes Son of Barlow there, Mrs. Scaresb: was Lying Inn of her Son Thomas. Mr. John Blundells Widdow lodged there.

July 8th.   I met Ri: Tatlock and sold him some of Dr Lathoms Chirurgicall Instruments.

July 12th.   I Lodged at Ditton at yᵉ Bank at Wᵐ Athertons, Fanny rid behind me.

July 13th.   Hen: Heys went with me to Mr. Writs of Cranton, I discoursed him about seeking for Coles in Ditton. Will: Weed: had a Reering of one bay of Shipponing all or most of my Servants were at it pritty late.

July 17th.   Mr. Plumb kept my Court at Will: Davys before dinner. When he was gon I went to John Farers. We adiusted the Difference between George Cottom and Jo: Tickley about a Tup.

July 19th.   Coz: Tho: Gelib: his Father and I went to Chorley to Cowlings, I drunk there wᵗʰ Mr. Char: Townley and Mr. Charls Chorley; Coz: Jo: Gelib: and Mr. Chorley met there upon the Townes Business.

In *Baines' Lancashire*, vol. 2, p. 126, the following inscription is given from a gravestone in Chorley Churchyard:—" Hic jacet Corpus Thomœ Gillibrand de Chorley Hall, Gen. Qui obiit 19° die

Octobrs A.D. 1733." Within three years of the Diarist's visit, both Mr. Charles Chorley and his father had perished in the Jacobite rebellion. Mr. Richard Chorley was executed at Preston, February 9, 1715-6, whilst his son Charles died in a Liverpool prison. Their estate was forfeited, and sold to Mr. Abraham Crompton, a banker, of Derby, for £5,653 18s. 1d. Mr. John Gillibrand, an upright and conscientious lawyer, lived at Astley Hall.

Coz: Tho: Gelib: I and oure Wives went to Preston, July 20th. dined wth my Lady Eliz^h Eyre, after dinner I went to the Bowling Green at ye Signe of ye Whit-Hors. I drunk at ye whit Bull with Coz: Tho Gelib: Mr. Tho: Singleton Mr. Edm Ashton &c. I made a Viset to ye two Mrs. Blundells Ann and Bridg: and to old Mrs. Walmesley.

Mrs. Bradley and Betty Wastley played on the Vir- July 22nd. ginells at my Coz: Gelibronds.

Sr Will: Gerard, Mr. Swinbourn, Mr. Rob: Fazak: Aug. 19th. and his Wife dined here.

"Rev. John Swinburne, S.J., alias or *vere* Savage, born in Derbyshire, March 21, 1660-1. Served the Lancashire district, where he died September 11, 1716."—*Foley's Collectanea.*

I went to Lever: and saw Sr Thomas Johnson come Aug. 22nd. into Town from London his Party had Tobacco Gilded in their Hats and the opposit Party viz: Mr. Clayton and Mr. Cleaveland had the Myter, there was great squabling about the Election of some of them for Parleament Men.

The members returned on this occasion were Sir Thomas Johnson and Mr. Clayton.

I went to ye Hall of Sefton to ye Buriall of Wm Aug. 26th. Thelwall there was Mr. Smith the Malster, Mr. Peter Morton, Mr. Bower, Mr. Crisp &c.

William Thelwall had broken his leg, and died in consequence of his hurt, after making a verbal will in presence of the squire, who says that Rev. Thomas Wolfall of the Grange attended him.

Coz: Molineux of Mosburgh, his Lady and Brother Sept. 2nd. lodged here.

1713.
Sept. 4th. Mr. Wm Moline: being this day 44 years old I gave a Bowl of Punsh to solemnize his Birth day.

Sept. 15th. I was at Ince Green when ye six Matches every one different were bowled by Mr. Burton, Mr. Formby and Parson Darbyshire, against Mr. Ald: Parson Letus and Parson Wairing, Mr. Nich: Fazakerley was there.

Sept. 18th. I Bowled at Ince Green against Parson Letus &c there was Mr. Nich: Fazak: Mr. Formby, Mr. Tatlock of ye Bank and his Brother &c.

Sept. 20th. I gave Hen: Sefton a Note to shew to ye Parish that it was agreed that he and his Partners should have Aile allowed them when they poynted ye Steeple.

Sept. 23rd. Samuel Clark, Jo: Cooper and Mr. Jo: Fletcher had ben in Great Crosby about an exchange of Part of Taylors Teneament, they are Trustees for ye Poore of Windle it being left to them, they came hither and discourced me about it and about a mistake as is in that Surrender.

Sept. 26th. I sent three Cart Load of Beanes to Lev: they are to goe to Guinea.

Mr. Gildas was the merchant who bought the beans.

Sept. 27th. I sent Wm Ainsw: towards Preston to Mrs. Walmesley the Younger of Showley who was Lying in of her Doughter Mary.

Sept. 28th. I helped to set some Tulop Roots as were dresed with Ink after different manners and some as were order'd otherwayes in hops to change their cullor but to no good effect. The rich Posy sent from hence to Will: Weedows Breaking.

It may be folly to "paint the lily," but an experimentalist has steeped white hyacinth plants in water tinged with aniline dyes, and some beautiful flowers, of colours not yet produced by the gardener, have been the result.—See *Cassell's Magazine*, vol. 8, p. 639.

1713.

Coz: Scarisb: I and oure Wives dined at Croston, old Oct. 8th.
Mr. Standley of Preston was there.

Coz: Scarisb: and I made a Viset to Gorsuch, our Oct. 9th.
Wives made a Viset to Parson Brownhills of Holsold.

I began my Journey towards Stockhild with Mally. Oct. 15th.
Called at Runshaw to see Miss Farnworth, bated at
Fletchers yᵉ Signe of the Bucks Heads in Brindle. I there
discoursed Geor: Abb: about being my Steward, we lost our
way and went to Rushton where we got a Guide towards
Great Harwood, we lodged there at Christo: Fieldings the
Signe of the three Pigeons.

Went to Gisbourn where we dined at yᵉ Signe of yᵉ Oct. 16th.
Dove, thence to Skipton and Lodged at Gilbe: Johnsons
yᵉ Signe of yᵉ Black Horse.

Called at yᵉ George in Long Adington, thence to Oct. 17th.
Stockhild.

Mr. Witham formerly of the Bass and his two Sons Oct. 18th.
dined at Stockhild.

My Brother Midleton took me in his Coach to Wetherby Oct. 19th.
where we dined at yᵉ Talbot with yᵉ Fox Hunters viz: Mr.
Henry Stapleton, Mr. Plaxton, Mr. Ned Tompson &c. My
Brother Joseph came.

Rev. Joseph Blundell, S.J., a younger brother of the Diarist,
born May 2, 1686, entered the Society of Jesus 1703, and was then
serving the Yorkshire Missions. He was afterwards at Spinkhill,
Derbyshire, and died at Watten, July 27, 1759, aged 73.

Made a Viset to Mr. Plumpton. Oct. 21st.

I left Mally at Stockhild and began my Journey Hom- Oct. 22nd.
wards. I lodged at Will: Heaks yᵉ Red Lyon in Yellom.

Came through Berry, Bolton &c and so to Wigan. Oct. 23rd.

Hen: Kerfoot shot a Herrón. Oct. 30th.

1713.
Nov. 5th.
Mr. Tho: Walm: I and our Wives went in yͤ Coach to Leverp: saw yͤ new Church and made a Viset to Mr. Morecroft.

Nov. 13th.
Mr. Worthing: Doughter Ursula came to be my Wives Maid.

Nov. 14th.
Mr. Ald: went out a Coursing with me, we went to Whartons in Ince to drink where we found Pat: Tasburgh, Pat: Barton and Chattering John Rimer.

Nov. 16th.
Rich: Webster took possession of my new Smithy.

Nov. 17th.
I took some of yͤ Picturs as were Dr Lathoms to Ned Howerds, some of them I hung up there in yͤ Chappell.

Nov. 20th.
Coz: Scarisb: his Lady and Mr. Traps the Younger &c dined here. Geor: Abbot came to be my Steward.

George Abbott had been in the service of the famous Cavalier, Caryll, Viscount Molyneux, and on attempting a passage to Ireland in 1689 was taken prisoner at Liverpool, and carried to London. The narrative of his imprisonment, called *Abbott's Journal,* was edited for the Chetham Society by the late Bishop Goss. (No. 61).

Nov 24th.
A Rat ran up Jo: Banisters Coat Sleeve, we killed it.

Dec. 1st.
I found Mary Holme and Hen: Bridge in yͤ Gatehouse Chamber about four in the morning for which I turned her out of my Service.

Dec. 19th.
Nutty's (Ursula's) Brother Mr. Will: Worthington came hither to see her.

Dec. 24th.
I Painted a Pair of Little Wheels for yͤ Coach.

Dec. 29th.
Mr. Tho: Worthington yͤ Saylor dined here.

1714.
Jan. 2nd.
My Wife and I Lodged at Wᵐ Athertons at Ditton. I played some tricks of Legerdemesney to his Gests and Neighbours.

Jan. 3rd.
My Wife and I went to Mr. Maiers to Prayers.

I Removed y⁰ Ship in y⁰ Hall and charg'd y⁰ Gunns against tomorrow.

Mr. Plumb, Doctor Lancaster and I &c. was at Mrs. Anns Cocking, there were three Battles. Tatlock was here, we had a Merry-Night and Fier'd y⁰ Gunns of my Ship.

Mr. Tatlock, Mr. Smith of Maile, Mr. Aspinwall &c were a Hunting this way. I invited them hither and made yᵐ drink at y⁰ Gates. I took in hand to cure Ginnet Blundells Legg but she did not long continew my Pasient.

Came to Ch: Howerds where I found Mr. Tatlock of y⁰ Bank, his Brother Thomas, Tatlock y⁰ Dier, Parson Becket of Kerkby, Mr. Smith of Maile, Mr. Aspinwall &c. We went a Coursing.

I sent Geor: Abb: to y⁰ Saile at Peele but he bought nothing. I met Parson Wairing, Mr. Crisp, Thomas Syer, Ned Hatton &c at Thomas Heskeths to consider about y⁰ Inclosing of Great Crosby Marsh, then I went to a Cocking as was in y⁰ Pinfold.

Lord Molin: his Sons Carroll and Tho: and Doughters Ann and Bridget dined here, so did Coz: Scarisb: and his Lady.

I was at a Cocking at Mrs. An Rothwells there were four Battles Play'd and this Town lost every one of them.

I went part of y⁰ Way towards Formby with Mr. Brana: and Patrick Norris to look at y⁰ Road as Walt: Thel: has set out over Ince Mosses for Mr. Branagans Gallaway that is to Run 3 times between Formby and Leverp: in 4 Hours Time, which he performed; and finished his Course in less time by above a quarter of an Hour, I was at y⁰ Race and Rid with Mr. Branagan from y⁰ Town to Formby and from

1714.

thence back to Lever: Sands. Duke Maltus, Walt: Thelwall, Mr. James Tildesley &c Rid part of ye Rase a long wth me.

Mar. 23rd.

I went to Leverp: and heard Prayers at Mrs. Brownbills thence I went to Mrs. Ladys with Mr. Branagan &c I bought a Hat of Widdow Leversage.

Mar. 25th.

I went to Charles Howerds and drunk with Mr. Wm Clayton the Master of the Suckcess Brigantine as had suffered Ship-rack.

Mar. 29th.

I went in the forenoone to Edm: Lathoms in Speak Town in hopes to have heard Prayers, I found Mr. Maor there but he had done ere I came.

Mar. 30th.

I came from Ditton to Lever: where I served Mr. Phillipson at Mrs. Browbills. Came home and then went to Sefton to ye Parish meeting but all business was over and found ye Parish had chosen me to be their Church Warden.

April 1st.

Went to Ormskirk and advised with Mr. Brooks about my being Chosen a Church-Warden of Sefton Parish. I drunk at ye Griffan with Dr Lancaster. Pat: Ald: broke his Collar Bone with a Fawl of his Horse.

April 2nd.

Went to Sefton and told Parson Letus, I would not Stand as Church-Warden.

April 5th.

I lodged in Chester at Mr. Pantons ye Signe of the Whit-Bull out of Norgate.

April 11th.

My Wife and I went to Eckleston we heard Mr. Swinbourn hold forth, there was present Mr. Holland of Sutton, Mr. Complin &c.

April 12th.

Cha: Howerd, Will: Wignold and I devided some Timber amongst us, it was Part of ye Suckcess Brigantine, we cast Lots and I had two very large Load to my Share for 20ˢ

I drunk at Mrs. Lady's (Liverpool) with Parson Walsh, April 17th. Parson Orme, Parson Wairing and his Uncle &c.

I met Tho: Syer at Harsnops, 'tis the first time we met April 21st. to consult of yᵉ Parish Affaires, since we were Church-Wardens, we caused a Chest over yᵉ Church Pourch to be brock open as had not ben open'd of very many years.

My Wife rid part of yᵉ way behind me towards Leverp: April 23rd. but the Hors flung her so she walked home on foot, and I went to Leverp: but Mr. Plumb being Just ready to goe to Bank-hall to shoot young Rooks I had very little discours with him.

Cap: Rob: Faz: called here as he was going from April 27th. Leverp: towards Formby to shoot Dotterell.

Thoˢ Syer and I looked at yᵉ Legasy Table in yᵉ Old April 30th. Church in Leverpoole.

Thoˢ Syer and I looked to see in what Repaire yᵉ Leads May 1st. were in and yᵉ Windows (at Sefton Church).

I dined at Scarisb: to take leave of Mr. Scarisbricks May 3rd. Son William who was going to Blandike. I smoked in Maynards Chamber with Mr. Gorsuch.

I went to Wigan to yᵉ Funerall of my old Lady May 8th. Bradshaw, there was at yᵉ Funerall or at least in the Roome, Sʳ Tho: Standish Mr. Banks of Winstanley, Mr. Standish, Mr. Scarisb: Mr. John Gerard, Dʳ Tho: Worthington &c.

I was at yᵉ Bishops Court in Ormskerk, the Chancellor May 13th. gave me leave in yᵉ Presence of Mr. Roberts and Mr.

1714.

Sankey to put Doars without Locks, to my Pew in Farnworth Chappell. Being Tho: Syer and I are yᵉ Church-Wardens we dined at yᵉ Talbot in Ormsk: wᵗʰ Parson Letus, Parson Wairing &c.

May 17th. My Wife went to Aigbourth to Condole yᵉ Death of Mr. Harington, she dined there. Richard Westhead and Wil: Tarlton told me they had taken seaven Young Foxes to day in a Denn in the Warand, I think they will bring them all alive to Wooton to Mr. Molin:

May 18th. I was at Ch: Howerds where there was a Battle Victory fought for a Saddle by eight Cocks, t'was wone by a Leverp: Cock as belong'd I think to Jack Whit.

May 22nd. Pat: Ald: lodged here upon Account of a fals Allarum that there were some People Searching at yᵉ Grange for Pat: Wofold.

May 29th. Wᵐ Tarlton went with me to Southard to yᵉ Funerall of Mr. Golding, he was buried at Winick there was at his Buriall Mr. Gerard of Highfild, Mr. Culcheth, Mr. Johnson of Warington, Parson Alanson, Mr. Blackbourn of Orford &c.

June 1st. I went to Orrell to Wᵐ Tarltons Marlers and made them shout.

June 17th. My Wife, I and Fanny began our Journey towards Stockhild, we called at Tho: Places in Ormsk: his Wife gave us a drink at the doar, we bated at Fletchers, yᵉ Signe of yᵉ Bucks Heads in Brindle, thence to Gisbourn where we lodged at John Yates yᵉ Spoted Hind.

June 19th. Walked with my Lord Langd: to my Brother Midletons Bath.

Mally began to drink the Sulfure Spaw-Water. Went to York where we Lodged at Mrs. Hawksworths in Little Blake Street.

Mrs. Naper dined with us at our Lodgings and then made a Viset with us by Coach to Mrs. Pastons, to Mrs. Eringtons &c.

Made a Viset to my Coz: Tho: Selby thence we wènt to yᵉ Whit-Bear Coffy-Hous where we drunk with Pat: Bostock and one Mr. Brigham.

My Wife and I made a Viset to my Lady Smithson thence she went with us to Viset Mrs. Ferfax. Went to Coggrave or St Mungoes. I lodged there but my Wife went back to Loftus-Hill to Mr. Hodgsons.

Sir Hugh Smithson, of Stanwick, Bart., married Elizabeth, daughter of Marmaduke, Lord Langdale. Their grandson, Sir Hugh, son of Langdale Smithson and his wife Philadelphia, daughter of Wm. Reveley, Esq., of Newby-Wisk, Co. York, married, in 1740, Lady Elizabeth, daughter of the Duke of Somerset, and eventually sole heiress of the Percies, Earls of Northumberland. In 1749-50 he became Earl of Northumberland, of which title he was in remainder by the letters patent obtained by his father-in-law a few months before his death. From this marriage the present duke traces his descent.

Dr Craythorne and I went into yᵉ Baith or St Mungows Well, after dinner he and I played at Cards with my Wife, Mrs. Doleman of Pocklington and the two Sisters Mrs. Dolmans.

Dined at Coggrave wᵗʰ yᵉ three Mrs. Dolman, Mr. Wilks and his Wife, Mrs. Bullock &c.

Young Mr. Plumton, Mr. Chumley of Bransby and Pat: Phisipson dined at Stockhild.

Mr. Hammond and Pat: Cass dined at Stockhild.

1714.

June 29th.   Mr. Cha: Ferfax, Sr Tho: Tankerds eldest son, Pat: Medcalf and Pat Wm Fenwick dined at Stock:

June 30th.   Pat: Graves, Pat: Smith and Mr. Plumton Senior dined at Stockh: Sister Midleton took my Wife and me in her Coach to Harragate or Knesburrow Spawes, I went chiefly to see my Coz: Joe Ingleby who was at ye Royall Oak, thence to the Green Dragon, then to the Sulfure Spaw.

July 1st.   My Wife I and my Children came to Burghwallice where we lodged.

July 2nd.   Coz Ann of Frickley and his Wife dined at Burg-wallice. My Lady Smithson lodged at Burgwallice.

July 3rd.   Edw: Fletcher the Fidler played to us, Lady Smithson I &c danced Country D̄aces &c.

July 4th.   Cozen Duke Ann of Frickley and his Wife dined at Burgwallis.

July 5th.   We came to Henry Nowells in Duesbury where we dined, it is an extraordinary dear house, thence to the George at Holcroft Head, then to Sampson Sunderlands the Black Lyon in Rippondale where we lodged, tiss a very Cheap Inn and sivell oblidging People but ye Lodging very ordinary.

July 6th.   Came to Bolton where we dined at Hen: Wilkinsons the Signe of ye Swan with two Necks.

July 11th.   My Brother Joseph held forth at Mr. Aldreds and then went to dine at Ince.

His brother had returned with him out of Yorkshire.

July 12th.   My Brother Jos: and Pat Ald: went to dine at Mos-burgh thence to goe lodg at Garswood.

My Wife and Brother Joseph and Mally walked to Lidiat Hall and the Coach went to Fetch them home.

I went to Leverp: with my Brother Jos: on Purpose to shew him the Town, we drunk at ye Woolpack wth Mr. Simpson, and then we went to ye Golden Fleece where I treated them with Perry.

I drunk at ye Crown in Water Street with Mr. Morphew, Mr. Rob: Faz: I saw the Show of the Waterworks at ye Griffan, there was Mr. Dugdale &c.

I went with Sr James Poole to the New Hous to prayers to Pat: Tasb: there was Mr. Crisp, Mr. Shepheard &c.

Went to Cha: Howerds where we had a Silly-bub. There came an Express from Stockhild to invite me to my Brother Midletons Funerall, I began my Journey towards Stockhild about 11 of ye Clock at Night.

I came to ye Swan with two Necks in Bolton about Six in ye Morning, thence to Bradford where I lodged at Geo: Fletchers ye Signe of ye Black Swan, I drunk there with his Brother who they called Captain Fletcher he had ben at St. Omers.

Came to Stockhild before Dinner, found my Brother Langdale. Mr. Plumpton and his wife came, Pat: Graton and Pat: Powell Dined here.

Came to Preston, lodged at Rich: Jacksons.

Heard Mr. Knights Mass, there was at it old Mr. Walmesley (of Showley) Mr. Standley and their Wives.

Tho: Kerklington ye old Simpler of Herbs, and Picture seller lodged here.

Mr. Gilb: Barrows Pothecary of Leverp: Dined here.

Aug. 7th.　My Brot: Jos: Married Mich: Mackdaniell to Catherine Taylor.

Aug. 10th.　I made a Viset to Mr. Woodrove at Low-Hill.

Aug. 19th.　I began my Journey with Walt: Thelwall towards Lancaster, Mr. Plumb and we met upon y⁰ Road and went together to Garstang, bated at y⁰ Kings Head.

Aug. 20th.　We went to Lawyer Bootle for his Opinion. Judges Powell and Trecy. Dined at my Lodging (Kings Armes) wth Mr. Brockolds.

Aug. 21st.　Heard y⁰ Tryall between Williamson and Rushton and £160 damage given to Williamson.

Aug. 22nd.　I came from Preston to y⁰ Hall of Boscow where Pat: Gorsu: selebrated.

Aug. 28th.　I went to Leverp: and was at y⁰ Funerall of one Wall a Quacker School-Mistress and heard Rob: Hadock Preach, coming home I light and let my Mare over goe me, I walked home and she was brought to me next Morning.

Aug. 30th.　My Wife, I and Children dined at Mrs. Barkers it being Ormsk: Fair, I shewed my Children y⁰ Strange Creatures as were to be seen, a Tyger, a Sivet Cat &c.

Sept. 11th.　I went to Leverp: with Mally and got a Rotton Tooth of hers pulled out by a Mountebank.

Sept. 12th.　Mr. Daniel Morphew and Mr. Ward came to prayers to Mr. Aldreds, they dined here.

Sept. 14th.　I had a great Breaking of Flax, there was 12 Breakers, 12 Scutchers, 11 Slansers, 4 to tend two Gigs and one to take up y⁰ Flax, in all 40 Persons, I gave a Good Supper to my own Breakers and Swinglers. Tatlock played to y^m at Night, we had 4 Disgisers and a Garland from Great Crosby and a deal of Dansing.

Mr. Scarisb: Young Mr. Trafford and I played at Cut and Trante Carrant at Night. Sept. 21st.

Mr. Heskaine and Cap: Rob: Faz: dined here. Sept. 24th.

My Wife sent a large Lives of Sants to Lidiat as she had borrowed of Mr. Moston. Sept. 26th.

I hung up one Stalk on my Indion Wheat in yᵉ Hall, it grew in my own Garden and was above 9 Feet 1 Insh long. Oct. 6th.

I intercepted a Peece of Beef as Marg: Ridgat was sending to her Mother for which I turned her out of my hous for this Night, but upon her great Submission I took her yᵉ next day. Oct. 9th.

I made a Viset to Croxtath where I found Mr. Molin: of Wooton and his Lady, Coz: Molin: of Mosb: and his Lady, Mr. Massy of Pudington, Sʳ James Poole &c. Oct. 10th.

One from Leverp: brought a Ticket for my Wife of the Play as is to be acted there to-morrow. Oct. 12th.

My Wife, Mally and I dined at Wooton, there also dined Mr. Jo: Gerard, My Lady Gerard and her Doughter Mary, Mr. Wᵐ Pools Wife &c, then went to yᵉ New-Market where we saw a Play Acted called Mackbeth. Oct. 13th.

I went to Leverpoole there Tho: Syer and I discoursed Richard Eckleston and made him give us a more moderate Bill of work done by him for Sefton Church. Oct. 16th.

James Davy yᵉ Cunstable came hither to carry Margarit Ridgate before Sʳ Thom: Johnson, but my Wife beged me to pardon her. Oct. 22nd.

1714.

Oct. 15th.   Tho: Syer and I had Rich: Eckleston and the Clark under examination about the Plumbers Bill before Parson Letus at his own Hous.

Oct. 30th.   I met Rob: Tompson at his Mothers in order to make them Friends.

Oct. 31st.   I discoursed Wm Abbot about making Stayers for ye Pulpet of Sefton Church.

Nov. 9th.   I dined at the New-hous it being Pat: Tasburghs Solemnizing of his Jubely, there was at Dinner Mr. Scarisb: Sr Fra: Anderton, Mr. Wofold, Pat Tasburgh, Pat Babthrop Pat Gelibrond &c.

Nov. 14th.   I made a Shutle-Cock for my Children but they could not play with it.

Dec. 4th.   Coz: Gelibrond sent his Servant to desire my Wife would be God-Mother to his Son Tho: who was borne ye 2^d Inst.

Dec. 6th.   I met Lord Molin: his Son Carol, Coz: Rob: Molineux of Mosburgh &c at Dukes in Great Crosby, we drunk Wine there and a Bowl of Punsh. Pat Aldred treated us with five Bottles of Claret.

Dec. 13th.   I went to Leverp: and as I was going I saw a Bote coming a Shoar wth ye Keel upwards, I told Sr Thos: Johnson of it. As I was vewing ye Dock I met Mr. Blund: and I think young Mr. Willis they desir'd my Interest to vote for Parleament-Men.

Dec. 22nd.   I killed a Hogg as I had fed with Ackhorns but it was not very Fat.

Dec. 24th.   Being Mrs. Molineux died yesterday, I went this Morning to ye Grange to pray for her, I heard three Mas: and helped to say y⁰ Offi: Defunct:. I sent to see Mrs. Scarisbrick who was Lying in of her Doughter Mary.

I went to y⁰ Grange to Mrs. Molineux his Buriall, Dec. 25th. there was Mr. Wofold, Mr. Gorsuch Yeomond of the Goar-Houses &c.

Mrs. Ann Molineux and her Sister Bridget lodged here Dec. 27th. so did Mr. Molineux of Mitch Wootons two Doughters.

Mr. Carroll Moline: and Brother Will: dined and Dec. 29th. Lodged here.

Mr. Carrol Molyneux became Viscount Molyneux in 1738 on the death of his brother Richard, and, dying without issue in 1745, was succeeded by the above brother, Rev. William Molyneux, S.J., who died in 1750, at Scholes Hall, near Prescot, where he had resided many years.

1715.

I was at a Parish Meeting at Harsnops where we agreed Jan. 5th. there should be twelve Representatives or Consultors Chosen for this Parish. There was Parson Letus, Mr. Bower, Tho: Syer of y⁰ Ford, John Tyrer, Anthony Fleetwood &c we then chose the 12 Representatives but since that time we have waived that affair.

We had a throng Carding Night at Cut. Jan. 6th.

Pat: Wofold was here beging Charity for Lisbon Collage, Jan. 12th. I gave him some.

I saw Pat: Ald: set a Hen-Egg upon an end, on a Jan. 13th. Looking Glass, he shew'd me y⁰ way.

I set an Egg upon one End tis y⁰ first time I did it. Jan. 21st.

I gave a Poore Woman a Doce for y⁰ Falling Sickness. Jan. 26th.

There was a most prodigious Wind it did more Feb. 1st. dammage in this Town than has ever ben knone done by Wind here.

This storm was general. The Diarist says 14 barns were blown down in one parish of Lancashire.

1715.

Feb. 3rd. Mr. Turvill made a Viset here he brought the Cuning Purs as was somthing hard to be opened.

Feb. 11th I was very busy most of the afternoone drawing out a Table of Fees the first time over, which when approved of and Writ Fair over is to be hung up in Sefton Church.

Feb. 22nd. Pat: Aldred and I dined at Dukes with Mr. Molin: of Mosburgh. I gave him my Picture of the Woman and Pale.

Feb. 26th. I went to Leverp: and paid Mr. Plumb £28 in presence of his Son William, a great part of it was upon Account of my Sute with Ince about yᵉ Water courses: I was at Wᵐ Griffiths Cock-pit I saw some Battles played, there was present Rich: Thorp, Mr. Holsold &c.

Feb. 27th. My Wife and I went to prayers to Lidiat but came full late enough. I dined there with Mr. Moston and my Wife went to Ormsk: she made a Viset to Mrs. Barker and Collonell Russells Lady.

Feb. 28th. I put yᵉ Harnish as were fited up and bought for the Parish Hears, on two of my Horses and drue them in yᵉ Harnish and rectifyed what was a Miss.

Mar. 1st. My Wife made a Viset to Mrs. Wairing who was Lying in of her Son John.

Mar. 10th. My Lord Molin: his two Sons Mr. Carroll and Mr. William dined here. I bought Mr. Aldreds Sword.

Mar. 13th. Being Pat: Ald: prayed to day at Leverp: Pat: Tasburg supplied his place in yᵉ Town. John Rose, young Rob: Bootle, Jo: Bart: of Ormsk: came hither to see my Bottle and Reel.

Mar. 26th. I drunk at yᵉ Woolpack with Patrick Norriss and Mr. Becket the Cork Cutter.

Nelly Sergeant came home from Lancast: she had been there, yᵉ time of yᵉ Assizes emproving herself in Cookery.

From Ditton Mally and I went by Runkhorn Bote and so by Helsby to Chester where we lodged at Edwᵈ Parsonidge his yᵉ Signe of yᵉ Golden Lyon.

From Chester we came to Eastom and came over in yᵉ Boat. Mr. Plumb proposed to me to buy Sʳ Cleavs Land in yᵉ Morehouses.

I met Parson Richmond at Sefton Church where he proposed that 12 Representatives should be chosen for yᵉ good of this Parish.

Tho: Syer and I met at Sefton we order'd how yᵉ Table of the Benefactors was to be hung and gave the Painter orders about it.

Hen: Kerfoot fought a Cock of mine in Lidiat. My Children and the Maids went in yᵉ Coach to Formby Faire, there was a Stage Play Acted there.

Tho: Syer and I deliverd up our Accounts as Church Wardens they were read in the Church and severall Stints were set for the better Regulating the Affairs of the Parish, there was Present Parson Wairing, Thomas Syer of yᵉ Ford, Mr. Williamson of Litherland, Tho: Bradley &c. I gave Parson Latus £5 towards the Augmentation of yᵉ Parish Stock. Hen: Kerfoot fought a Red Cock of mine at Alker against Mr. Edw: Molineux.

Parson Wairing and his Uncle Henry Wairing called here as they were going to Ince Green. I went with them, we and Parson Darbyshire bowled three Rubbers.

Pat: Gelibrond and I &c observed the great Eclips of the Sun.

1715.

April 23rd.   I shewed Dr Only my Reel and Bottle and my Little Calf and some other of my Curiossitiss.

April 28th.   My Lord Molineux was at Great Crosby and being he wanted Licker Pat: Aldred who was wth him sent hither for Brandy I lent him two Bottles and some Sugar.

May 6th.   I went to Leverp: and contracted wth Mr. Plumb for one Aicker of Sr Clave Mores Land.

May 9th.   Ann Thelw: was here and had a Sevear Scoulding Bout concerning her Doughter Margarits Truth and Honesty.

May 10th.   Pat: Norris my Lord Ferfax Sacerd: made a Viset here.

This seems to have been Rev. Andrew Norris, S.J., belonging to a younger branch of the Speke family. Was son of John and Elizabeth Norris (Beauvoye), born at Speke, 1656. On entering the English College, Rome, 1673, he says—"My parents and relations are of the higher class and are all Catholics. I have three brothers, but no sister. My father and friends suffered much for religion." This must have been before the defection of the chief family from the Catholic faith. At the revolution of 1688 he was imprisoned for a short time in York Castle. Was at one period Superior of his brethren, and died January 26, 1721.—See *Foley's Records*, vol. 5, p. 616.

May 14th.   The Young Folks of this Town had a Merry-Night at James Davis, Tatlock played to them; the Young Weomen treated y^e Men with a Tandsey as they had lost to them, at a Game at Stoole Balle.

May 22nd.   Pat: Holsold and I called at Holsold and went into y^e Church, we drunk at y^e Ailes-Hous with the Parson.

Holsold = Halsall.

May 28th.   I was at y^e Bishops Court at Ormsk: I dined at y^e Angell wth Mr. Prescot of Leverp: Parson Latus, Parson Wairing, Mr. Wofold &c.

May 30th.   My Teame and severall of y^e Neighbours led Coles for Parson Latus from Blay-Gate.

After Supper we played at Cards at Loo.

I went to Ince Green and Bowled there with Mr.
Formby, Mr. Tatlock of y° Bank &c. Parson Latus, Parson
Wairing, Mr. Aspinwall of Leverp:, Pothacary Lathom &c
were there.

I went to Leverp: and dined at Alderman Tyrers. I
was at Mr. Sherlocks Schoole and saw Mally Dance.

Parson Wairing called here and I went with him to
Ince Green, there was Parson Letus, Wairing, Darbishire,
Mr. Formby, Mr. Tatlock &c. Young Parson Brownell and
I bowled against Parson Latus and Mr. Bayron.

We saw y° Morris Dansers of Sefton as were going
their Round in order to Rear a May-Pole in Sefton.

I gave a great many Flowers towards y° Flowring of
Ince Cross. I was at Ince Bowling Green, there was Mr.
Nich° Fazak: Mr. Formby, Mr. Tatlock, Mr. Lancelet of
Ormsk: &c.

My Children went to y° Flowering of Ince Cross.

I went to Leverp: with my Brot: Lang: We went to
Low-Hill Bowling Green there was Alderman Tyrer, Mr.
Danvers, Young Mr. Write, Young Mr. Cleaveland, Dr
Fabius &c. When my Brother Langdale had done Bowling
I went with him to the Talbot where we and Mr. Heskaine
took a Glass of Wine together.

I went with my Brother Langdale to Croxtath to wate
of my Lord Molin: who was newly come from the Bath.

My Brother Langdale, my Wife and I went to Wooton,
we dined there wth my Lord Molineux.

July 5th.　I was at Harsnops at a Parish Meeting I found Mr. Jos: Poole and some others there from Leverp: the Aile being very bad we went to Tho: Tickleys.

July 9th.　The Little Boyes and Girles of this Town diverted themselves with Rearing a May-pole in the West-Lane they had Morrys dansing and a great many came to it both old and young chiefly out of ye end of the Town.

July 10th.　Alderman Tyrer sent to invite me to-morrow to ye Buriall of his Father in Law Alderman Clayton.

July 11th.　My Children and I went on Bord Mr. Lancasters Ship the Planter. I drunk at ye Woolpack with Cap: Lancaster, Mr. Sherlock &c. I was at ye Funerall of Cap: Clayton, there was in ye Roome with me Parson Richmond, Parson Becket, Mr. Green, and Mr. Blundell of Prescot &c.

July 13th.　I went to Ince Greene and Bowled there wth Parson Latus, Parson Wairing, Mr. Tatlock &c Mr. Formby, Mr. Smith of Maile &c was there.

July 15th.　I went to Mr. Hursts Buriall there was at his Hous Alderman Tyrer, Mr. Rich: Norris, Parson Richmond &c.

Aug. 2nd.　Mrs. Bootle late of Peele sent to see if I would sell her any of my goods or Furniture.

Aug. 10th.　The Constables John Sumner and James Scarisb: summonsed me to Appear at Ormskerk on Fryday next to take ye Oaths.

Aug. 14th.　I dined at Mosburgh wth Black Dr Lanc: and Cap: Rob: Faz: Parson Low came to us.

Aug. 18th.　Henry Valentine ye High Constable serched here for Horses, Armes and Gunpowder.

Parson Brownhills Wife and his Doughter Tatlock
made a Viset here.

I turned some out of the Wheat-hey as were Songoing
without Leave and took their Corn from them and gave it
to those as were there by my Leave.

I went to Leverp: and saw the Mulbury, the Batchlor
and the Robert all in yᵉ Dock, they came in this Morning
and were yᵉ first Ships as ever went into it; the Mulbury
was yᵉ first. I Breakfasted at Mr. Owens, he went wᵗʰ
me to a Smithy at yᵉ lower end of Red-Cross-Street where
I saw an Ox Rosting.

I went to Prescot and gave Lawyer Blund: direcsions
to draw a Deed for yᵉ Farther setling my Estate. I
drunk at yᵉ Bull wᵗʰ Alex: Holland and Wᵐ Case, thence
we went to yᵉ Ship. I made a Viset to Mr. Oliver Lime.

My Wife went to Leverp: she light at yᵉ Black Horce
and heard yᵉ Singing there, she saw yᵉ Great Ship and
severall others in yᵉ Dock.

My Wife and I heard Mr. Hardesty Preach, we dined
at Mr. Lancasters, I drūk at yᵉ Woolpack with Mr. Lancaster and his Brother yᵉ Doctor &c.

I dined at Dukes in Great Crosby wᵗʰ my Lord Molin:
his Son Carroll, Mr. Laybourn, Cap: Penny &c.

I went into Rob: Blansherds and there eat some thing,
being they were Breaking.

I went to Prescot and dined at Lawyer Blundells; I
light at the Ship and drunk there with Mr. Boyer, Mr.
Golding of Heartshey &c.

1715.

Sept. 28th. I Bowled at Ince Greene wth Mr. Tatlock, Parson Wairing &c Mr. Whitley &c was there.

Sept. 29th. My Wife and I went to the Scones to wish Mr. Harington Joy, it was his Birthday, tis the first time we have seen them since they were Married.

> Scones = Scholes Hall.

Oct. 5th. This being the finishing day of Bowling I dined at Whartons in Ince with Parson Brownhill Junior Mr. Whittle &c.

Oct. 17th. My Wife and I dined at Thom: Syers.

Oct. 19th. Duke let my Wife blood in her Arme.

Oct. 29th. We expected the Hors Militia to come Serch here.

Oct. 31st. I came not in till dark Night expecting a Call.

Nov. 5th. They began to fortify Leverpool by Kasting up great Banks for feer of my Lord Danwinwater.

Nov. 12th. The Fight at Preston was begun.

Nov. 13th. This Hous was twice sirched by some Foot as came from Leverpoole, I think the first party were about twenty-six.

Nov. 16th. I set in a Streat place for a fat Man.

Nov. 17th. I took a Nap between four of ye clock and five and then went to seek my Lodging.

Nov. 18th. I made an End of Reading a Book called Englands Jests.

Nov. 19th. I made an End of Reading the Book called ye English Rogue. This Hous was sirched to day by some from

Leverp: Mr. Huson and Mr. Robinson was amongst
them.

English Rogue,—a history of the most eminent cheats of both
sexes, 4 vols, published 1665, reprinted 1874.

I was in the Boys Chamber and heard him talk. I Nov. 20th.
had a Bed-Fellow.

This would probably be his chaplain, Mr. Aldred.

My Bed-fellow and I parted. I began to read the Nov. 21st.
Unparalled Adventures writ by R. Burton.

I Rid over in y⁰ Boat at Runkhorn and did not light Nov. 24th.
till I came to the Ail-hous, where we baited, thence to
Cole-brook where we lodged at Robert Pickerings y⁰ Signe
of y⁰ Cock.

At Newport I lodged at Justice Stantons the Signe of Nov. 25th.
the White Swan.

Mr. Tully Oneall and I came to Wolverhampton where Nov. 26th.
we bated at Widdow Bembows y⁰ Signe of the Cock, thence
we went to Bermidgham and lodged at Rob: Corbits the
Hen and Chickings.

From Rowington Mr. Stamford went with me to his Nov. 28th.
Hous Sawford where I Lodg'd.

From Wickham I came to London and set up my Dec. 2nd.
Mare at Mr. Ogles the Signe of y⁰ Whit Hors at y⁰ End
of Little Wild Street.

I dined at Mr. Aldreds near Lincolns Inn Arch in Dec. 3rd.
Duke Street.

This Mr. Aldred was brother to his chaplain.

1715.
Dec. 5th.   I Removed my Horses to yᵉ Cock and Dolfin in Grays Inn Laine.

Dec. 9th.   I saw yᵉ Preston Prisoners come into Town.

Dec. 12th.   I made a Viset to my Lady Darwend-water in Lester Street.

Dec. 13th.   I mended yᵉ Clock upon yᵉ Stayers at my Landladys.

Dec. 16th.   I went to Cliftons the Bull and Gate in Holbourn and to other places to sell Ginny but to no purpose.

Dec. 17th.   I saw the Wax work in Fleet Street and the Birds and Beace.

Dec. 19th.   I drunk at John a Gaunts with Mr. John Gorsuch and Mr. Renolds.   I saw yᵉ English Opera Acted called Dioclesian.

Dec. 23rd.   I saw five Men and two Women carted towards Tibourn there to be Executed.   I was in Smithfield in hopes to sell Ginny but could not.

Dec. 24th.   I bought a Gold Laced Hat of Mr. Renolds.

Dec. 29th.   I saw the Antilop and other Beasts in Holbourne.

Dec. 30th.   The Ostler sold Ginny in Smithfield and paid me the Money.   I saw the moving Picturs in Smithfield.

1716.
Jan. 6th.   I made a viset to Mrs. Bridget and Mrs. Dorothy Standley at Mr. Ormanbys near Little-burn Stile.

Jan. 9th.   I began to learn French of Mr. George Barton over against the Sun in Great Wild-Street.

Jan. 11th.   I took yᵉ Clock upon yᵉ Stayers in peeces.

Jan. 12th.   I sat in the Chear of State upon the Themes, I danced on yᵉ Themes in a Booth, and at yᵉ Warwick-Shire Booth

I got a Dish of Sausages Fryed. I walked over the Themes from Temple Stayers to Southerick and back again.

I put y⁴ Lock again on my Closet doar and have got Jan. 17th. a new Key made for it.

I made a Viset to Mrs. Br: Butler at y⁴ blew Ball in Jan. 18th. Little Wild Street.

I was upon the Themes and there saw an Ox Rosting Jan. 19th. I eat a part of it as I saw cut of y⁴ Spit, they say there were two Oxes Rosted on the Themes to day. I was at y⁴ New Exchange and there saw a Looking Glass as was in one peece 86 Inshes Long and 44 Insh wide Valewed at £130.

I dined at Mr. Berrys and treated that Family there Jan. 26th. wth a Shew of Monstures.

I saw y⁴ Moving Images in Shanlow Street, it was the Feb. 13th. first time they were shewed.

I presented Mr. Plumb with a Snuff Box. Feb. 19th.

Lord Derwinwater and Kenmure were Executed. Feb. 24th.

There was High-Mass for Lord Derwinwater at y⁴ Feb. 27th. French Envoys, severall Persons of Note were there.

Our Street Doar Lock was picked and y⁴ Doar opened. Feb. 28th.

I saw a Woman whiped at y⁴ Carts —— twice round Feb. 29th. Red Lyon Squaire.

I made my first Viset to Sr John Curson. Mar. 2nd.

Mrs. Ann Aldred helped me to buy a Roclore and a Mar. 3rd Tissu Waiscot at Thomas Stevens y⁴ Signe of y⁴ Duke of Ormond on Horsback.

1716.
Mar. 5th.   I received my Pass.

Mar. 6th.   I gave Mrs. Bridget Standley and her Sister Dorothy a small collation at their Lodging, they and I went out to see the Apparitions in yᵉ Air lick Clouds of Fier and Smoke.

Mar. 7th.   I drank my Farewell with Counsellor Eyr and his two Brothers and Mr. John Culcheth at yᵉ Castle Tavern in Holbourn near Fullers Rant.

Mar 8th.   Came from my Lodging in a Coach to Billing-Gate, then in yᵉ Tilt Bote (in about 3 Hours and a half wᶜʰ is twenty miles) to Gravesend.

Mar. 12th.   I went on Bord the Sᵗ John of Bridges a Smack of 50 Tunn.

After being on the sea three nights he lands at Ostend on March 15, and makes a long stay abroad. He goes from place to place, visiting and describing various churches and sights. He meets English Jesuit Fathers and other priests, several Catholic families living abroad for the quiet practice of their religion. Amongst these were many Jacobites, escaped from England after the perils of "'15." His wife and children followed him in the summer, and the two girls were taken to Gravelines for their education.

1717.
Aug. 3rd.   We went on Bord Mr. Galloways Vessell the Betty Yot and Sailed out of the Harbour of Callis to Ramsgate where we Ancored.

Aug. 4th.   We Sail'd to Braud-Stairs alias Brad-Star where we cast Ancor. My Wife and I walked to Margarit where we lodged at yᵉ Whit Hart.

Aug. 5th.   We went from Margarit by Bote on Bord yᵉ Betty and came to London. My Wife and I lodged at the Cross Keys in Gratius Street.

Aug. 20th.   My Wife bought a Red Satine Sute and I Dove Colour Cloath-Sute.

I took my Wife and Mrs. An Aldred to Tatnam Fair
where we saw a Play acted called Jane Shore.

My Wife and I made a Viset to Mr. Scarisb: in New
gate.

I went to make a Viset to Sr Tho: Johnson but he was
not at home. My Wife and I saw a Play called Titus
Andronicus acted at ye Play house in Drury Lain. Mary
Woodcock had her Pockets plucked from her.

My Wife and I made severall Visets in the Coach viz
to the Mrs. Standleys, to Mrs. Dalton, to Mr. Blevin and
to my Lady Hailes, but my Lady being lately delivered we
saw her not, onely saw her Mother Mrs. Bagnoll.

This being Bartholemew Fair I went to Smithfield and
saw a Fars acted which was called Argulus and Parthenia
and a Poppy Play called Earl of Essex. I met Mr.
John Culcheth, Mr. Francis Poole, Mr. Thornton, Mr.
Tompson &c at the Brittish Coffy Hous.

I went with my Wife to Bartholemew Fair, we saw
a Farce Acted as is called Robin Hudd and Little John,
and Poppy Play called Patient Grissell and the Babes in
the Wood.

Walked thorrow St James Park where we saw some of
the Trees as were Blowed up by the Roots and some as
were snaped of 7 or 8 Foot from ye Ground by the Great
Storme of Wind upon 21st Instant some of ye Trees were
about 3 yards in circumference.

Went to Malburgh Hous, 'tis a pritty little Hous
and some good Pictures drawn by L'Garr, thence to
Buckingham Hous wch is really Noble and fine.

1717.

Aug. 30th. I went to Wills Coffy-hous near Covent Garden. I made a visit to Mr. Scarisb: in Newgate and drank there with Mr. Blackbourne who has been a Prisoner there as I take it above 21 years, Mr. Gregson and Mr. Ashton was also with us.

In *Pink's Antiquarian Notes*, part i., p. 45, will be found an interesting account of the extraordinary case of Robert Blackburne, imprisoned for half a century for a political offence. The Editor is indebted to the writer (Mr. W. A. Abram) for the following note regarding the others:—" 1717, July 23—Robert Scarisbrick, Esq., Mr. John Ashton, and Mr. John Gregson, who were said to have been engaged in the late Rebellion, and had never been apprehended, surrendered themselves to the Lord Chief Justice Parker, who committed them to Newgate."—*Historical Register.* Mr. Scarisbrick was afterwards tried at Lancaster and released on bail.

Sept. 1st. I treated Dr Gerningham, Mr. Sauthcote &c. with Wine. There was a Bone Fier and Illuminations in St Jamses Squaire for the Victory obtained by Prince Eugaine over the Turks.

Sept. 2nd. We began our Journey in y⁵ Stage Coach from London.

Sept. 13th. Mr. Harington drove Ince Charriot, he came a Nuting.

Oct. 1st. I went to Leverp: and made a Viset to Mrs. Clayton, to Mrs. Houghton and Mrs. Tyarer. I dined at y⁵ Woolpack wᵗʰ Sʳ Clave Moar &c. I payed £18 to Mr. Plumbe for a Purchas of one Aiker of Land from Sʳ Clave Moar.

Oct. 6th. It being near Full Moon I cut my Wives Hair off.

Oct. 7th. I dined at Dukes in Great Crosby with Lord Molin:, Mr. Tho: Whittle, Parson Wairing, Joly Brown of Leverp: and layed a Waiger with Mr. Whitley wᶜʰ is not to be paid of some time.

Oct. 13th. It being Crosby Goosfeast I went to Dukes where I drunk with Mr. Rodes and Mr. Tatlock of Leverp:

I Registered my Reall Estate at the Sessions in the Oct. 15th. Town-Hall (Wigan) before Mr. Case and Mr. Owen.

This was in pursuance of a recent Act requiring all Recusants to register their estates. The annual value of the Diarist's estate was given as £482 12s. 2½d.

My Wife went to Condole Ailes Tickle for y⁰ loss of Oct. 16th. her Husband who was found this Morning drowned near his own Hous.

I was at Sefton at y⁰ Buriall of Rich: Tickley, there Oct. 18th. was at his Hous, Yeomon of y⁰ Gore Houses, Mr. Formby, Mr. Cottom of Leverp: Mr. Wofold &c.

Will: Fleetw: of Simons Wood was here to have Oct. 20th. ben Married to his Fourth Wife but was disapointed.

My wife and I went with Mrs. Blund: &c on Bord the Oct. 23rd. Barbadas Merchant and dined on Bord her, Capt: Bryan Harding is Master, he gave us some Guns.

We delt Saw-loves to the Poore, it being the first Nov. 2nd. time any Saw Loves were given here as I remember; of 2 Buss: of Barly we made 420 Loves, but they were too little, if three had been made into two they would have ben pritty well. Althŏ it was a fine day and the ways very good, yet I believe there was about one third part of y⁰ Saw-loves left and very few came as were not Inhabitants of this Parish.

I went to Parson Wairings in y⁰ Morning and got y⁰ Nov. 13th. Boys leave to play and then went a coursing with Parson Letus, Parson Wairing, Mr. Syer of the Ford, &c.

I went to see y⁰ Iron Forge in Aintry. Mr. Poole of Nov. 20th. Burchley and his Son Lodged here.

Ellen Rigby brought me word that there was a Ship Dec. 5th. loaded with Butter as had Sufferd dammage y⁰ last

Night, some of it was brought up to Great Crosby, she bought us three Muggs of it.

Dec. 19th.   I went to Lidiat to see Pat: Moston, I made a Viset to Dennats Wife, she told me that for above these 12 years last past she has not eaten anything but spoone Meat, not so much as a peece of Bread or Puding.

Dec. 23rd.   Mr. Burtles of Leverp: and his Friend dined here I shewed them my Picture of yᵉ old Man and Candle.

> If this was Hogarth's "Politician" it must have been produced early, as he was then only about to finish his apprenticeship with Ellis Gamble.

1718.
Jan. 3rd.   Coz: Tho: Gelib:, Mr. Tho: Walmesley and I went to Leverp: and dined at yᵉ Wool-pack we went to look at the Dock and the Charity Schoole. I tasted some very good Wine in Mr. Ginks Seller.

Jan. 11th.   I went to Astley to wish Coz: Gelib: joy, its yᵉ first time I have ben there since he was maried.

Jan. 12th.   Coz: Gelib: and I walked in the Morning to Coz: Tho: Gelibronds to prayers.

Jan. 14th.   We went from Astley to Coz Tho: Gelibronds where we dined with Mr. Tho: Walmesley, Will: Low &c. Coz: Tho: Gelib: shewed me his Gardens, Fishary, Fountain &c. I gave some small Rings and Spaw Crosses to my Little Cozens there.

Jan. 22nd   My Wife and I were present when Mr. Turvill made his Prof: I eat of a very good Chees as was twelve years old and made by Tho: Foolers Wife of Great Crosby. I drank Punsh in the Hall at Ince wᵗʰ Mr. Turvill who treated us, Pat: Smith of Culcheth, Pat: Wᵐ Molineux, Pat: Rich: More &c.

My Wife and I went to the New-Hous to pray for Mr. Tasburgh. I was in my Mill w^n Mr. Tasb: was carried past to be buried.

Rev. Henry Tasburgh, S.J., a native of Suffolk, born 1641-2, entered the Society of Jesus 1664-5, and was sent on the Lancashire Mission 1673. Was rector in 1701, and died at the New house in Ince Blundell, January 27, 1717-8. He was buried the following day at the Harkirke. See *Foley's Collectanea*, where he is said to have died February 6th.

I went to Morehall to attend the Funerall of Mr. Wofold there was there Sr Edw: Standley, Mr. Brooks of Ormskerk, Mr. Formby, Mr. Molin: of Wooton, Mr. Standley of Hooton &c I did not goe with ye Corps to Highton Church.

I dined at the New-hous wth Pat: Billinge and Mr. Sail &c I flung a Trash after Mr. Saile.

I went to Parson Wairings to wish his Sister Kelsey Joy. Parson Kelsey was there, we had a Bowl of Push.

I went to ye Hall of Male and got some Cutings or Imps of ye Apple Called ye Summer Queening.

Mr. Saile of Hopkar came to Tho: Syers.

I was one of the Bearers at the Funerall of my Lord Molineux, there was then at Croxtath Mr. Case of ye Red Hasles, Lawyer Gibson, Atturney Hulme, Mr. Nich: Fazak: &c., Mr. Culcheth came with me from Sefton Church.

I treated at the Talbot Mr. Hulme the Atturney, Mr. Byron of the Edge, Yeomon of the Gore Houses &c.

Talbot, in Ormskirk.

Pat: Needham held forth at Mr. Ald:

1718.

Mar. 29th.   Mr. R: Fazak: the Father gave me Bond at the Wool-pack for £270 Principall with Interest.

April 4th.   I went to wish Mr. Scarisbrick wellcome home from y⁰ Assizes.

April 5th.   I Bought some Hugaback and Diaper from Mr. Hen: Tatlock and some Wine of Mr. Ginks, I dined with them at the Wool-pack.

April 11th.   I cut Rob. Weedows Hair and his Brother Henrys Hair.

April 15th.   Tho: Syer and I went to the Saile of Quick Goods at Croxtath.

April 22nd.   Mr. Saile was Married.

April 25th.   Mr. Ald: and I went to Formby wᵗʰ Coz: Moli: of Mosb: and Mr. Tankerd we expected to find Dotterell and onely one was seen.

May 8th.   I went to look at Parson Hindleys Garden but he being ill of the Gout I could not see him, thence I went to Ormsk: and dined at Doctor Lancasters.

May 10th.   I went to Prescot and light at the Ship Tho: Moss his, I went to Mrs. Glovers to look at Mr. Limes Quondom Garden.

May 13th.   I went to Leverp: and paid all to Mr. Crumpton the Uphoulstarer as I ought him.

May 16th.   I went to Leverp: for a Livery Sute for Rob: Weedon at Mr. Cottoms Shop, he treated me at his Hous and gave me a dooble Snuff Box. I bought a Swine in Daile Street.

May 29th.   Pat Ald: shewed me how to clense or Purify Quick Silver.

Doctor Gerards Brother William dined here.

I went to wate of my Lord Darby at Knowsley, I June 16th.
dined there with him, Mr. Windam, Parson Antwistley
and his Brother, and young Mr. Case; after dinner all of
us played at Bowls except Mr. Windam.

I went to yᵉ Sail of Goods at Croxtath and bought June 17th.
some of Thomas Syer &c.

I went to Leverp: and bought some open Silver Lace June 21st.
of Mr. Maior for my Wives Hat.

My Wife and I went to Leverp: and heard Pat: June 22nd.
Doodell hold forth at Mr. Hardestys, we dined there with
Mr. Tute and his Nephew Mr. Nugent &c.

I fixed the Sedar Chest of Drawers as I bought at June 23rd.
Croxtath in my Closet.

My Broth: Jos: went hence, I went with him as far June 28th.
as Blind-Leg, where we found Coz: Molin: of Mosb: and
his Brother, Mr. Percy and Ned Farnworth &c.

Pat: Gelib: came very late and brought word we July 5th.
might soone expect a sevear Serch for Priests.

My Lord Lang: Mr. Ald: and I went a Seting and July 15th.
Shooting. There was an impudent disbanded Souldior
carried hence by the Cunstable to Leverp: where the
Maior ordered him to be whiped. I had a Merrinight
Tatlock play'd here.

My Lord Lang: Sister Midleton &c intended to have July 18th.
gon to Leverp: but were prevented by hearing of the
death of my Nephew Peter Midleton.

My Lady Molin: her Doughters and Mrs. Mary July 23rd.
Molin: dined here, I also expected Lord Molin: and

1718.

Lord Cardigan. Lord Lang: and I went to Ince Greene I bowled there; there was Parson Darbyshire and Wairing Mr. Formby, Mr. Bayron of the Edge, Tho: Whitle &c.

July 24th.

Lord Langdale and I dined at Mosburgh, we bowled there after dinner. Coz: Gelibrond of Astley sent a large Salmon hither of a Present.

July 28th.

My Lord Lang: went hence, I went wth him to Astley.

July 29th.

Coz: Jo: Gelibrond and I went with my Lord Langd: to Coz: Tho: Gelibronds where we heard three of his Doughters play on the Harpiscolls. Coz: Tho: Gelibronds Wife and Mr. Rich: Chorley din'd with us at Astley.

Aug. 5th.

Mr. Smarley the Atturney was here I paid him what I ough him upon Account of ye Purchas of Jacksons Land. My Brother Langdale, Dr. Traps and Mr. Heskaine made a Viset here, I gave a Guiney to Mr. Heskaine towards Crosby Race.

Aug. 6th.

I ' went to Ince Green and Bowled with Parson Darbyshire, Mr. Formby and Thomas Whitley; Parson Wairing and Mr. Bayron were there.

Aug. 8th.

Tho: Syer and I went to Crosby Marsh to see where was proper to set out Ground for a Hors Race.

Aug. 15th.

I went to Great Crosby where I saw a good part of Don Quick-sot Acted.

Aug. 16th.

Mr. Carroll Molineux dined here and then I went with him to Crosby Marsh and helped to set out the Cours.

Aug. 21st.

My Sister Middleton, my Wife and I dined at Mosbourgh with Mr. Harington and his Lady.

1718.

My Wife and Sister Midleton made a Viset to the Aug. 24th.
Ladys of Magull.

I went to Crosby Marsh and ordered where the Aug. 26th.
Distance Post should stand and saw them fixing the
Chear.

My Wife Sister Middleton and I dined at the Scous Aug. 27th.
at Mr. Haringtons with Mr. Molin: of Mosbourgh and his
Lady, Ned Ogles &c. Mr. Percy came home with us.

Scous = Scholes Hall, near Prescot.

My Lord Molineux sent his Keeper to me with a side Aug. 31st.
of Venison.

I was at the Gallaway Race on Crosby Marsh and Sept. 1st.
was in the Chear with my Lord Darby and my Lord
Molineux &c four Horses ran and Mr. Bosloms wan the
Plate.

Emb: Blansherd brought us word that Coz: Scarisb: Sept. 10th.
was discharged at Lancaster.

I Rode out in the Morning with my Sister Middleton Sept. 11th.
into my Lord Molineux his New Park and looked at the
Deer and Whit Beasts, thence we went to yͤ Iron Forge,
then to Mr. Bowers.

I went to Scarisbrick to-congratulate Mr. Scarisb: for Sept. 15th.
his good Suckcess at yͤ Assizes.

Mr. Nich: Faza: and his London Brother were here, Sept. 20th.

We dined at the Scows with Mrs. Cath: Standley and Sept. 22nd.
Mrs. Eckleston and lodged at the Red Lyon in Warington
a very good Inn.

I went to Leverp: and drank at Mrs. Ladys with Oct. 5th.
Mr. Smarley and Berry two Atturneys.

1718.
Oct. 18th. I Brought home some Withen Stakes for Pat: Gelibronds Arbor.

Nov. 2nd. I made a Viset to yᵉ Hall of Ince and stayed there pritty late expecting the News-paper.

Nov. 21st. Tho: Syer came home from Hopker after having composed Matters between the Mother and Son.

Nov. 25th. I went to yᵉ Mugg-hous and congratulated Capt: Fazak: for his Post there, young Mr. Faz: gave me a Bowl of Punsh.

Nov. 27th. Mr. Saile and his Wife came to lodge at Tho: Syers they intend to Table with him for some time.

Dec. 9th. Mr. Bower and John Tyrer met me at my Lords Arms in Aintry. Mr. Bower made some proposalls to me for the Purchass of Dʳ Lathoms Fifteen Aiker.

Dec. 13th. I went to Leverp: and drank with Mr. Rech at yᵉ Wool-pack he is to be Land-Lord there. Pothecarry Par gave Jolly Brown and me a Bottle of Wine at his Hous.

Dec. 17th. Mr. Turvill Came to Condole my Wife for the Death of my Lord Langdale.

1719.
Jan. 1st. Coz: Tho: Gelibrond and I and our Wives dined at Astley. Mr. Willi: Brooks was there.

Jan. 2nd. I walked to Coz: Gelibronds Cole Pit. My Wife and Coz: Gelibronds met old Coz: Gelibronds Wife at Chorley.

Jan. 3rd. We came home from my Cozen Gelibronds of Chorley.

Jan. 23rd. Mrs. Saile was delivered of her first Child, Richard.

Jan. 27th. Mr. Saile and his Kinsmen made my Workmen in yᵉ Ackers to shout.

1719.

I sent of a how-do-you to Scarisbrick to bid the young Feb. 1st. Master welcome home.

My Wife and I made a Viset to y° Hall of Ince, it Feb. 10th. being Srofe Tuesday we eat Pan kakes there.

I saw a Man that eat Fier but I did not see him eat it. Feb. 24th.

My Wife and I went to Ormsk: to meet Dame Standley, Mar. 9th. Mrs. Fra: Traford came with her, we all dined at the Wheat Sheafe.

John Fletcher told me that he saw yester Night a Mar. 20th. Strang and unusuall Light proceed from y° Moone somthing like a Commet and shooting downwards till it disapeered it cast an extraordinary light but did not last above one Minnet it happened between 8 and 9 of the Clock.

Mr. Jackson paid me in full for the Purchas of his Mar. 31st. Land in Great Crosby.

Great Crosby Jury and my Jury met Mr. Crisp and April 7th. me at the Sea-side where we Staked out y° Bonderys between Great Crosby and the Morehouses that each Town might know their Liberty to fish in.

I went to Mr. Hindleys the Parson of Oughton his April 11th. Curate Mr. Loxdale shewed me several od sorts of Flowers, he went with me to the Aile-Hous where we smoked a Pipe.

I was at Great Crosby Race where five Hunters Ran April 19th. for a Plate, a Hors of Mr. Cleevelands wan it.

Mr. Saile, his Wife and Family removed from Tho: April 28th. Syers and went hence to live at Hopkar. I sent some Clay to the Mugg Hous and Pip-Makers to be tryed there.

Parson Loxdale and John Aspinwall came to see my May 5th. Flowers I showed them my best and also my Cheane Pump.

I went to Mr. Case his, but he was not at home so I smoaked a Pipe wth his Son Henry and then went to ye New Engin as is to draw up Water from one of ye Cole-pits, thence I went to ye New Glass-hous, Mr. Case came past whilst I was there so I followed him to his Hous where I stayed awhile and desired him to be one of my Executors.

May 7th.   The Play of Don Quicksot was Acted at James Davys.

May 13th.   I went to Crosby Court where I proposed to ye Jury to Joyne with them in Prosecuting of those who Fished on our Coast but it was not Accepted.

May 14th.   I went to Ormsk: and shoed my Toe to the Mounte-bank Dr. Fry, I drank at the Swan with Dr. Lancaster.

May 15th.   I met Mr. Shepperd at the Hall of Sefton and bought some old Wainscoting of him.

May 18th.   My Wife and I dined at Lidiat with Mr. Moston, thence we went to Mickering where we found Mrs. Wofold and Mrs. Bridget Blundell, Pat: Blackbourn was there.

May 27th.   Mr. Taylor of Ormsk: brought a New Clock to Tho: Syers for Mr. Saile.

May 30th.   I went to Leverp: I drank part of a Bowl of Punsh at Mr. Cottoms, ye Riding Parson was there.

June 9th.   I fetched home from ye Hall of Sefton the old Glass as I had bought of Mr. Shepperd.

June 14th.   Wm Davy the Skinner refused to show me his Leas, we fell out about his geting Turves.

June 17th.   Went to Whartons in Ince where we had a Meeting concerning geting a Rode to be made over the Key at Leverp:, and severall Sign'd to a paper for Raising Money viz, Mr. Formby, Mr. Syer of the Ford, Mr. Will: Williamson, Ed: Darwin, Yeomon of the Goar-houses myself and others.

Mr. Formby, Mr. Tho: Whitle, Yeomon of y⁰ Goar- June 20th. houses I &c met at the Woolpack about making a Road over the Key at Leverp: I showed the Deputy Mayor what we intended to doe in that affair.

I gave a great many Flowers to two young Women for June 21st. Flowering of a May-Powl.

I went to y⁰ Golden Hors-Shoe by Darby Chappell. June 22nd.

I was at Mr. Aldreds where he made up a falling out June 25th. as was between Thomas Syer and Edward Hatton.

I drew out part of a Modell for Mr. Aldreds new Hous. July 2nd.

Mr. James Tildesley and his Wife and Sister with the July 3rd. Famoly of Ince made a Viset here.

I drank a Glass at Mr. Cottoms with him, Mr. John July 4th. Bolton and Captain Fazakerley.

My God-Son Tho: Syer claped me Blessing, 'tis the July 5th. first time.

I went to Ince Green and Bowled with Mr. Formby July 8th. Whittle and Mr. Oldfield. I gave one Guiney to Mr. Whittle upon Account of a second Mart.

I went to Leverp: and bought a Comicall Drinking July 17th. Glass.

I went with my Wife to Leverpool thence she went to July 19th. Wooton to wate of my Lady Westmoreland. I dined at Mr. Fazakerleys and drank at y⁰ Woolpack with Dr. Tarlton, Mr. Darcy Chantrell &c.

Mrs. Scaresbrick, her son James and her Doughter July 21st. Frances &c dined here.

1719.
July 22nd.   Pothecary Lathom, Mr. Cottom and his Wife and her Sister Mrs. Mary Yates dined here.

Aug. 2nd.   Dorothy Blundell came hither and began to prepair against to-morrow, all Hands were as busy as was proper.

Aug. 3rd.   My Lord Molineux his Keeper brought me a Present of a Side of Venison. My Lord and Lady Molineux, my Lady Westmoreland, my Lord Belew, the Ladys of Maghull, Mr. Trentham, Mr. Turvill &c. dined here. Coz: Gillib: of Chorley, his Wife, his Son John and Doughters Margarit and Jane lodged here.

> This Jane, daughter of Thomas Gillibrand, Esq., married John Hawarden, gentleman, who held the manor of Widnes—Lower House in Widnes, and Lea Green in Sutton. His will is dated January 16, 1741-2. Their son, Thomas Hawarden, of Liverpool, Esq., took the name of Gillibrand, of Gillibrand Hall, and ob. May 28, 1787. He sold land in Sutton, August 2, 1768.

Aug. 7th.   Coz: Gillibrands two Doughters played upon yᵉ Organ at Leverp:

Aug. 13th.   My Teame brought two Bolster Load of Timber for Mr. Aldred out of my Lord Molineux his New Park, there were five other Teames.

Aug. 25th.   Mr. Scarisb: and his Son James dined here and then we went to Great Crosby Race were six Ran for yᵉ Plate, a Croped Hors of my Lord Molineux his wan it; Coz: Rowly Poole, Mr. Henry Tyrer &c. was there. I drank in a Booth with my Lord Molineux, Mr. Molin: of Mosb: Mr. Wᵐ Wofold &c. I gave one Guiney to Mr. Syer being what I had Subscribed towards yᵉ Plate.

Aug. 26th.   We went to the Gallaway Race at Great Crosby My Lord Molin: his Brack Rowly and a Mare of Mr. Heskeths ran for yᵉ Plate, my Lord Molin: wan it.

1719.

I sent a Present of young Pigeons to Mr. Plumb to Sept. 1st. stoar his New Dove-Coat in Wartery with.

This house, which Mr. Plumbe had then recently built, was afterwards called Plumbe's Hall; and here resided, at one time, Sir Joshua Walmsley, Kt., Mayor of Liverpool, 1839-40. The Corporation bought it in 1843, and pulled it down with the view of utilising the site for a borough gaol. The site being pronounced unsuitable, after the lapse of a few years it was converted into ornamental grounds, called Victoria Park. (See *Picton's Memorials.*) Mr. Plumbe was an intimate friend of Mr. Blundell, and kept his Court Baron at Crosby, where he was a frequent visitor. He was fond of both coursing and fishing, and had many opportunities of enjoying these amusements in company with the squire. Mr. Plumbe was successful in his profession, and purchased, in 1718, Alexander Hesketh's estate, viz., Uplitherland and one-third share of Aughton, which is still in possession of the family. At the beginning of this century the Plumbes acquired, in marriage, the estate of Sir George Tempest, of Tong Hall, Yorkshire, and took the name of Tempest. The late Colonel Plumbe Tempest, who died July 27, 1881, was succeeded by his sister, Catherine E. P. Tempest.

Pat: Kannell made a Viset here. Sept. 3rd.

Rev. James Cannell, S.J., was a son of Mrs. Cannell, of the Isle of Man, who suffered much persecution for religion, as may be seen from her letter to William Blundell, Esq. (*A Cavalier's Note Book*, p. 163.) He was born 1649, and chiefly laboured at Wigan, where he is said to have been the earliest missioner. He died there in 1722, aged 73.

I went to Ince to wate of Sr Lawrence Anderton he Sept. 6th. being come from London.

Pat: Gillib: my Wife and I rode out to see ye Land Sept. 17th. Mark as is building at the Grange.

Pat: Gillib: went hence, my Wife and I brought him Sept. 18th. past Maile-Clent.

Joh: Vose began to build the West Laine Hous, I Sept. 30th. layed the first Stone wth my Coat of Armes and ye first Letters of my Wives Name and mine engraved of it, it is the Foundation Stone of the most Westerly Corner.

This house is still the residence of the priest, but has been re-fronted, and the stone referred to inserted in the wall on the eastern side.

1719.

Oct. 11th.   I sent William Carefoot to see if he could harken me out a Miller but he could not.

Oct. 19th.   I was at the Funerall of Parson Letus but yᵉ Corps was carried to yᵉ Church ere I came, so I stayed in yᵉ Ailehous till yᵉ Sermon was over and drank with Mr. Crisp, Mr. Bower, Thom: Fleetwood &c. Parson Becket, Mr. Byron &c were at the Funerall.

Oct. 22nd.   I went to Tho: Tickleys and drank there with Mr. Molineux of yᶜ Grange, there was some Drunken troblesome Company in yᵉ Hous.

Oct. 26th.   My Wife went to condole Mrs. Letus for the death of her Husband.

Oct. 25th.   I went to Ditton and lodged at the Bank at Will: Athertons, I played them some tricks of Leger-de-mesne, and set them upon some Chrismass Tricks, we were extreamly Merry.

Nov. 9th.   William Carefoot went to the Bare-Bate at Formby.

Nov. 10th.   The West-Lain-Hous was Rear'd.

Nov. 14th.   I dined at the Wool-pack in Lev: with four Strangers, I suppose they were Londoners. I saw Matthew Buckinger who was born without Hands or Feet, I saw him writ very well with his Stumps and tipe very dexterously some nine Pins down and play Tricks of Leger-de-Mesne, Mr. Whitley and Mr. Bayron went with me to see the Little Man play his Tricks.

Nov. 27th.   I sent my Coach Carriage to carry yᵉ Corps of Cicily Lea to Sefton.

Dec. 8th.   Hen: Swift and Roger Marser asked me leave to fish on the Sea Cost within my libertyes.

I Burned half a Groce of Pipes.

Tho: Bigarstraff came hither wth a Petission for me to signe to the Barleament to make ye River Wever Navigable, I did sign it.

The first Act for rendering the Weaver navigable from Frodsham Bridge to Winsford was passed in 1720. The other Acts were dated 1759 and 1807.

I went to ye Buriall of Wm Bawer but came too late so that I met ye Corps and went to Sefton, when the Buriall was over I stayed drinking at the Aile-Hous with Dr. Lancaster, Selsby of Ormskerk, Young John Yates.

It being Christmas day my Wife and I went in ye Night to Mr. Aldreds, we also went thither about tenn of the Clock this Morning, my Wife was extreamly ill and I was not very well.

Ned Howerd came to desire I would deside a difference between him and Mr. Aldred.

My Wife dined at Ailes Tickleys. I went into Tho: Syers where he gave us a Bowl of Punsh, we were seaven in all viz Mr. Syer of ye Ford, James Berry the Atturney, Mr. Byron &c.

I went to Preston, I set up my Horses at the Miter and dined there, they got me lodging in a privat Hous. I made a Viset to the three Sisters the Mrs. Blundells.

It being the Great-Saturday I exchanged my small Coach-Hors Jack with Henry Heys for a large Bay Gelding not five year old I calle him Stag. I called at Gris'es and smoked a Pipe there with Dr. Lancaster.

My Wife and I went in ye Coach to Ince with my New Hors Stagg he performs extraordinary well.

1720.
Jan. 25th.

I went to Ince Green when Parson Wairing flang a
Lead over yᵉ Green but it not being very fairly done we
had a small squable about it; Mr. Cottom came to us
when the Throw was over. Parson Wairing and I bowled
against Mr. Ald: and Mr. Bayron.

They afterwards adjourned to " Ned Wharton's," where Mr.
Cottom, who had been coursing, entertained the company with the
following anecdote, related by the Diarist :—" 1719-20, January 25—
Mr. Henry Cottom of Leverp: Mr. Turville of Ince, and several
others were a coursing. The hare being very closely pursued took
refuge under an ass which was in the lane. When the dogs came
near the ass, it began to bray and make such an ugly noise that
the dogs ran away from it and by that means the hare saved its life."

Feb. 6th.

This Town and Thornton had a Tryall before Mr.
Maior of Leverpoole and Mr. Rich: Norris for yᵉ Setlement
of Rich: Webster and his Famoly, our Atturneys were Mr.
Plumbe and Mr. Peters, Thornton had Mr. Brownsword. I
drank at yᵉ Wool-pack with Mr. Jenks, Captain Tarlton &c.

Feb. 20th.

I went to Mr. Cottoms and paid him what I ought
him for Fustion &c for a Frock, I went to Mr. Maior of
Leverp: and Mr. Norris to yᵉ Bird in yᵉ Hand where I
discoursed them concerning yᵉ Setlement of Ri: Webster
and his Famoly. I drank at yᵉ Wool-pack with Thom:
Hurst, young Rob: Bootle, &c. Rich: Westhead pretended
to be my Guide home but lost his way and brought me
thorrow Litherland Town.

Feb. 21st.

I was at yᵉ Buriall of Rich: Tristrams Wife and
Doughter, there was at yᵉ Buriall Hous Mr. Cottom, Mr.
Bower, John Tyrer and his Wife &c.

She died in childbirth. Mrs. Blundell had gone to visit her
when she heard of her danger.

Mar. 1st.

This being Shrove Tuesday I saw Rich: Syer, John
Ainsworth &c throwing at a Cock before my Gaites in yᵉ
Foulds.

1720.

I went to Mr. Cottoms, I dined there with Mr. Billing Mar. 5th. My Lord Molineux his Gentleman. Mr. Peters brought me an Order to the Wool-pack for the Setlement of Richard Webster and his Famoly in Thornton. Coming home I fell upon the Sands and Hurt my Hip very ill and my Hand.

Rev. Richard Billinge, S.J., was then priest at Croxteth Hall. He died 1732-3, aged 58.

I gave a Comfortable Drink to my Hors Stagg. I sent Mar. 13th. a How-do-you to Mr. Scarisbrick.

I went to yᵉ Edge. Mr. Bayron was gon to the Ford Mar. 18th. but his Wife sent for him he soone came back and Mr. Syer along with him, I stayed and Smoaked a pipe with them.

Ailes Tickley, Dorothy Blundell and Betty Blund: dined Mar. 20th. here. I went part of the way towards Sefton wᵗʰ the Corps of Rob: Tompson and then Mr. Rich: Molineux the Saylor came back with me.

My Closet being very unready, I put it into better Order. Mar. 24th.

I set about one Buss of Rufford Potatows in the April 9th. Oat-Croft without any Muck or Straw.

Coz: John Gelibrond went to Leverp: and put in his April 14th. Clame for a Debt owing to him by Mr. Earle.

My Wife and I went to Mathew Withingtons in Derby April 18th thence we went to Mr. Carters of Blacklow in Roby where we called and looked at his pritty Hous and Gardens.

I sent to the Scous (Scholes Hall) to condole Mrs. April 20th. Harington for the Death of her husband.

Charles Harrington, of Huyton Hey, Esq., buried at Huyton Church, March 12, 1719-20.

April 21st.

My Wife and I called at Mr. Plumbs new Hous in Wartery he was there and shewed it to us, we went to Leverp: Sera Ather: went with us, I bought her some Whit-Mettle waire at the end of Daile Street and a Hat for her at Mrs. Rumsys. We all dined at the Wool-pack I drank there with Mr. Rob: Tatlock, Mr. Whitle, Will: Hulme the Atturney &c.

April 23rd.

My Wife and I walked to Sefton to make a Viset to Parson Acton and his Wife, 'tis the first time either of us went since they came thither.

April 26th.

I was at the farther end of the Barbary Walk with Tho: Howerd and his Brother John &c and furnished them with two good Kasks. Patrick Norris was here to heare what News Thomas Howerd brought out of yᵉ Island.

April 27th.

Mr. Thomas cerched the West-Lain-Hous and a deale of the Out-Housing of this Hous for Brandy as he heard was conceiled here.

April 29th.

Rich: Jump came to buy my Black Mare Bess but we could not bargan.

April 30th.

Mr. Williamson the Wine-Cooper came hither and Ordered two Kasks of Clarret for Tho: Howerd.

May 1st.

My Wife sent Ned Howerd to Wooton to wish my Lady well-come-home.

May 2nd.

I dined with Henry Tyrer at Widow Barrows in Orms-kirk and drank there with Mr. Ashurst, Justis Walmesley &c. I was at part of the Tryall between Thornton and our Town concerning the setlement of Richard Webster and his Famoly there was Mr. Entwisley yᵉ Chancellor, Mr. Ric: Norris &c upon the Bensh.

1720.

Parson Acton Mr. Bayron and young Rob: Bootle were May 3rd.
here a beging towards the rebuilding of St Johns Church
in Chester, I gave them something.

I went to John Aspinwalls and to Parson Hindleys to May 6th.
get some Roots of Flowers.

I set them and the Flowers as Parson Loxley gave me May 7th.
yesterday.

I fetched Mrs. Lettonby hither from Leverp: she is May 8th.
shortly for going to Madam Bagnolls. Pat: Turvill was
here.

Mr. Ald: removed from Ned Howerds to live at the May 9th.
West-Lain Hous. I went thither this afternoon and took
a pipe with him.

I Brought Mrs. Letonbys Will to Lev: as I had drawn May 11th.
for her, she signed it.

Mr. Ald: said Mass the first time at the West-Lain- May 13th.
Hous I served him.

I sent a few old Pigeons and young ones to Mr. May 18th.
Plumbe to store his Dovecoat with at Wartery.

It being Mr. Aldreds Birth-day he gave a Bowl of May 19th.
Punsh at his hous to Parson Wairing, Mr. Bayron and
me &c we were seaven of us.

I Removed the Great Stone as has time out of Mind May 23rd.
stood neare the lower Bark-Gate and fixed it at yᵉ turning
of the Cawsey in ye West-laine.

My Wife and I dined at Scarisbrick the three Sister May. 26th.
Blundells from Preston were there, coming home we made
a short Viset at Gorsuch.

1720.
May 28th.

It is supposed that Will: Thelwall is run his Country becaus 'tis publickly known he had a false Key of my Seller.

May 29th.

Mr. Turvill called here and smoaked a Pipe and then went to Crosby Marsh to see y° Runing Horses.

May 30th.

Coz: Scaris: and his Son James dined here, we went together to Crosby Race where my Lord Molineux his Crop beat a Whit Hors called Crutches.   Mr. Plumbe and his Son were upon y° Ground.

May. 31st.

Young Mr. Clifton and Doc: Traps were at Mr. Aldreds.

June 2nd.

Being Ni: Davy dyed today my Wife and I went to pray by him.

June 5th.

I went to Astley where I Lodged.

June 6th.

Coz: Gilib: and I went to prayers to his Sons, Coz: Tho: Gilib: shewed me his Water Engin for Cherning with &c.   Mr. George Clifton came to Astley.

June 7th.

Went to Cowlings to Read y° News.

June 9th.

My Wife and I went to Leverp: we looked at the Charrity Schoole.

June 11th.

Being Rob: Bootle Junior finished his Marling to day I went to his Hous and gave something to his Marlors, I drank there with Jo: Rose, Bryon Fleetwood &c.   I proposed to them to set an Egg on y° end upon a Looking Glass, Wm Harrison the Clark did it.

June 12th.

We were as busy as was proper prepairing against to-morrow.

June 13th.

Coz: Scarisb: and her Son James, the three Sister Blundells from Preston &c dined here.

I went with Pat: Gel: to Lidiat to see Mr. Moston.

Mr. Ald: came hither to borrow some things against to-morrow.

My Wife and I dined at Mr. Ald: with my Lord and Lady Molineux the Famoly of Ince &c: we were eighteen in all.

This was the house-warming given by Father Aldred, now settled in his new abode.

I Bowled at Ince Greene with Will: Harrison the new Schoole-Master who came thither today.

Old Mr. Walmesle of Showley dined here.

My Wife and I began our Journey towards York. We dined at the Leggs of Man in Wigan with Coz: Gelib: of Astley and his Brother W^m we lodged at the Row Buck in Ratchdale.

At Leeds we lodged at the Queens Armes a very good Hous and very oblidging People and very reasonable.

I saw Mr. Thursbys Collection of Curiositys which are very well worth seeing. At York my Wife and I lodged at my Sister Middletons, I sent my Men and Horses to the Falcon.

My Lady Smithson dined wth us, I bowled with Mr. Naper &c.

Mr. Menell of Kilvington dined with us, Mr. Rob: Dolman made us a viset. I made a Viset to Mrs. Medcalf the Widow.

My Wife and I heard part of a Sermon at Mrs. Pastons. Coz: Barbara Dolman, Mr. Naper and his Wife &c dined with us.

1720.

July 11th.   I went from York to Hallifax where I Lodged at yᵉ Signe of the Cross, a large but nasty Hous.

July 12th.   From Hallyfax I went to Burnley where I dined at the Spar Halk it was the worst way I ever rode for so long together.

July 13th.   From Showley I came past the Lower Hall of Sambsbury and Curedley Hall and so to Astley, thence to Ormskerk where I took a Pipe at yᵉ Swan wᵗʰ Parson Loxdall.

July 17th.   I shewed Ben: (Brancker) my Picture of yᵉ Old Man and yᵉ Candle.

July 19th.   I went to Crosby Marsh and saw five of my Lord Molineux his Horses sweat, viz, Fox-hunter, Stroaker, Sobryety, Crop, and his Black Gallaway Darcy. My Lord Molin: and his two Brothers Mr. Carroll and Mr. Thomas were there, being it rained before the Horses came to the Ground we went into the Warand-House where we stayed a good while and took a Glass of Wine.

July 20th.   I went to Ince Green and Bowled with Mr. Rob: Heys, Parson Wairing &c. Mr. Sandford whom they call my Lord Mar was there.

July 22nd.   I went to Viset the sick in this Town.

July 25th.   I dined at the New-hous with the Famoly of Ince and the Ladys of Maile &c. I sent of a How-do-you to my Lady Peters and of Business to Mr. John Culcheth.

The Rev. William Clifton, S.J., had recently come to serve the Catholics of Formby, and this was his house-warming. Nearly thirty years later he was buried in the Harkirke, and is thus registered:—" Mr. William Clifton Pr: of the S J, dyed the 18 August, 1749, at 5 in yᵉ morning at Newhouse in Ince Blundell, was bury'd in the Harkk the 19th between 8 and 9 in the morning."

I began my Journey towards York to fetch my Wife
home, but before I got to yᵉ Bark Gate Stagg flung Hen:
Curedon off and also my Maile Trunk and Rufler refused
to goe forwards wᵗʰ me, wᶜʰ stayed me a good while but all
things being mended we set forwards and dined at the
Black Bulls Head in Manchester a very good Inn.

At Sheffield I lodged at the Golden Crown a very
good and cheap Inn.

I heard Mass at Mr. Sherbourns and dined there.

I came to York and dined at my Cozen Irelands with
my Sister Middleton, my Wife and Mrs. Frances Plumpton;
at Night we went to the Assembly where I doe believe
there were above 200 Gentlemen and Ladys and I counted
in one Roome 15 Cupples in one Company dansing
Country Dances.

Mr. Stanfield and I were at Mr. Brighams, we went
thence to the Black Swan where we drank wᵗʰ Sʳ Carnaby
Haggerston, Sʳ John Swinbourne &c.

Sister Midleton and I &c: dined at Mr. Standfields;
after dinner Sir Car: Haggerston, Mr. Solvin Junior &c
came to us, we Carded by Turnes and sometimes drank.

Sʳ Carno: Hag: Mr. Solvin Junior and Mr. Fosor
Junior dined here.

I dined at yᵉ Falcon. I saw the Play acted called the
Commity.

Sir Carnaby Hag: made his first viset to my Neece
Midleton, Sʳ John Swinbourne was here.

I was at the Horse Raice where four Ran for the
Kings Golden Cup as they called it, but it was for a Purs

1720.

of one Hundred Guineys, Mr. Wettys Bay Hors called Merry-Man wan it.   My Wife and I were at y⁰ Play called The Devills to doe about her.   Sister Midleton &c went to the Assembly.

Aug. 9th.

I went to the Tennis Court and saw Mr. Ireland &c play at Tennis.   I saw Mr. Dashwoods Gray Hors True-blew ride over the Ground by himself for a Silver Soap Dish of £30 Vallew.   I was at a Puppy Play.

Aug. 10th.

I was at the Hors-race where Foure Horses ran for a Silver Tea Cettle Vallew £40 it was woone by Mr. Dashwoods bay Mare Harmeless.

Aug. 11th.

We all dined at Mr. Dolmans wᵗʰ Mr. Craythorn and his Lady &c I was at the Horse-Race where twelve Ran for the Ladys £60 Gold Cup it was woon by Mr. Chetwins Gray Hors Trout.

Aug. 12th.

I was at the Cock-pit where I think I saw 4 or 5 Battles.   I was at the Hors-Race where nine Gallaways Ran for a Silver Cup and Cover for it of £20 Vallew. Mr. Nicholsons Gray Mare Annaka wan it.

Aug. 15th.

Pat: Townley prayed here, he and Mr. Dolman dined here.

Aug. 16th.

My Wife and I began our Journey homewards.   We Lodged at y⁰ George in Otley, a very good Inn but noe good outside.

Aug. 17th.

We called at Mr. Atkinsons and dined there, then went to Gisbourn but there not being a good Inn, we went to the Signe of the Boot in Sola (Salley) Abbey but none of us went into Bed.

Aug. 18th.

We went to Preston and dined and Lodged at the Miter, we made a Viset to the three Sister Blundells and to Mrs. Fleetwood Butler. I saw the Man eat Fier and saw a peece of Mill-Stone-Greet about foure Inshes thick broke upon his Brest with a Hammer.

I went to Ormsk: in expectation to have swaped away Aug. 25th. my Black Mare Bess, Mr. Traffords Man Mr. More met me there with a Bay Gelding but he was not for my Purpose. I drāk at the Swan with Mr. Smith of Maile &c Coming home I called at Parson Hindleys, I walked with Parson Loxley into his Flower Garden.

I went to Leverp: and dined at Mr. Cottoms. I Aug. 27th. drank at yᵉ Wool-pack wᵗʰ Mr. Rob: Faz: Senior and at Will Rolins his with Mr. Boyer.

My Wife and Pat: Gillib: went to Ince to condole Sept. 1st. Mrs. Blund: for the death of my Lady Anderton.

Mrs. Blundell's son Robert eventually came into possession of the Anderton property. See *Lydiate Hall* for an account of the family and of Lady Anderton's will.

I was at the Buriall of Mr. Fazak: of the Hill-Hous, Sept. 3rd. I went with the Corps to Walton Church, there was Parson Loxdale, Parson Wairing, Yeomon of the Gore Houses, Mr. Whittle &c.

My Wife and I went to yᵉ Hall of Maile, Mr. Tho: Sept. 4th. Molin: was there, so was Mr. Whittle.

Pat: Wofold being dead my Wife and I went to yᵉ Sept. 6th. Grange to prayers.

I went to Garswood to wish Esqr: Gerard wel-come- Sept. 7th. -home from his Travells abroad, I dined there wᵗʰ Mr. Sturton, Mr. Poole of Burchley &c.

My Wife and I dined at Mr. Cottoms with Parson Sept. 13th. Mallery.

1720.

Sept. 14th. The Famoly of Ince dined here, so did Mr. Plumb and Mr. Cottom, Mr. Burton and Pat: Edw: Scarisbrick.

Sept. 17th. At Leverp: Mrs. Ginks shewed me her Hous, I drank at Mrs. Lady's with Mr. Allonson &c.

Sept. 27th. I went to look at Tho: Syers New Hous in Crosby.

Sept. 30th. Nelly Howerd cut my Haire off my Head.

Oct. 1st. My Wife went to the Carr Side to see her God-Doughter Frances Blun: who is dangerously ill.

Oct. 4th. My Wife was at the Labouring of Will: Tarltons Doughter when she was Delivered of her first Child. I Rode out to Sefton to look at the new Diall-post.

Oct. 5th. My Wife overtooke the corps of her God-doughter Fra: Blundell and went along with it to yᵉ Church.

Oct. 6th. I took the Hous-Clock a peeses.

Oct. 12th. I Attended the Corps of Mr. William Wofold from Leverp: to Highton where he was Buried. I was one of yᵉ Bearers, so was Mr. Molineux of Mosburgh, Mr. Smarley the Atturney &c.

Oct. 13th. I was at a Race on Crosby Marsh between a Bay Mare of Mr. Heskains and a Gray Mare of Mr. Entwistleys, Mr. Heskaine wan the Race.

Oct. 17th. This being Crosby Goos-feast I went to Nicholas Johnsons and drank there with Ned Hatton, Wᵐ Gray &c then I went to Margarit Lurtings and drank there with Mr. Cottom, young Mr. Pepper, Mr. John Gerard, Junior &c.

This is the first mention of Mr. Peppard, who afterwards married the Diarist's daughter Frances.

This being Crosby Goos-Feast I went to Tho: Heskeths _{Oct. 18th.} and drank there with Mr. Williamson of Litherland, Parson Wairing, Mr. Bayron &c.

I went to wish Mr. Scarisb: welcome home from _{Oct. 24th.} London.

I took the Jack to peeces and helped to dress it. _{Oct. 31st.}

This day being my Wives Birthday the Famoly of _{Nov. 1st.} Ince dined here, so did Ailes Tickley and Betty Blun: Betty Thomas of Priestons Row in Leverp: came hither to sell some Forraine goods.

Preesons Row, called so from Alderman Preeson.

Mrs. Blund: came hither in her Charriot and took _{Nov. 15th.} my Wife with her to Leverp, they dined at ye Talbot.

I closed up the Mouths of my Bee Hives and began _{Nov. 19th.} to feed them with hard Biskets made of Bean Flower and sweet Wort, it had not ben amiss if I had don it two Months sooner.

I Rode out to the Sea side to see if there were any _{Nov. 23rd.} Rack upon my Coast. John Harrison sent me a long Reed as he had found, there being great quantity of them all along this Coste.

I sent my Carriage to Carry the Corps of Bryan Leas _{Nov. 25th.} second wife to Sefton.

My Wife and I went to prayers to the Grange and _{Nov. 30th.} heard Pat: Munson preach.

He had succeeded Rev. T. Wolfall as priest there.

I went to Garswood to wish Joy to Es^{qr} Gerard and _{Dec. 5th.} his Lady.

1720.
Dec. 7th.   I helped Arthor Wilson to Remove the Jack out of the Dary into the old Kitchen but we did not quit fix it right.

Dec. 10th.   Being yᵉ Jack would not goe well I undertook it and made it doe very well.

Dec. 14th.   Mr. Lovell being dead at yᵉ New Hous I went thither to prayers and Dined there with Pat: Will: Molyneux, Pat: Gelib: &c I came part of the way with the Corps, it was Buried in the Har-kerk.

Dec. 23rd.   Owen Mackdanell was here and gave me his Fathers Will to Keep.

Dec. 24th.   We went in the Night to Prayers to Mr. Aldreds and when we came back we found the Turf Stack in the Bake-Hous on Fyer which probably in a very little time would have set the Hous on Fyer.

> "That only night in all the year,
> Saw the stoled priest the chalice rear."

It is no longer customary in country places to celebrate midnight Mass at Christmas.

Dec. 26th.   Mrs. Blundell being this day 42 years old, My Wife and I dined at Ince, we carded and supped there.

Dec. 28th.   The Famoly of Ince dined and suped here, so did Betty Blundell of the Carrside, we played at Cards both after Dinner and Super.

1721.
Jan. 2nd.   I fixed up the Jawbone of a Sherk in the Hall.

Jan. 3rd.   My Wife and I dined and suped at the New hous with yᵉ Famoly of Ince and Pat: Munson; Ailes Tickley and Betty Blund: dined there. Hen: Curedon Killed four Misse as were in one of my Bee Hives.

My Wife and I were at yᵉ Buriall of Mr. Rob: Fazakerleys Wife, Mr. Molin: of Mosb: Mr. Scarisb: Junior and I &c were Bearers.

John Tickley yᵉ Overseeor of yᵉ Poore, Gab: Norris, John Molin: &c came hither and desired I would hinder any Strangers from coming to live in this Town.

I Scoaped 30 Leomonds, yᵉ Juce of them made one Pint, and about the fourth of a Pint, I put to it one pint of Brandy. I also made some Shrub; the proportion was Brandy 2 Qts, Crab Vargious 1½ pt, Leomonds 6, Dubble Refined Sugar 1 lb. The proportion of Mixture for my last Brue of Aqua Cœlestis was Brandy 2 Qts, Crab Vargeus 1 Pt and $1/5^{th}$ of a Quart, Lime Juce $1/5^{th}$ of a Qt, Lisbon Sugar 1 lb, Leomonds 3, and being the Brandy was very good I put to it 4 Qts and 1 pt of Water, the water was first bouled, the outward Rine of the Leomonds was infuesed into it, so they were also in the Shrub, but the Brandy and Leomond Juce had not any Rine infuesed in it. This Night I had a Cargo of 16 Larg ones brought to Whit Hall.

Out of many entries relating to such compounds this is retained, on account of the precise particulars it gives. From the last note it appears that the Diarist followed the example of his Liverpool neighbours, some of whom had doubtless arranged this contraband affair. As James Williamson, the wine cooper of Liverpool, had spoken for two casks of claret on behalf of Charles Howerd, he must have been well aware of the expected consignment.

W: Ca: covered the Cargo very well with straw.

Cha: Ho: brought me a good provision for Aqua Cœlestis, I shewed him his goods well stowed in Whit Hall.

I went to Pat: Cliftons and Turned my Pancake there, I found my Wife Mrs. Margarit and Mrs. Mary Blundell &c there, we all played at Cards.

1721.

Feb. 18th.   Being Dorothy Blundells Son Henry of Ince Town was dead I sent my Coach Carriage to carry him to be buried.

Feb. 19th.   Mrs. Margarit and Mrs. Mary Blun: dined here and so did Ailes Tickley, Betty Blundell and Ginnet Jump.

Feb. 26th.   My Wife made a Viset to Dorothy Blundell to condole yᵉ Death of her son Henry.

Feb. 28th.   I dined at Mr. Shepperds in Darby with Mr. Molin: of yᵉ Grange and Rich: Blundell of the Carr-Side.

Mar. 13th.   I went to Leverpoole and drāk at Evis'es with the Maior, Mr. Taylor, Pothocary Barrows &c and at yᵉ Wool-pack with Mr. Cottom and Mr. Plumb Junior.

Mar. 17th.   I went to the Grange to Mr. Molineux his Coppers and gave them somthing to make them to shout.

April 3rd.   I was at the Funerall of Widdow Maile of Maile the Bearers were Mr. Rigby of Hadolk Mr. Clayton of Adlington Junior, Coz: Molineux of Mosburgh &c. My Coach carried two of Widdow Mailes Doughters &c: to and from the Church. I stayed drinking at yᵉ Ail-Hous in Sefton Church Yard a good while with Doctor Lancaster, Richard More &c.

April 5th.   My Lord Langdale sent his Servant hither from my Lord Molineux'es of a how-do-you. I began in good earnest to spin Hay and made a good part of one Leafe of a Screene.

April 8th.   I went to Leverpoole and had Thomas Taylor and his Wife before Mr. Mayor of Leverpoole. Mr. William Plumbe and Mr. Peters were present.

April 10th.   My Wife sent Ned Howerd to Wooton to welcom-home my Lady Molineux. My Wife and I dined at

Scarisb: with Mr. Trafford of Croston and his Brother
Richard, Mr. Nelson of Fairest and Mr. Ashton &c.

Lady Molineux, after the death of her husband in 1738, spent
a long widowhood at Woolton Hall, where she died March 20, 1766.
She was a great benefactress to the Catholic mission there.

My Lord Langdale and Mr. Th: Heskaine Lodged here. _{April 11th}

I Rode out with my Lord Langdale to look at the _{April 12th.}
Land Mark at the Grange.

Mr. Carrol Molin: and Mr. Heskaine went to Wallowsy _{April 15th}
and saw my Lord Molineux his Horses sweat.

Mr. Taylor the Mayor of Lev: and Mr. Rich: Norris _{April 21st.}
came to vew Formoss-poole Plat. Tho: Syer I &c were
there with them. Mr. Peters swore foure Witneses in
Order to get a better Bridg there.

Mr. Hen: Blund: was at Prayers at Mr. Aldreds 'tis _{April 23rd.}
y⁰ first time I have seen him since he came from beyond
y⁰ Seas.

Henry Blundell, a younger brother of the squire of Ince, had
been to St. Omer's College for education.

I went to Ormsk: Sessions and dined at the Kings _{April 24th.}
Armes with Mr. Antwisley the Vice Chancellor, Mr. Case,
Lawyor Blundell &c, at Night I drank at y⁰ Swan w^th
John Crook, of Scarisb: John Wilm of Martins Croft,
John Merry &c.

It being a White-Meat day I dined at a Table by _{April 25th.}
myself at the Swan.

I went to the New-Hall and Spoke to Mr. Shepperd &c. _{May 3rd.}

Went to Oughton where I Light of Parson Loxdale at _{May 5th.}
the Claks and smoaked a Pipe there.

1721.
May 6th. At Lever: I made a Bargan with Mr. Turner for some Lime Stone and Glass-Bottles. I went to look at Mr. Willes his Flower Garden and at Mr. James Tildesleys. I drank at Night wth Mr. Peters, Mr. Williamson of Litherland &c.

May 8th. I dined at Char: Howerds with Mr. Taylor the Mayor of Leverp: Mr. Rich: Norris, Mr. Smith ye Collector, Dr Diggans &c. Mr. Corleys should have met us there to have discoursed about building a Bridg over Formoss-poole Gutter but he came not. Mr. Peters was there so was Edw: Litherland.

May 10th. Esqr Gerard and Pat Norris dined here. Pat: Gorsuch and his Sister Ann lodged here. I sowed some Cowcomber Seeds they had been steeped in New-Milk about twenty four Hours.

May 13th. Mr. Ald: Reared his Stable and Shippon.

May 15th. My Wife went with Cozen Nanny Gorsuch to make a Viset to Mrs. Williamson (of Litherland).

May 18th. I Walked to Crosby Hors Rase it was three heats for a Sadle Mr. Syer of the Ford wan it.

May 20th. Mr. Cottom gave me a Bowl of Extraordinary good Punsh at his Hous Mr. Hugh Patton was with us. I bought some Wine of Mr. Williamson.

May 25th. Coz: Scarisbricks Son Josep: came to take leave of me, he is going to St Omers.

May 27th. My Wife and I called at the Signe of Sr William Gerards Crest in Ashton, thence to Gravock where we Lodged.

Grave Oak Farm may still be found close to Hopcar, near Leigh, formerly the seat of the ancient Catholic family of Sale.

William, son of Gilbert Sale, of Hopcar, Esq., deceased, lived here, having married Jane, daughter of Edmund Tristram, of Ince Blundell, yeoman. His mother was then residing at Hopcar, which was finally sold by her son, Gilbert Sale, of Liverpool, in 1770.

My Wife and I went to Hopker, Mr. Colcheth and Mr. Tompson made us a Viset. *May 26th.*

Mr. Rich: Saile and I went to Leigh and looked at the Church, I saw there some remarkable Bones. We went to Garswood and attended the Funerall of Sʳ Wᵐ Gerard to Winwick Church, there was at Garswood, Mr. Banks of Winstanley, Mr. Antwisley &c. Went to Culcheth with Mr. Culcheth and made a Viset to the Laydys. *May 29th.*

My Wife and I came from Gravock we dined with Pat: Billing at Brinn thence to Mr. Lanctons of the Low I drank there with Mr. Bradshaw the three Mr. Diconsons then to Holland where we stayed awhile at the Agle and Child and so home. *May 30th.*

I went to Ince Green there was Parson Wairing, old Rob: Bootle &c: I bowled hand to fist with Mr. Harington each four Bowles. *June 14th.*

I went to Lev: and discoursed Mr. Massy yᵉ Painter about Painting Benshes in yᵉ Garden &c. *June 17th.*

Will: Carefoot came home with some Glass Bottles from Thatway Heath. *June 22nd.*

I took the Jack in peeces and mended it againe. *June 23rd.*

I went to More-hall to wate of my Lord Biss: I dined there with Pat Roydon, Mrs. Barker &c coming home I overtook the Morris Dansers as were going to Flower the May-Pole in Magull. *June 24th.*

My Lord Biss: Witham, Pat Roydon &c lodged here. *June 26th.*

1721.
July 1st.   My Lord Biss: has Confirmed here in all 284. I went to Ince with him.

July 2nd.   My Wife and I dined at yᵉ Hall of Eckleston.

July 3rd.   I went to Mr. Bayrons Marlors and made them to shout. Pat: Rivers came from Ince and Lodged here.

The Rt. Rev. George Witham, Bishop of Mareopolis and V.A. of Northern District, died April 16, 1725, aged 70, at the family seat, Cliffe Hall, in Yorkshire, and was buried at Mansfield Church. The Rev. John Savage had been, since 1712, 5th and last Earl Rivers. He was living at Liege in 1733, and held a canonry. As he was at Douay in 1735, he could not have died as early as 1728, the date assigned by Sir Harris Nicolas. Soon after his accession to the peerage, in a law contest with a relative, to give himself a *locus standi,* he made a temporary act of conformity. The Duke of Shrewsbury urged him to take the oaths and enter the House of Lords, where justice would be done to his claims. He replied, "My lord, I have already gone too far." "Then," rejoined the Duke, "I will not press a tender conscience."

July 5th.   Parson Wairing and I bowled at Ince Green against Mr. Heys Junior and Tho: Kennion.

July 6th.   Mr. Bayron had his Finishing day for his Marling, I went to his Hous wʳ I met severall of my Neighbours viz, Parson Acton, Parson Wairing, two Robert Bootles, Mr. Syer, Yeomon of yᵉ Gorehouses, &c.

July 8th.   My Wife and I began our Journey towards Holy-well but no Ferry Bote being on this Side, I hiered the Sower-Milk Gallay she carried us and our three Horses over at twice and Landed us at yᵉ Wood-Side, thence we went to Shotwick, at Holly-Well we Lodged at the Starr.

July 9th.   My Wife and I went into yᵉ Well, I was much out of Order after I came out and Continewed so for some Hours. I went with my Wife to Mrs. Crews.

We came from Holliwell to Flīt, thence to Shotwick *July 10th.* where I Rode over without a Guide and came back agin with one to fetch my Wife over, then to Eastom where I left my Servant and Horses, My Wife and I went over in the Sower-Milk Galley and Landed about eleaven of ye Clock at Night at Leverp: we lodged at the Wool-pack.

Mrs. Lettonby dined with my Wife and me at the *July 11th.* Wool-pack. Being the Dock was let drye I went to see it as also did severall Hundreds of People.

I sent a How-do-you to Cozen Tho: Gelibronds six *July 23rd.* Children who were ill of ye Small Pox.

I was at Ormskerk Race, there was Mr. Molin: of *July 24th.* Mosbourgh, Old Mr. Walmesley of Showley, Mr. John Gorsuch, Mr. Plumb: Mr. Maior of Lever: Wm. Atherton &c: there were three Horses ran for the Plate, a Hors Called Mr. Listers wan it.

My Wife and I made a Viset to Mrs. Clinton, Mrs. *July 26th.* Wharton and Mrs. Alanson (at Liverpool) I drank at ye Wool-Pack with Mr. Branker and Mr. Allonson.

I went with Pat: Acton to Leverp: and Procured him *Aug. 2nd.* a Place to lodg at and a Conveniency for Baithing in the Sea.

I was at Crosby Race; Crop, Whit-Stockings and a *Aug. 8th.* Gray Mare Ran; Whit-Stockings got ye Plate, viz, £20. I should have desided a Dispute between Pat: Turvill and Mr. Cottom but could not doe it.

I made a Viset to Mr. Taylor the Maior of Lever: *Aug. 15th.* he gave me a Bottle of Wine. I drank at ye Wool-pack with Mr. Rob: Fazak: and Mr. Whittle.

1721
Aug. 24th.
My Wife, Mrs. Wilding and I went to Lidiat to Prayers, Mr. Blund: was there.

This was no doubt on occasion of the funeral of Rev. John Mostyn, S.J., priest of Lydiate, who was buried within the Abbey walls, where part of the tombstone was formerly visible, as mentioned in the first edition of *Baines' Lancashire*. It is somewhat curious that the Diarist makes no allusion to his death.

Aug. 28th.
My Wife and I went to Lodg at Astley, we called at Fran: Farers he shewed me a Place in his Ground where 'tis supposed there formerly stood a small Castle and in takeing up the Foundation (for that was all as was left of it) he found a Largē Mugg-Bottle which I suppose held about three Gallons, the Mouth was large enough for a Girle to put her Hand into it, it had two large Bows as came from the Mouth of it, to the Belly to carry it by; it was of Cource brown Clay and seemed not to be nicely made nor well burned, 'twas so broke in Digging it up that I could onely Judge at the size of it; he also shewed me a peece of a Mug wᶜʰ seemed to be yᵉ Bottom of a Quart Jugg and had Stāped upon it in yᵉ inside of yᵉ Bottom these Words in this Caracture OF BASSI.

Francis Farrer seems to have lived at Downholland. Close to the high road leading through Halsall and Scarisbrick to Southport is a very appropriate site for a castle or fort, commanding as it does all the adjacent country. Although the Editor lived in the neighbourhood for many years, he never heard of any discovery of Roman remains at Downholland. (See *Watkin's Roman Lancashire*, p. 214).

Aug. 29th.
This being my Coz: Gelibro: Weding day his son Thom: came to Astley and Coz: Tho: his Wife dined at Astley.

Aug. 30th.
I went to Yarow Bridg Green and Bowled with Mr. Robert Lee, Parson Rawley &c. Young Mr. Trafford was there.

Coz: Gelibrond and I dined at Coz: Tho: Gelibronds Aug. 31st. and then we three went to Mr. George Cliftons.

Coz: Gelib: and I went to look at Mr. Crumptons New Sept. 1st. Hous, thence we went to Chorley.

Mr. Crompton's house, built of stone, stood a little to the north of Chorley, and was removed in 1817 by R. T. Parker, Esq., of Cuerden, to whom his great-grandson had sold it. Crompton's house was usually called Higher Chorley Hall. Lower Chorley Hall, a fortress-like edifice, was superseded in 1807-8 by the present Gillibrand Hall, erected by Thos. Gillibrand, Esq.

We called at Ormskerk and wished Joy to Dr. Lancaster Sept. 2nd. and his Wife recently married.

I Bowled at Ince Green with Mr. Blundell Mr. Haring- Sept. 6th. ton &c. Parson Wairing Tho: Kennion &c were there.

I gave Pat: Clifton some Eye-Balsom being one of his Sept. 15th. Eyes is very bad.

I took some Young Pigeons for Parson Acton. My Sept. 18th. Lord Molin: sent me a Side of a Stagg.

Robert called at Garswood from me to congratulate Sr Sept. 20th. Will: Gerard for the Birth of his Son.

I was at the Funerall of Parson Richmond of Walton, Sept. 21st. that is I attended the Corps to the Church, there was Parson Acton, Clayton and Wairing &c. I drank at the Ail-hous with Mr. Yates, Cottom, and Mr. William Nelson, &c.

I was at ye Funerall of Cap: Rob: Fazakerley in the Sept. 22nd. New Church Yard. The Bearers were Mr. Will: Holly-well, Mr. Jam: Tildesley, myself, &c.

I went to Prayers to ye Hall of Wood, thence to Sept. 24th. Mosburgh.

1721.

Sept. 25th.   I was at yᵉ Funerall of Jane Bryanson there was her Brother - in - Law Thom : Spensar, Tho : Blanshard, Wᵐ Weedon &c. as we were going with the Corps (which was carried on my Coach Carriage) the Famoly of Scarisb : and the 3 Sisters Mrs. Blundells of Preston overtook us.

Sept. 27th.   I bowled at Ince Greene with Mr. Rigby of Cowley-Hill, Mr. Yaits of Maile, &c.

Oct. 4th.   My Wife went to Rich : Moss to wish Joy to Mrs. Molin : of the Grange. Pat Bartlet went hence.

Oct. 5th.   I attended yᵉ Corps of old Rob : Bootle to yᵉ Church, there was at yᵉ Buriall Hous, Mr. Byron, Mr. Cottom, Yeomon of the Goar-houses &c.

Oct. 6th.   I dined at Dr. Lancasters (at Ormskirk) and went to Mr. Tyrers and wished his Wife Joy. I set up my horses at the Seaven Starrs.

Oct. 12th.   Being Pat : Gelib : took Phisick to-day we dined with him in his Roome.

Oct. 16th.   It being the Goosfeast I went to Parson Wairings where we had a very good Bowl of Punsh, there was Parson Acton, Parson Bell, Parson Balden, Mr. Rigby of Cowley Hill &c.

Oct. 18th.   I met Parson Wairing, Mr. Tho : Whittle and his Brother, two Tho : Syer, Mr. Molineux yᵉ Groser of Leverp : Mr. Byron &c at Tho : Heskeths.

Oct. 25th.   I made up my Bee-hives and poynted them well to keep out Mice. Rob : Weedow went to Alker to his Sisters Braiking, and Wᵐ Carefoot to his Fathers Braiking.

Oct. 26th.   Mrs. Allonson and her two Sons dined here.

Nov. 26th.   Pat : Ald : perceived that yᵉ Hall Chimney was on Fire and came to tell us but no dammage was done.

1721.

I was at Tho: Farers and heard the Quarrell between Dec. 4th.
him and Mr. Sadler. Mr. Sadler dined here.

Pat: Gorsuch lodged here, he came to help my Wife Dec. 19th.
for the Jubyly.

My Wife and I dined at Mrs. Parrs (it being her Dec. 27th.
Doughters Birth-day) with Mr. Plumbe of Heskaine, Rich:
More, Mr. Molineux of yᵉ Grange and their Wives &c.

Mr. Dugdell yᵉ Painter came to see if I would employ Dec. 28th.
him to paint for me.

1722.

My Wife and Mrs. Wilding went to Mrs. Lettonby's, Jan. 1st.
they Lodged there. My Servants all went to yᵉ Hall of
Ince there being Musick there.

I Played at Cards at Rob: Bootles with Parson Acton, Jan. 6th.
Parson Wairing Mr. Byron &c, we were invited thither.

Mr. Blundell, his Brother Henry, Pat: Turvill and Mr. Jan. 9th.
Harington dined here. Mr. Hardesty Marryed a Cupple in
my Chappel as came from Leverp: George and Jane ———.

The Rev. John Hardesty *vere* Tempest, S.J., was then priest
at Liverpool, and had walked to Crosby the previous day. Some
account of him is given in *Lydiate Hall and its Associations*.

Two men who said they came from Coventry left each Jan. 15th.
a very Rich Pack here to be kept for them till tomorrow.

I saw young Mr. Yats and Doctor Orme set William Jan. 16th.
Marrows Thigh, he broke it yesterday coming from Preston
Faire.

Humphrey Darwin shewed me Jane Bryansons last Will Jan. 21st.
concerning five pounds left to the Poore of the Morehouses.

I helped John Vose to shape out my Coate of Armes Jan. 23rd.
with Brick and to contrive how it is to be made at the
Higher End of the Gravell Walk.

1722.

Jan. 27th.   I Lent my Carriage to carry the Corps of Ned Blansherd to Sefton.

Feb. 5th.   Being Ellin Harrison dyed to day I went in the Evening to pray by her Corps.

Feb. 6th.   My Wif and I were at the Funerall of Ellin Harrison, her Corps was carried on my Coach Carriage.

Feb. 10th.   Mr. Dugdale and his Son began to Paint the Back-Parlor they did it over with Clear-Cole the first time. The Punsh Bowl being fixed in the middle of yᵉ Arch over my Coat of Armes and it and the two Pine Apples being Plaistered I gave the Brick-men a Drink upon the Scaffold.

Feb. 12th.   I saw Mr. Dugdall draw out a Lyon Rampand for Will: Thelwall to cut out for part of my Crest.

Feb. 18th.   This being the first time Mr. Hardesty began to pray Monthly at Lidiat my Wife and I went thither we dined there; Mr. Molineux of the Grange and his Wife were at Prayers there.

Feb. 19th.   My Wife and I dined at yᵉ Grange with Mrs. Parr, Rich: More &c.

Mar. 7th.   I was in Sefton Church where there should have ben a Tryall between Parson Egerton and Parson Hartley but Parson Hartley soone gave it up. Lawyer Blund: and Lawyer Starkey were there; there were Nine Clergy Men and nine Lay-Men on the Jury, they gave the cause to Parson Egerton, so that he is now to be the Rector of Sefton.

The cause was decided in favour of the claim of the Earl of Cardigan, but the right of presentation was subsequently sold to the Rothwells, who still possess it. Rev. Richard Rothwell and his son, Rev. Richard Rainshaw Rothwell, held the living for the unprecedented term of 100 years, viz.: from 1763 to 1863.

1722.

I attended the Corps of Tho: Bradley to the Church Mar. 19th. there was Parson Walker, Mr. Smith of Maile, Mr. Byron &c.

I Grafted the Leomond Apple the highest Miss Dimple Mar. 20th. next and yᵉ Blossom Russet the Lowest all between the Wood and Bark on the Hodg-podg Tree in the New-Grounds.

I fixed a Sun Dyall upon the Wall at yᵉ End of yᵉ Mar. 23rd. West Laine.

I went after my Wife and Pat: Gorsuch to Henry Mar. 29th. Norrys'es where we had a Formby Sod.

The Editor has tried in vain to discover the meaning of this term, but apparently no inhabitant of Formby can now explain it. It occurs nowhere else in the *Diary*.

Coz: Gillibrond and I walked along yᵉ Division Ditch April 6th. from the Bridg to Orill-Hill-Plat where we met old John Sumner and William Weedon they went with us to look at Gabriell Norris his Plat &c. Rich: Molin: and John Molineux went with us to what is Called Lady-Green Water-Cours, we followed it from Orill-Hill Laine almost all along, to yᵉ Plat in Ince Braud Laine.

I drank at yᵉ Wool-pack with Rigby the Glass Grinder, April 7th. young Hadock the Quaieker, Tho: Hurst &c: the Dispute about the Word Synonimus.

I made an Agreement between Rich: Jump and Bryan April 11th. Lea for what Trespas shall be done by Rich: Jumps Rabets during his Terme of 4 years at yᵉ Grange.

Hen: Gray and all my Servants were merry at April 12th. Margarit Lurtings.

I Bought a Druget Sute of Mr. Cottom, I dined at his April 14th. Hous with Mr. Pepper &c. I drank at Mrs. Ladys wᵗʰ Mr. Plumbe &c.

1722.

April 18th.   Mr. Cottom, Mrs. Acton, Mrs. Byron &c dined here. I Bowled at Crosby Green with Parson Wairing, Mr. Byron, &c.

April 20th.   I gave Mr. Peters Orders to get a Warant for Ann Ballard for Cuting the Starr.

> Starr grass is of great use to keep the sand from drifting, and in the old leases days were specified for the planting of starr.

May 2nd.   I Bowled at Crosby with Parson Wairing; Pothocary Lathom &c Mr. Formby, Mr. Cottom &c were there.

May 5th.   I went to Leverp: and payed Edmūd Gee for Daile-Boards.

May 7th.   I began my Journey towards Ashburne Faire in Darby-Shire. I dined at Starkeys the Agle and Child in Warington, I called at Barbington Bowling Green Hous but did not light.

May 8th.   I went from Congleton to Leek then to Jeromy Groves yᵉ Talbot in Ashburne in the Peak in Darby-Shire where I dined wᵗʰ Hollys of Moss-lee in Staffordshire and Mr. Burhall who came along with me for some Miles, they shewed me where the River Jurnet sinks under the Ground and continews to run under Ground for about three Miles.

May 9th.   I went to see Mr. Blundell's four Black Mares as he had bought for his Coach.

> Black horses were then the fashion, and the squire had gone to Ashbourne Fair to buy some. He only succeeded in getting one black and one bay.

May 15th.   I went to Prayers to Stony-Hurst, I saw yᵉ Hous and Gardens, I dined there with Pat: Brinkhurst, I came from thence to Ribchester where I saw two Remarkable Stones for Antiquity the one is the Corner-Stone of a Building and supposed to have ben part of a Roman Alter on which they Offerd up Sacrifize, &c. I light at yᵉ Unicorns Head and drank there wᵗʰ Mr. Walmesley of Showley and his Son Thomas.

See *Watkin's Roman Lancashire*, p. 128.

As we came home from Preston we called at Dr. Lancasters in Orms:. *May 16th.*

I sent two Doz: yong Pigeons to Mr. Plumbe to Store his Dove-Coat. *May 22nd.*

Mat: Morris the Germon came from Leverp: and mended my Jack. *May 28th.*

I Bowled with Parson Richmond, Mr. Formby, &c. at Crosby I drank at Heskeths with Pothecary Lathom, Mr. Green the Atturney &c. *May 30th.*

Tho: Marrow, Junior shewed Betty Bolton his Thumb and Rob: Weedow his Foot, I had them both in Cuar. *June 8th.*

I drank part of a Bowl of Punsh at Tho: Hesk: wᵗʰ Mr. George Tyrer, Young Mr. Case, Old Mr. Stokes, Mr. Jackson, &c. I Bowled with Mr. Williamson who married Mrs. Hurst, Parson Wairing, &c. I drank with Parson Acton, Mr. Thomas, &c. *June 11th.*

I Bowled at Crosby with Parson Wairing, Mr. Barton of Walton, &c. *June 13th.*

My Wife walked to Mr. Williamson's of Litherland to look at their New Parlor. I went to Edw: Rothwells' Marlors and made yᵐ to shout. *June 14th.*

This being Mr. Munson's Birth-day, I went to the Grange to Solemnize it, we were eleven, viz.: Rich: More and his Brother-in-Law John Plumb, Mr. Byron, John Rose, &c. *June 15th.*

1722.

June 17th.

My Wife and I heard Pat: Hardesty hold forth at Lidiat we dined there with Mr. James Clinton, his Wife and her Sister, we all went to look at Mr. Poole's Hous and then to Francis Farers we saw his Doughter Ailes who had seen her Angell Gardian.

Francis Farrer has been spoken of before as living at Down-holland. His daughter, Alice, died a few months later, and was buried December 9, 1722, on the north side of Halsall Church. Her tombstone was seen by the Editor a few years ago, but has been removed by the present rector to make room for improvements. The inscription describes her as the daughter of Francis Farrer, yeoman, and Elizabeth his wife, of Downholland.

June 20th.

Parson Acton, Mr. Syer and Mr. Byron the Church-Wardens &c. were here abeging upon Account of the Great Losses sustained in Lacashire in Dec: An: Do: 172/0/ by the violent overflowing of yᵉ Sea; the Sea had overflowed 6600 Aikers of Land, had washed down 157 Houses, and damnifyed 200 more, the whole loss was computed to be more than £10,227.

The Diarist says in his *Anecdote Book* that this flood did very great damage in the Fylde, in Meols, and at Alt-Grange. In the Fylde a man got up a tree to save his life, and a hare swam to the same tree for refuge while he was in it. In the Meols a swine of 40s. value got up to the top of a turf stack, where he lay till he was fetched down.

June 22nd.

Will: Carefoot went with my Coach Carriage to Leverp: and carried the Corps of Mr. Taylor (late Mayor) to Preston where he was Buried.

June 24th.

My Lord Langdale and Mr. Carroll Molineux dined here.

June 25th.

My Wife and I did not goe into Leverp: but went directly over in the Rock Boat and so to Chester where we Lodged at the Golden Lyon.

June 26th.

My Wife and I made a Viset to Mrs. Blundell of Ince at her Lodgings. After dinner we came to Eastom and

Came over in yᵉ Boat but did not come on Shoar of near
an Hour after yᵉ Boat ran on Ground, becaus the Horses
could not be got out.

My Lord Langdale and Mr. Heskaine Lodged here. July 3rd.

Mr. Eckleston Gors: dined and Lodged here. July 4th.

I went with my Lord Langdale to the Stand and dined July 5th.
there with Lord Molineux, Mr. Richard Lee, &c.

Parson Acton, Mr. Cottom and Pat: Bartlet dined here, July 6th.
I went wᵗʰ my Gests to Crosby Green and Bowled with
my Lord Langdale Hand to Fist, Mr. Thomas, Mr. Byron,
&c. were there.

My Lord Langdale went hence. I went with him to July 7th.
yᵉ Sea-side and stayed there whilst he was Baithing. Mr.
Heskaine and I came to Thomas Heskeths, Parson
Richmond, Parson Martin, &c. came to us.

My Wife and I went to Ince to wish Mr. Blundell and July 22nd.
his Lady welcom to their own Home.

Mr. Robert Blundell had just married Katharine, daughter of
Sir Rowland Stanley, of Hooton, Co. Chester, Bart. Their arms
may be seen over the entrance to Ince Blundell Hall, which he
restored.

My Wife and I went in yᵉ Coach to Leverp: we took July 26th.
up Mrs. Cottom and then went to Wooton where we dined
with Dr. Lawson of Chester, Mr. Richard Lee, &c.

Mr. Blundell and his Lady, Mr. Stanley and his Lady, July 30th.
Widdow Blundell and her two Doughters &c dined here.

My Wife and I dined at Ince, there was my Lord Aug. 2nd
and Lady Molineux, &c. we were in all about Twenty at
both Tables.

1722.
Aug. 7th. I began to uese Spectacles but not as a Constansy, onely when ye Print is too Small for me or that it is rather too dark to see my Letters plaine without y^m for now they are of advantage to me, thô formerly they were not.

Aug. 8th. I Bowled at Crosby Greene with Mr. Swettenham Mr. Cottom and Alderman Tyrer.

Aug. 10th. My Wife went to Lidiat to Prayers and went to Conf: She designs now to make use of Pat: Hardesty.

Aug. 13th. Will: Fleetwood of Simons Wood brought me a Passion Flower to look at.

Aug. 14th. I Bowled at Crosby with Apothecary Lathom &c there were severall Great Matches Played and a Deale of Company upon ye Greene. Lawyer Bootles youngest Brother was there so was Mr. Whittle &c. Pat: Al: and Mr. Crisp Bowled a Match by Moone Light and one Candle. There was present at it Parson Wairing, Young Mr. Swettenham Mr. Bayron I &c.

Aug. 15th. My Wife and I went to Mr. Sheperds. I saw Darby Plate run for by seaven Horses, it was wan by one Spensers; Mr. Cottom, Andrew Barton, John Rose &c were there.

Aug. 19th. Widdow Blund: and her two Doughters, Mrs. Blundell and her Sister Harington &c made a Viset here.

Aug. 20th. Mat: Morrison ye Germain Smith came to borrow some Money of me, I would lend him none but promised to lay out som with him.

Aug. 22nd. Mr. Carol Molineux and Mr. Syer were at Tho: Hesketh taking ye Naimes of the Horses wch were to run for Crosby Plaite, I drank there with Mr. Whittle Mr. Byron &c. The Squabble between And: Barton and Thom: Fleetwood about a Guiney Bet of throwing a Bowl.

Pat: Williams pray'd at Mr. Aldreds and din'd here, its y⁰ first time he has been here since he came to live at Ince.

Father Williams, S.J., had succeeded Rev. C. Turville. He was brother to Rt. Rev. T. D. Williams, O.P., consecrated Bishop of Tiberiopolis December 30, 1725, who was V.A. of Northern District till his death, April 3, 1740, aged 80.

Miss Jenny Gillib: came to Lodg here, she went with my Wife to Crosby Race, there were four Ran for the Plaite it was wan by Mr. Watkin William's Bay Mare Stairing Dolly. I layed a Waiger and Mr. Jo: Poole held the stakes.

My Lady Molin: and her Doughters, Coz: Scarisbrick and his Son James, Mr. Trafford &c dined here. I saw the Match Runn upon Crosby Marsh between my Lord Darby's Mare Stockings and Lord Molineux his Black Gallaway, Lord Darby wan. Mr. Plumbe and his Son &c were there.

I Burned above one Groce of Pipes in y⁰ Washhous Grate. I mixed some Pouders togethir for Convultion Fits.

Nelly Byron came to play with Miss Gellib:, she Lodg'd here.

I Bowled at Crosby with Mr. Hulme the Atturney Hand to Fist, four Bowles out of a Hand. Mr. Whittle, Byron and Andrew Barton were there.

Jane Withington went wᵗʰ a Present of Pigeons to y⁰ Ladys at the Scones but they were not at home.

Mr. Will: Plumbe, Lawyer Radcliff &c made a Viset here.

My Wife went to Wigan to see Widdow Harington, she Lodged at y⁰ Legg of Man.

1722.

Oct. 8th.   I went to Leverp: and made a Viset to Mrs. Hollywell. I pay'd Mr. Ward for Lime Juce and discours'd Mr. Seel about the price of Daile Boards.

Oct. 10th.   I Bowled at Crosby with Mr. Amory, John Blansherd &c.   I drāk with Apothocary Parr, Mr. Molineux of Leverp: the Grosor, Mr. Syer &c: Alexander Lever sold two Peeses of Fustion by Auxion.

Oct. 15th.   My Wife went to Ince to wate of Mrs. Townley and to Condole Mrs. Blu: for the death of her Sister Harington. I saw (at Nich: Johnsons) the Child which was born (as I think in Garston) without Legs or Armes.

Oct. 28th.   I went to Leverp: to yᵉ Buriall of Mr. Rensh the Land-Lord at the Wool-pack, there were at the Buriall Hous Mr. Cottom, Mr. Syer &c I attended yᵉ Corps to yᵉ old Church.

Oct. 31st.   John Meadow and And: Bar: played in Hesketh's at Breaking yᵉ Seeling.

Nov. 4th.   My Wife went in yᵉ Morning to Lidiat to Mr. Hardesty, she dined at Mr. Crisps.

Nov. 7th.   I was at Crosby Green.   This is supposed to be the finishing day of Bowling this Season, there was Parson Wairing, Mr. Whittle, John Rose &c.

Nov. 21st.   Mrs. Shepherd, her two Sons and Dorothy Blund: dined here.

Nov. 30th.   Mr. Blundell Doctor Molyneux and their Wives &c made a Viset here so did Mr. John Haring: and Mr. Aldred.

Dec. 4th.   I Faulted Mr. Blund: for shooting neare my Wood, Dʳ Moline: and Pat: Bartlet were with him, but they were got as far as to the Cross Field ere I spoke to Mr. Blund: .

1722.

I went to Lever: I brought home a Handsome Grate Dec. 8th. for y⁰ Great Parlor wᶜʰ the Germain Smith made me.

I went to see Coz: Molineux of Mosburgh, he having Dec. 13th. ben ill of the Siatica, I dined there with Mr. Hesketh of the Maines, Parson Peplow of Rainford &c.

I paid Mr. Seele for one Hundred of Daile Bords. Dec. 22nd.

My Wife and I dined at y⁰ New Hous with Mr. Dec. 26th. Blund: and his Lady his two Sisters Margarit and Mary, Betty Blund: of y⁰ Car-side &c.

Mr. Blundell of Ince.

1723.

I met Mr. Bretter at y⁰ Towns Meeting in Ditton we Jan. 2nd. prevented our being put on to be Cunstables, there was Mr. Chadock Steward to Mr. Dalton, Daniell Eckleston &c.

As I came home from Ditton I called at Mr. Plumbs Jan. 3rd. in Wavertree and dined there with Mr. Smarlay and his Wife &c. Parson Kelsey came to us in the after Noone.

A Night or two Since, my Hen-hous was Robed of Jan. 9th. about a Dozine Hens.

I went and wished Joy to Bryan Leas third Wife. Jan. 10th.

My Wife went to Leverp: to shew her Finger to Betty Jan. 31st. Bolton.

My Wife and I heard Mr. Munson hold forth at Mr. Feb. 2nd. Crisps, we dined there. Parson Acton came to Mr. Crisps—we took a pipe together.

My Wife and I were at y⁰ Funerall of Mrs. Rachell Feb. 3rd. Smith, she was Carried upon my Coach Carriage and buried in Walton Church.

My Wife and I dined at Ince We heard Pat: Williams Feb. 10th. hold forth.

1723.

Feb. 11th.   I sent a Servant to Mr. Scarisbrick with a Condoling Letter upon Accounts of his Sons Misdemeanour.

Feb. 13th.   My Wife dined at More-hall. I was at yᵉ Saile of Goods at the lait Mrs. Smiths in Aintry.

Feb. 20th.   John Tyrer and I went to my Lords Armes (Aintree) and tooke a Pipe.

Feb. 22nd.   I made my Incomperable Salve for a Cut or a Bruse.

Feb. 24th.   Mrs. Hawley dined here, my Wife went with her to Sefton and then she went to Lidiat to Pat: Hardesty.

Feb. 25th.   I fetched home my Irish Chears from Leverp: wᶜʰ were in the Custom Hous.

Feb. 26th.   My Wife and I dined at Mr. Actons with Mr. Syer, Ben Branker, and their Wives &c: after dinner we were twelve of us who drank there, the Occation was yᵉ Christoning of Mr. Actons Son Robert.

Mar. 2nd.   I discoursed Mr. Peters concerning removing Will: Sumners Doughter out of yᵉ town ere she be deliver'd.

Mar. 5th.   Mr. Pursell came to us with his Petistion.

Mar. 6th.   This being a Saile Day at the Parsonage of Sefton I went thither and bought some old Slates of Mr. Pusy. I went in with Mr. Acton and took a Pipe with him.

Mar. 10th.   I dined at Scarisbrick. Mr. Gorsuch and Mr. Wadsworth came thither after dinner.

Mar. 15th.   I went to Mr. Sheperds with my Wife and Coz: Gellibrond they were Gossops to his Doughter Frances. Mr. Green yᵉ Atturney Came thither after Dinner.

Mar. 19th.   My Wife and I &c dined at Mr. Syers with Parson Acton and his Wife, Mrs. Wairing &c. I drank part of a

Bowl of Punsh there with Mr. Bixter of Leverp: Mr. Byron Tatlock the Dyer &c the Occation was y⁰ Christoning of Mr. Syers (7th) Doughter Rachell.

Mr. Plumbe and I dined at the Talbot (Liverpool).   Mar. 22nd.

Mr. Sadler payed me £50 for y⁰ Purchas of D⁰ Lathoms   Mar. 23rd.
late Hous and Teneament.

My Wife went to y⁰ Wood and proposed Ann Buckleys   April 7th.
Doughter to Mrs. Sadlor for a Servant.

Yeomond of the Goar was here and Acquainted me   April 10th.
that my Lord Molin: desired y⁰ River of Alt might be
Scour'd as usuall.

I Counted the Crow-Nests in my Wood—94, the last   April 11th.
year I had but two Nests.

Mr. Ned Molineux was here to know whether I should   April 18th.
see his Son at Doway.

My Wife went to see Mr. Williamsons Doughter who   May 12th.
was Married to Tatlock, Son to Tatlock the Dier, she was
liing In of her first Child.

My Wife and Mrs. Wilding walked to Lidiate and back   May 15th.
againe.

I Sent my Luggage to y⁰ Carrior at Leverp: to be   May 21st.
carried to London. I gave Wᵐ Carefoot full directions
what to do in my Absence and read my Orders to him.

We went over from Leaverp: in Eastom Boat and dined   May 26th.
at Hooton with Doctor Low, thence to Chester.

My Wife and her Maid Ellen Howerd, Coz: Jane   May 27th.
Gillib: Lieftenant Barker, Liefte: Sole and I began our
Journey towards London in y⁰ Stage Coach from Chester.

1723.

May 29th.   From Coventry we came to Northampton a very pritty Town, the Market place large, the Streets broad and a very handsom Church.

May 30th.   To the George in Alders Gate London, where Mr. Parks met us and brought us to Mr. Haltons Wax Chandlor at the Golden Ball in Great Duke-Street where we Lodged.

June 2nd.   I drank with Mr. Hanson at the Holy-Lambe.

June 3rd.   My Wife, I, Miss Gillib: and Mrs. Aldred saw Cartooch Acted at the New Play-Hous.

June 4th.   I made choice of some Cloth at Mr. Humph: Traffords for a sute of Cloths for me.

June 8th.   Mr. John Culcheth lent me fourty Guineys.

June 10th.   Went by Boat to Greenwich where we went on Bord the Duke of Charos (Chandos) Captain Knight Master and sailed thence to Graivsend.

June 12th.   Landed at Calis about 3 and went to Table Royall.

The Diarist and his lady made this journey to fetch their daughters from school. They visited sundry places, saw many English priests, and dined at Brussels with the widowed Lady Derwentwater, who resided there with her chaplain, Father Wakeman, but died very shortly after this visit. Their daughter, Francis Blundell, was confirmed by the Bishop of St. Omers.

Aug. 4th.   Went on Bord the Duke of Shandos and set saile towards London.

Aug. 8th.   My Luggage was sirched and some Spirituall Books and Pictures taken from me to be burned.

Aug. 26th.   I went with my Doughters to Bartholemew Fair, we saw a Droll, a Little Man and a Popit Play. I met Lawyer

Culcheth, Dr Eyre and Sr Franc: Anderton at the Castle Tavern in Drury Laine.

Pat: Richardson and Mr. Will: Scarisbrick din'd Sept. 3rd. with us.

I was at ye Lancashire Club in Fleet Street with Mr. Sept. 4th. Lee of the Bank, two Mr. Traffords &c.

My Wife and I saw Humphrey Anger and Joseph Sept. 9th. Midleton Hanged at Tyburn.

We four made a Viset to my Lady Westmoreland at Sept. 10th. Twitnam and dined there, coming home we were over-turned, Fanny's Arme and my Side was hurt, Surgeon Gihee let me blood.

We saw the Consious Lovers Acted at Drury Laine Sept. 14th. Theatur.

Steele's most successful play, "The Conscious Lovers," was first acted on November 7th, 1722, and was published by Tonson on December 1st, with the date 1723 on the title page.—*Athenæum,* 5th December, 1891.

My Doughters and I were at the Quaikers Meeting in Sept. 15th. the Strand.

Mally and I saw the Corps of Mr. Fetherson carried Sept. 16th. in Forme by ye undertaiker.

I was at Mrs. Standleys when four Paters said y Sept. 18th. Office of the dead for Mrs. Bridget Standley. I was at ye Lancashire Clubb at the Legg wth Mr. Nich: Parker, Mr. Fleetwood Leigh &c.

My Wife and I were at Pankarage at the Buriall of Sept. 19th. Mrs. Bridget Standley, Mally was a Pall Bearer.

I was at the Jews Sinegogg by Leadon-Hall Market. Sept. 21st.

1723.

Sept. 25th.   I was at yᵉ Cockbit-Bowling Green. I was Chearman at yᵉ Legg Club there was Mr. Parker, two Traffords, &c.

Sept. 27th.   We four went to make my Lady Gerard a Viset then we went to see the Duke of Norfolks Fine Hous in St James' Squaire.

Sept. 28th.   Mr. Medcalf went with us four to the Play called Hamlet Prince of Denmark.

Oct. 3rd.   To Chester where we Lodged at yᵉ Golden Raven a very Cheap Hous, my Horses met me there.

Oct. 4th.   Came over in Eastom Boat but there not being Roome in it for my Horses, I left them and my Men in Chesshire.

Oct. 14th.   Mr. Tho: Standley late of Preston din'd here.

Oct. 23rd.   Mr. Gorsuch and his Son Eckleston lodged here.

Oct. 29th.   Pothecary Livlesley came hither and desired I would make use of him being I had made use of Mr. Latham his Master for my Apothecary.

Oct. 30th.   The Overseeors of the Parish (Sefton) bargaaned with Mr. Crisp in behalf of my Lord Molineux and with Alderman Tyrer for some of their Land to be added to yᵉ Road in Arnolds Reanes.

Nov. 14th.   My Wife and I dined at Ince with the Ladys of yᵉ Scones.

     Scones = Scholes Hall.

Nov. 20th.   I drank at John Tarletons with Lawyer Radcliff, Mr. Plumbe and his Son.

Nov. 27th.   I shewed my Doughters yᵉ Glass-hous and Charity Schoole.

Mr. Tho: Whitley called here and discoursed some Nov. 28th.
little about what is owing by Mr. Rob: Fazak: to me.

Antony Bulfinsh came to try two Pair of stays wh: he Nov. 29th.
had made for my Doughters.

Mr. Standley of Hooton and Parson Poole came hither Dec. 1st.
wth Mr. Blund:

Mr. Plump and Mr. Wittle met me at Lever: we Dec. 6th.
looked at some of Mr. Fazakerleys Houses in Union
Street in Order for me to have some of them for what
Money Mr. Faza: owes me, but I thought them too deare.
I dined at ye Wool-pack with Mr. Plumbe and Mr. Whitley.

Mr. Roger Diconson came hither, he discours'd me Dec. 9th.
concerning Lawyer Culcheth and Sr James Standley.

I pay'd for some Glass Bottles which I had from Dec. 12th.
Thatway Heath.

Parson Wairing, Pat Ald: and I made a Viset to Mr. Dec. 23rd.
Brooks ye Vicker of Walton, his Curat Parson Davis was
there and Mr. Whittle.

There was a Riding for Ann Norris who had beaton Dec. 31st.
her Husband, they called here in their Round, Henry
Swift was their Ridor.

My Wife rode dubble on Jewell to Mrs. Sadlors 'tis Mar. 22nd.
the first time he carried Dubble.

Mrs. Sadlor's at Aintree.

I was at the Buriall of Mrs. Molin: of the New Hall. April 9th.
I met the Corps upon ye Moss behind Ellethon Hunters.
When the Funerall was over I went in and drank with
Mr. Hulme the Atturney, George Smith, Rich: More &c.

1724.

April 13th. I went to Leverp: and Attended the Corps of Mr. William Cleaveland from his House to y⁰ Old Church there was at the Funerall Hous Lawyer Bootle, Mr. Peters &c.

April 22nd. Pat Bartlett let Mally blood.

April 24th. I went to Mr. Sheperds he helped me to look over and valew Mr. Fazakerleys Teneament called the New Hous in Fazakerley, thence we went to Walton and drank wᵗʰ Parson Richmond and the School-master.

May 6th. I went with Thomas Brownbill and his Kinsman Mr. Toping to Sephton, I shewed them y⁰ Seller at y⁰ Hall and the Church. I went to Pa: Windles on account of a Meeting about Scouring Alt, there was Mr. Tyrer of Ormsk: Yeomond of y⁰ Goar-Houses, Mr. Smith of Maile, Parson Acton &c.

May 20th. I bowled at Crosby with Parson Harrison Mr. Byron &c Parson Brooks Parson Davis &c were there.

May 23rd. My Doughters and I dined at the Legs of Man in Wigan thence we went to the New-Hall of Atherton wᶜʰ is in Building and then to Manchester where we Lodg'd at the Bulls Head a very good Inn.

May 24th. We saw the old and New Church, we were at the Quaickers Meeting and in Mr. Edwards his Pritty Garden. We made a Viset to Mr. Yates.

May 25th. It being Salford Fair I light of a Paising Gelding there, I rode him into Manchester and bought him, I call him Pesient Grissell.

May 27th. I went to Crosby Green there was Parson Egerton t'was the first time I was acquainted with him.

Went to Crosby Greene, there was Mr. Byron, Mr. June 3rd.
Richard Molin: Rob: Boo: &c.

I sent to Wooton to welcom home my Lord and June 8th.
Lady Molineux.

I Bowled at Crosby wth a younger son of Atturney June 10th.
Tyrer, Yeomon of ye Goar &c. Mr. Tatlock of ye Bank
his Brother Thomas and Tatlock the Dier were on y^e
Green.

Parson Richmond, Parson Davis, Mr. Tho: Tatlock June 12th.
and Mr. Tho: Whitley made a Viset they Lodged here.

Dined at Eckleston, coming home Parson Davis and June 14th.
Tatlock ye Dyer stop'd me a little at Jack Seftons. I
called at Tatlocks of ye Pear-Tree, he gave me £20 for
his Sons first years Pention and thirty Shillings for his
Private Expences.

Rev. Henry Tatlock, S.J., then a student at St. Omers' College,
was for the most part of his life priest at Lydiate and Fazakerley,
residing chiefly at the latter place, where he died 1771, aged 62.

Dined at More-hall, thence went to Oughton Moss and June 16th.
saw three run for the Great Plate, a Gray Hors of my
Lord Darbys wann.

My Wife Doughters and I dined at Wooton.   June 19th.

Lodged at the Whit Bull in Preston.   June 20th.

Walked with my Wife and Doughters to Enom June 21st.
(Auenham) Walk and to ye Gardens, We made a Viset
to the Sister Blundells and to Mrs. Butler.

I Bowled at Crosby with Parson Harrison, Mr. Byron June 29th.
&c. Parson Egerton came in the evening, we had a Bowl
of Punsh upon account of a Waiger lost.

1724.

July 1st.   My Wife Doughters and I went to Mr. Yates of Maile who was very oblidging to us.

July 19th.   George Smith came in the evening to look at my Gardens. Mr. Livesley the Chirurgeon came along with him.

July 27th.   My Doughters and I went to Knowsley to see the Hous and Gardens we met Mr. Sheperd and his Wife there, we dined there with Mr. Rich: Norris Mr. Jo Poole and his Son David.

July 28th.   I was at the Race on Leverp: Sands, five horses Ran for the Plate and Spencers Bay Mare wan it.

July 30th.   Fanny stood God-mother to Mr. Crisp's Doughter Frances.

Aug. 4th.   John Voce began to build yᵉ Summerhous at yᵉ farther corner in the New-Grounds.

Aug. 8th.   Mr. Standley of Hooton, Collon: Collumbine, Mr. Blundell and their Ladys and Sʳ Fran: Anderton &c made a Viset here.

Aug. 12th.   Went to Crosby Greene where I found Sʳ Fran: Anderton, Coll: Columbine &c I Bowled with Apothecary Virnon &c: there was Parson Crosby, Parson Kelsey and Mr. Cottom.

Aug. 14th.   Before three this Morning I disturmbed two Cupple of Woosters Jane Withington, Nelly Howerd and their Sparks.

Aug. 15th.   Mat: Withington came to chapter his Doughter for Courting in yᵉ Night.

Aug. 17th.   Jane Withington and Nelly Howerd left their Service, they went to Darby Waikes.

Aug. 20th.   Mr. Eckleston sent his Servant to me with a Letter of Grand Apportance but to no Purpose.

I was at the Race on Crosby Marsh between a Gray <small>Aug. 27th.</small> Gelding of one Stirrops of Warington and a Black Darby-shire Mare, the latter wan. When the Race was over I went to Heskeths where young Mr. Standish Mr. Harington &c Bowled; when we went into y⁰ Hous Mr. Harington and I &c played at eaven and od.

Margarit Gray was seased this Morning very ill after <small>Aug. 30th.</small> the same Manner as several of the Neighbours are, and in the Evening she took a Vomit.

My Lady Phillipa Standish, Lady Molineux &c dined <small>Sept. 3rd.</small> here.

My Wife and Mally went to Ince to wish Mrs. Blundell <small>Nov. 1st.</small> Joy of her Son Henry, he was borne yesterday.

Mr. Henry Blundell was afterwards a patron of the fine arts, and made the collection of statues, etc., which now adorn Ince Blundell. He died in 1810, and on the marble entablature erected to his memory at Sefton Church by his admirers are some eulogistic verses by W. Roscoe, the historian.

D͏ʳ Angier came y⁰ first time to see me. <small>Nov. 2nd.</small>

Dr. Samuel Angier, an eminent physician, resided in Union Street—so called from the union of Sir Cleave More with Ann, daughter of Joseph Edmund, Esq. Edmund and Union Streets laid out about 1709.—*Picton's Memorials.*

A How-do-you sent from Mr. Harington and from <small>Nov. 5th.</small> Culcheth.

How-do-you's sent from Mr. Standley of Hooton, Widow <small>Nov. 6th.</small> Eckleston and the Lady's of the Scowes.

My Wife and Mally went to Mr. Crisps and heard Mr. <small>Nov. 30th.</small> Munson Preach.

Fanny and I went to Wigan to be under D͏ʳ Francis <small>Dec. 4th.</small> Worthing: our health being very bad, the Coach was

1724.

overturned and when we came neare Wigan it was laid fast y⁰ Rode being so deep, so we left it in y⁰ Laine all Night, and we went with our Horses to Wigan where we Lodged at Kendalls the Leggs of Man.

Dec. 5th.   I sent the Horses home but kept the Coach in Wigan. We dined at oure Inn and then Fanny and I went to Dʳ Fran: Worth: We suped at Mr. Goldings where we are to Bord, Fanny Lodges there and I lodg at Mrs. Heskeths.

Dec. 9th.   Mrs. Diconson of Wrightington sent a How-do-you to Fanny.

Dec. 11th.   Coz: Gillibrond of Astley Mr. Standish and his Son Howerd came to see us.

Dec. 16th.   Mr. Ned Molineux came in y⁰ Morning to see me.

Dec. 19th.   I made a Viset to Dʳ Fran: Worton, I found Pat: Mare there and his Neece the Widdow Harding (Hawarden).

Dec. 21st.   Mr. Culcheth and Pat: Smith came to see me.

Dec. 23rd.   I came home from Wigan, I baited at y⁰ four Laine Ends in Bigarstaff.

1725.
Jan. 2nd.   Mr. Pursell helped me to cleare and dry severall of my Books which were damnifyed by y⁰ wet in my Closet.

Jan. 5th.   They brought me word that Mr. Pursall was found drowned in Thornton.

Jan. 17th.   My Wife and Mally went to Leverpoole with Fanny she is to be under the care of Dʳ Bromfield she Lodges at Mrs. Williamsons.

Feb. 9th.   Mr. Blund: and his Lady, Mr. James Tildesley and his Wife, Pat: Curedon &c made a Viset here.

Fanny was so ill of ye Convultion Fits that Mr. Aldred Feb. 13th.
gave her the Holy Oyles. Dr Ferniho of Chester met D^r
Dickins here, they had a Consult.

Pat: Walmesley pray'd here. Feb. 19th.

Mrs. Blund: and Parson Poole's Doughter made a Viset Feb. 21st.
here, so did Mr. Will: Walmesley and his Wife.

Mr. Sadlor din'd here I gave him some Plate, for him Mar. 1st.
to Engrave my Coat of Armes on.

Mr. Cottom came to see Fanny he had ben at the Mar. 4th.
Christoning of Parson Wairing Son Gerard.

I was at ye Buriall Hous of Ailes Tickley there was Mar. 19th.
Mr. Shaw of Leverp: Mr. Byron, Mr. Formby Mr.
Williamsons Son of Litherland &c. I went to Wm Davys
and falted him for seting his Wives Teneament to Tho:
Johnson without my Consent, his Answer was he cair'd
not one Pin, he would set that and his other Teneament
to whom he list and I might doe my Worst.

Mrs. Blund: desir'd I would ues my Endeavour to Mar. 28th.
prevent her Husband being chosen Church Warden.

I went to Prayers to Mr. Crisps and then went to ye Mar. 30th.
Parish Meeting where Mr. Blund: was design'd to be
chosen Church-Warden, but we prevented it.

I gave Mr. Peters a Glass of Wine at ye George and April 17th
discoursed him concerning Skiner Davy, he got me a
Warant for him &c.

I try'd Skinner Davy before Mr. Goodwin the Maior of April 24th.
Lever: for Detracting me and saying severall scurrelous
things of me, Mr. Peters was my Atturney, Mr. Hulme
and Mr. Barron were Skinner Davys.

1725.

April 27th.   Coz: Tho: Gillib: came to Acquaint his Father with Miss Jenys Resolution.   Mr. Standish and his Son Ralf dined at Astley.   Mr. Standish made a Proposall to me.

May 1st.   The young Men of this Town Acted the Commedy Called The taiming of the Show in my Hall.   Mrs. Blund: &c were here, they Suped here.

May 5th.   It being the Opening of Great Crosby Bowling Green I went thither, there was Alderman Tyrer Mr. Cottom, Mr. Whittle &c.

May 11th.   I Bowl'd at Ince Green, there was Mr. Chappell, Olton and Standle ye Apothecary all of Ormschurch and Mr. Smith of Maile.

May 16th.   I met Skiner Davy in Sephton Church where he publickly beged my Pardon for talking Scurrilously of me, I drak at Pall Windles with Parson Harrison, John Rose, Rob: Bootle &c.

May 17th.   I saw part of ye Play called Taiming the Shrow Acted at Robert Blansherds, I drank there with Mr. Ned Molineux Rich: Tarlton &c: the Players came hither first to shew themselves before they went to ye Stage.

May 19th.   I went to Crosby where I Bowled with Mr. James Clenton &c: Alderman Cunlive was there, I drank wth Mr. Everet.

May 26th.   Mr. Nelson brought a Letter from Lady Molin: to my Wife in behalf of Ra: St:.

June 6th.   Fanny had one of her Violent Convultion Fits, it was Occasion'd by seeing a Mous in her Roome.

June 9th.   I went with Dr Bromfield and Pat: Hardesty to Crosby, I Bowled four Bowles out of a Hand against Mr. Crispe three. Mr. Hulme yᵉ Atturney Bowled a Match with Parson Harrison &c. Mr. Warbrick, Mr. Woodard &c: were there. I came directly home without going into the Aile-hous.

I fetched home my Coach which came by the Robert June 14th. from London and pay'd Cap: Howerd £5 for bringing it, Mr. Chadock was there.

I went to Crosby Greene and Bowled Hand to fist June 16th. with Mr. Ri: Molin: of yᵉ Grange; Hulme the Atturney and Mr. Byron were there.

Parson Egerton, Parson Acton and his Wife, Mr. June 21st. Cottom &c: dined here, After dinner we hansaled the New Summer hous.

To "hansell"—to open, to use for the first time. This word is still in common use, and generally implies more or less of festivity to celebrate the occasion.

Mr. Blund: Pat: Burton &c called here as they went July 7th to Crosby Green I went with them and Bowled with Parson Brooks, Parson Wairing &c: Mr. James Tildesley was there.

My Wife Doughters and I went to Ormsch: Race July 13th. there were three that Ran and the Bolton Mair wan, Mr. Plumbe and his Son and Mr. Cottom were .there. Mr. Strickland of Sizargh and Coz: Gillib: of Astley came home with me.

This Famoly and Ince met at Pat: Aldreds. He gave July 13th. yᵉ Ladys Coffy and we men had a Bowl of Punsh.

Mr. Strickland went hence, I went with him to Maile July 19th. Clent.

I Rode out with Fanny it is the first time she has July 20th. Rode out single this 8 Months as I think.

July 21st.　Pat: Turner and three Sons of Mr. Standley of Hooton was here, but. I was gon to Crosby Green, there was young crooked Blaise of Lever: Ashton a Draper of Ormschurch &c.

July 25th.　My Wife Doughters and I went in yᵉ Coach to yᵉ Grange, Mrs. Bl: her two Sisters-in-Law and three Sons of Mr. Standleys of Hooton came thither, coming home most of us prayed by the Corps of Mary Molineux.

July 26th.　The Wool-pack being very full Mr. Allonson, Mr. Crupton and some others who were drinking wᵗʰ me there, Adjourned all to Mr. Moss'es and sent for Aile to yᵉ Wool-pack.

July 27th.　Mrs. Bravarius came to look at my Wives Legg.

She was housekeeper at Ince Blundell.

July 28th.　I went to Crosby and Bowl'd with Parson Kelsey, Parson Harrison &c: The Maior of Leverp: Mr. Carr, Mr. Windsor &c: were there.

July 29th.　Coz Gili: sent an express with a Letter from Lady Phill

Aug. 2nd.　Wᵐ Carefoot brought me home two peeces of Timber wᶜʰ were Reck.

Aug. 7th.　I went to Leverp: and drank most extraordinary good Aile at Mr. Whawleys with Mr. Plūbe and his Son Will: and Mr. Cottom.

Aug. 11th.　Mr. Plumbe dined here I went with him to Crosby there was Dʳ Bromfield, James Williamsons Son James and I think both their Wives Par: Richmond Parson Davis, old Will Rollins Thom: Howerd &c:

Aug. 16th.　Mr. Standish made his 2ᵈ Viset to Mally.

Coming back (from Woolton), I looked at Mr. Plumbes _{Aug. 17th.} fine Flowers, then went to Leverp: and bought two Small Keggs of Wine of Mr. Williamson.

My Wife, Mally and I went to Ormschurch Race _{Aug. 25th.} where my Lord Molineux his Roan Hors beat Lord Darbys Gray Mare.

Lord Frederick Howerd dined and Lodg'd here. _{Aug. 26th.}

I sent Mrs. Fleetwood Butler to Scarisbrick. _{Aug. 28th.}

I went to Ormschurch Horse-Faire. I drank at the _{Aug. 30th.} Talbot wth Mr. Sanderson, Stewerd to Sr Wm Gerard, Francis Farer &c.

My Wife I and Mally din'd at Wooton with Lord _{Sept. 2nd.} Frederick, Lady Philippa Standish &c : Coming back we called at Leverp: and took Fanny and Mrs. Williamson to see the Commody Acted called the Busy Boddy.

Lady Phillipa Standish, first wife of Ralph Standish, of Standish, Esq., was daughter of Henry, 12th Duke of Norfolk, and sister of Lord Frederick Howard. She died 1731, and her husband married secondly Mary, daughter and co-heiress of Albert Hodgson, Esq., of Leighton Hall.

Sr Francis Anderton being at Ince Pat Ald: and I _{Sept. 5th.} went thither we Suped there.

I went to Crosby Greene, there was two of Lawyer _{Sept. 8th.} Bootle's Brothers, Mr. Cottom &c.

My Wife and I din'd at Ince, there was Lady _{Sept. 13th.} Molineux and her two Doughters &c : Stewerd the Book-Sellor was selling books in the Hall.

My Lord and Lady Molin: their Doughters, Mr. Tho: _{Sept. 16th.} Standley, Mr. Washbour &c : dined here.

1725.

Sept. 21st.   Mr. Standish and I went to Ince Green and bowl'd with Sr Francis Anderton and Mr. Blundell, Mr. Moli: of ye Grange and his Brother Rich: were there.

Sept. 22nd.   This being Mallys Birthday Mrs. Acton, Mrs. Byron &c: dined here. Tatlock played here and we dans'd till Morning, Sr Francis Anderton dans'd with us in ye after noone.

Sept. 25th.   It being Fanny's Birth day Tatloc play'd here, we danced both before and after Supper. Mr. Hen: Blund Sup'd here, we play'd with him at Chaising ye Whistle.

Sept. 27th.   She drank too much Burch Wine. Mr. Tho: Butler and his Neece Fleetwood Lodged here.

Oct. 4th.   I was at the Race on Crosby Marsh where four Horses Ran for a Sadle, Mr. Lowders Gray Gelding wann.

Oct. 6th.   Being Matters are now lickley to goe forwards Coz: Gillib: and I began to Consider what proposalls were proper to be made to Mr. Standish.

Oct. 11th.   My Doughters Mr. Standish and I went to the Hall of Formby, Mr. Formby was not at home.

Oct. 18th.   It being Crosby Goosfeast Mr. Standish and I dined at Parson Wairings, there was Parson Acton, Parson Harrison Mr. Cottom &c:

Oct. 19th.   Mr. Standish Coz Gillib: and I went to Ormesch: and took a Glass of Wine at the Queens Head.

Oct. 20th.   Coz: Gillib: and I din'd at Standish, Mr. John Gerard Junior was there; Old Mr. Stand: I &c: discoursed of Proposalls for my Doughter Marys Setlement &c:

Nov. 2nd.   Being Mr. Greene kept Crosby Court at Jacksons, I went thither and Order'd Rob: Johnson in Presence of

Edw: Hutton, Joh: Banister &c: to open me a Bridle Rode
thorrow the Bottom of his New Inclosed Field viz: to make
me a Rode to ride from y* Scab Laine thorrow his said
Field along y* Water-cource which runs between it and y*
Wheat Hey, I claiming a Hors rode that way for my
Customers to my Mill; According to my Command Robert
Johnson himself and his Tenants Son Joseph Newhous
made me a Rode, so I, young Mr. Standish and his
Servant James Hill Rode that way home from Great
Crosby.

My Wife and Doughters din'd at y* Talbot in Leverp: Nov. 3rd.
Young Mr. Standish went with them to the Play, they
saw Mary Queen of Scots Acted.

Pat: Smith the Superior dined here so did Pat: Nov. 12th.
Clifton, Hadesty &c: We toosed William Roostich in a
Blanket.

Mr. Standish and I rode out to the Sea-Side in Nov. 18th.
Expectation of Meeting Mr. Clifton and his Lady in their
way home to Lithom they being Married upon y* 16.

Mr. Standish went hence, this was his last Viset.   Nov. 20th.

Mr. Ralph Standish had not succeeded in winning the affections
of Mr. Blundell's daughter Mary. He subsequently married Mary,
daughter of George Butler, Esq., of Ballyraggat, Ireland.

Mr. Molin: of the Grang being dead, my Doughters Nov. 22nd.
and I went thither to pray, I heard three Mas: Mr.
Blund: and his Lady, Mr. Molin: of Mosburgh, Mr.
Rob: Chantrell &c: were there.

I was a Bearer at the Funerall of Mr. Molin: of y* Nov. 23rd.
Grange there was at the Grange Mr. Formby, Mr. Cottom,
Mr. Tho: Heskaine Apothecary Livesley &c:

1725.

Nov. 25th.   Mally discoursed seriously and told me her Mind.

Dec. 4th.   The Miller being uneasy upon some things which he heard were said of him told me he would leave my Service unless I would come upon a New Bargan with him.

Dec. 7th.   Mrs. Blundell being brought to Bed my Wife Stood God-mother to Miss Anna-Maria.

Dec. 14th.   I Began to make a Church of Pallatine Work and almost finished it.   Pat: Roydon Lodged here.

Dec. 21st.   I was at the Funerall of Mr. Gorsuch of Gorsuch, I was a Bearer so was Mr. Molineux of Mosb: &c: he was Buried at Ormschurch.   Pat: Curedons old Woman in ye Straw Hat.

Dec. 26th.   My Wife sent a Present to Mrs. Acton against ye Christoning tomorrow of her Son Tho:.   My Wife went to ye Hall of Lidiat and spoke to Jane Heys about her coming to be Chamber-Maide here, but they did not bargan.

Dec. 27th.   My Wife and Doughters made a Viset to Mrs. Molineux of ye Grange to Condole the Death of her Husband.

Dec. 31st.   I Hir'd Rich: Prescot to be my Millor am to give him £11 5/- ℔ ann: and he to find Lite and Licker.

The Diarist remarks that owing to the wet summer the roads were extremely bad, and coals had to be fetched on horseback in winter, a thing never before known. A horse-load sold in Liverpool for 2s. 6d., which was formerly 7d.

1726.

Jan. 2nd.   I went towards Ditton but ye Snow being so deep and the Rodes bad I got no farther than Childol where I Lodg'd at Longworths I made a Viset to Parson Kelsey and eat some Christmas Faire with him, I gave his Doughters some Span Rings.

I went to the Bank in Ditton where I Lodged. We Jan. 3rd. hunted the Whistle after Supper.

Pat Bartlet Lanced Mary Molineux in her Gumbs Jan. 16th. for the Tooth-Aich, and mixed some Powder of Roman Vitriall with her Blood.

Will: Davy Skinner came in a submissive Manner and Jan. 19th. desir'd I would be Friends with him.

Parson Poole's Doughter of Cheshire came hither wth Jan. 20th. Mr Blund: &c:

Wm Davy ye Skiner gave me £10 at Leverp: for which Jan. 22nd. I engaig'd not to prosecute him by Law and promised to forgive him all Misdemainors past which I knew of.

Mr Livlesley sent his Brother hither with some Phisick Jan. 23rd. he fell in Rimrose as he came.

Two Men were here who say'd they had ben Jan. 24th. Transported out of Scotland into Maryland and were now returning homewards.

Roscow went to Ince to shew her lame Arme to Mrs. Jan. 30th. Prevarius.

Mr. Strikland lodg'd here. Feb. 1st.

I was at the Buriall of Mr. Robo: Fazak: at Walton, Feb. 17th. so was Mr. Smarley, Mr. Cottom, Mr. Wm Plumbe &c: I was a Bearer so was Mr. Standley of Hooton, Old Mr. Trafford of Croston &c.

My Wife and Doughters made their first Viset to young Feb. 21st. Mrs. Williamson of Litherland.

The Little Boys of ye Town rann Blindfold after an Feb. 22nd. other who had a Bell, for a Cock; when that Sport was

1726.

over, they ran with their Hands ty'd on their Backs after yᵉ Cock and took him in their Mouth.

Mar. 2nd.   I bought half a doz: small Silver-Hafted Knives and as many Forks for a Desets, of a Rich Pedlor.

Mar. 13th.   Mr. Francis Walmesley came to see me he being for going to Sea in a few days.

Mar. 22nd.   I was at the Buriall of Henry Blund: of Ince that is to say I was at the Buriall Hous but not at the Church, onely went part of the way with the Corps.

Mar. 23rd.   I was a Bearer at the Funerall of Widdow Eckleston, so was Mr. John Gerard Junior, Mr. Culcheth &c: she was buried at Prescot, there was at Eckleston Mr. Cubbon, Mr. Bretton, Tho: Hurst the Ship Carpinder &c: When yᵉ Funerall was over most of us went into Lauransons.

Mar. 26th.   Mally Rode behind me to Lever:

April 1st.   We Began to make some Wine of 60 Sivell Oringes and 30 Leomons they cost 6ᵗ - 8ᵈ four doz: Pound of Lisbon Sugar cost £1. 4ᵗ   It made six dozen Bottles wᶜʰ comes to 5ᵗ 1¼ᵈ ℔ Doz.

April 7th.   I Visited the Chappell at yᵉ New-Hous and at Ince for the Jubily, coming home I met Mrs. Blundell &c: who had ben upon the licke Viset at Mr. Aldreds.

A Jubilee in the Catholic Church is a larger indulgence, or the plenary remission of temporal punishment due to sin, to be gained by the performance of prescribed penitential works. A certain number of visits to neighbouring churches are usually enjoined.

April 14th.   Mally play'd at Picket wᵗʰ Coz: Butler.

April 19th.   Mr. Blu: made a Viset here and took a Snap of Cold Meat with me.

I walked with Coz: Butler to the Dock, the Charity April 21st. Schoole &c (at Liverpool).

I sowed Cowcumber Seed which had ben steeped six April 25th. Hours in New Milk.

I went with Coz: Butler to Mr. Brooks'es the Vicker April 26th. of Walton.

Pat: Roydon dined here, I went with Coz: Butler to April 27th. Crosby Green, I Bowled Hand to Fist with Mr. Cottom, there was Pars: Brooks, Mr. Jaimes Tildeslay &c.

I Began my Journey towards Astley with Fanny we April 30th. Lodg'd, at the Queens Head in Ormeschurch I found Mr. Nelson of Fairest there.

From Orms: I went with Fanny to Coz Gillib of May 1st. Astley where she is to stay for some time for change of Aire in hopes to Cure her Ague-Fits.

I came from Astley to Ormsc: I light at Billing'es at May 2nd. his new Hous.

I Began my Journey towards Asburne Faire. May 6th.

I went with Mr. Taylor Steward to Mr. Eckleston to May 7th. the Cock in Leek, thence to Ashburne, I light at the Talbot and Lodged at a Privat Hous.

I Heard Mr. Laybours Mass at Madam Peggs the Hall May 8th. of Hildersley. I dined at the Ordinary at the Talbot.

The Diarist went to Asburne to buy black horses for his coach, which were then all the rage. He could only find two to suit him.

I began my Journey homewards, we baited at New- May 10th. Haven a Hous upon a Large Common in Derby-Shire very famous for a Sheep Faire; I observed their Fences in those

1726.

parts were all Walls from three Foot high to five Foot, built
of dry Cobling Stones and layed at such a distance, they
loock in some places like Lettises (? Lattices) and a Child
very readily may put his Arme through them, there are
few or no Gates into the Fields onely a Gap left in the
Wall wch they fill up and pull down as they have Occasion;
then we went to Buckston where I saw ye Warme Spring
and some of ye Baths, then went to Disley where we
Lodged at Swindals the Signe of ye Rams-Head, good
entertainment and not dear.

May 18th.   Mr. Plumbe of Down-holland brought a Black Gelding
for me to look at but I bought him not.   Coz: Butler
and I went to Crosby Green we drank Punsh with Parson
Egerton, Brooks, Parson Harrison, Mr. Cottom &c:

May 20th.   Coz: Butler and I went to Whit-Otter Mair in Holsold
a fishing where we met Mr. Rob: Fazak: Mr. Swettenham
&c: we dined and some of us Lodged at Wm Rigbys in
Holsold.

May 21st.   Coz: Butler and I went with Mr. Heskaine to his
Hous where we dined and then came home.

May 23rd.   Parson Egerton, Brooks and four other Parsons Suped
here.

May 25th.   I Bowled at Crosby with Parson Brooks, Parson
Harrison, Dr. Bromfield.

May 26th.   Mr. Stickland came but stayed not long being he had
received a Positive Denighall.

          Mr. Strickland of Sizergh, another suitor for the hand of Miss
Blundell.

May 28th.   Coz: Butler help'd me to choose some Wine at Mr.
Williamsons Seller.

Coming home we stay'd at a Barn in Thornton and Watched the Country People dance.

Coz: Butler dined at Parson Wairings, I went thither in y° evening there was Parson Brooks, Egerton and Davys; Mr. Heskaine, Cottom &c. Wm Carefoot came home from Derby-Faire with 3 Colts each 2 years old, I call them Buck, Buty, and Lovely.

Coz: Butler and I went with Mr. Blund: to Crosby Green, I bowled with Parson Wairing &c: Mr. Cragg was there. Dandy brought my New Coat and Waiscot and tryed it on, but it did not fit.

I went in the Coach with four Blacks in y° same order wth hereafter they are to goe in.

Coz: Butler and I dined at Tho: Howerds in Crosby with Mr. Heskaine and Young Mr. Hollywell.

Coz: Butler went in my Coach with my Wife and Mally to Orms: Race, the chief divertion was between Sr Ralph Ashtons and Mr. Egertons, the latter wan. I drank in Rigbys Booth with Mr. Heskaine, Mr. Wm Poole of Leverp: &c then went to y° Wheat Sheaf in Ormschurch where I drank with young Mr. Entwisley, Mr. Heskaine &c:

Coz: Butler and I dined at the Wheat Sheafe with my Lord Darby Sr Edw: Standley Sr Ralph Ashton, Mr. Rich: Norris &c: I was at y° Race on Oughton Moss, where Lord Darbys Ruflor beat Mr. Pilson's Bay.

Hen: Ascroft gave me the Jaw-Bone of a Beast which he had found in y° Growing Moss 5 Foot and a half deep; I take it to be the Jaw Bone of a Young Swine.

My Teame and 13 others Lead coles for Mr. Aldred.

1726.

June 25th.   I went to Leverp: I went with Mr. Molineux to look at some Lansskips which he has drawn.

June 26th.   My Wife and I dined at Eckleston tis y* first time we have seen Mr. Eckl: since he was Marryed.

June 29th.   I drank at Tho: Howerds with Parson Jackson, Egerton, Brooks and Lawyor Radcliff &c.

June 30th.   Coz: Butler and I dined at Knowsley with Mr. Scarisb: Will: Brownhill &c:

July 12th.   Sister Midleton my Wife Doughters and I went to Leverp: we went on Bord my Lord Droughadays Yatch the Old England.

July 22nd.   Mr. Holton come to invite my Sister Midleton to More-Hall. Pat: Edw: Scarisb: dined here. Mr. Sadlor drew out a Pattrom from Sister Midletons Apron.

July 23rd: Coz: Butlers Servant brought a Side of Venison from Rock-savage. Mr. Heskaine sent a Present of Venison.

July 27th.   I was at the Race wch Parson Wairing, Mr. Byron and Rob: Bootle Ran, for 3 Load of my Turves, Rob: Bootle wan them.

July 29th.   I had a Merry-Night we Danced in the Dining Roome viz: Mr. Faz: Young Mr. Holywell Mr. Heskaine &c: The Country People danced in y* Hall; my Musick was Anderton and Marsh.

July 30th.   We danced after dinner, and at Evening I discharg'd my Musick.

Aug. 2nd.   Apothecary Livsey and his Brother the Churcheon who is lately come out of France made me a Viset.

Coz: Butler Sister Midleton my Wife, Mally and I dined at Mrs. Hollywells in Leverp: and then went to the Assembly after that to the Talbot where we sup'd and so home the next Morning.

I went to Bank-Hall with Coz: Butler, Sister Midleton, my Wife and Mally; Mr. Heskaine was there, he went with us to my Lords Fountaine and New-Summer-hous.

The Earl of Derby had just purchased Bank Hall, the ancient seat of the Moores, who had fallen into difficulties.

Mr. Blundells two Sisters and his Aunt Bridg: and Dorot: made a Viset to Fanny.

I went to Crosby Race there were five start for ye Plate, a Mare of Maikins of Prescot wan it.

I fixed the Hous Bell better than it was and put a New Rope to it.

Coz: Butler and I dined at the Leggs of Man in Prescot with Mr. Cubbom, Mr. Windsor, Alderman Goodin &c: thence we went to Knowsley Park where we saw three Horses Run, Makings Mare of Prescot wan. I waited of my Lord Darby at his Summer-Hous. When the Race was over, We went to Mr. John Chantrells Standing and drank a Glass of Wine wth Mr. Hesketh of Rufford, young Mr. Trafford &c:

We went with Mr. Eckleston to Knowsley Park where we saw a Gallaway Race, Lord Darby's Munkey wann, there was at the Race, Sr Edw: Standley, Lawyer Standle Brother to Sr James Standle.

The Wind being very high in ye Night I got up towards Morning and went to look at my Mill.

1726.

Sept. 7th.   Coz: Butler and I dined and Lodg'd at Mr. Heskeths of Rufford, Old Mr. Standish, Mr. Rigby of Harrock and his Son made a Viset there.

Sept. 8th.   I Left Coz: Butler at Rufford and came to Pat: Gorsuch to the Hall of Boscol (Burscough), but being too late I stay'd but a small while and then came thorrow Ormschurch home.

Sept. 13th.   Dr Clayton, son to Daine Clayton in Ireland and Lawyer Radcliff dined here. Pat: Curedon went hence to live at Sefton and to help at Croxtath, he has ben a Gest here, I think neare one Yeare.

Sept. 15th.   Pat: Turbervill the Provin: dined here.

Sept. 18th.   Tho: Brown Servant to Mr. Houghton came to see if I would let his Master have two Thousand Thornes.

Sept. 19th.   I was at Crosby Race where Maikins Bay Mare beat Rob: Rigbys Black Mare, 'tis the third Race I have seen her win since ye 28 of last Month. I drank wth Mr. Standley of Cross-Hall, Mr. Heskaine, Mr. Berry ye Atturney &c: there was at ye Race Mr. Halsold of Leverp: Mr. Wm Plumbe, Wm Kennion &c:

Sept. 21st.   Coz: Butl: and I went with my Wife and Doughters to Low-Hill where we dined at Widdow Dailes and bought some things of a Scotchman who had a Chaimber there of Rich goods.

Sept. 27th.   I made Mr. James Clinton a Viset and drank there with Mr. Sherlock &c:

Sept. 28th.   Cozen Butler met my Lord Molineux a Fox Hunting, they killed one Brace of Foxes in Ince.

Sept. 29th.   Coz: Butler dined at ye Stand wth my Lord Molin:

Coz: Butler and I went a Fox-hunting with Lord- Sept. 30th.
Molin: there was Surgeon Livsey Dr Rice &c:

Coz: Butler and I met my Lord Molineux a Fox- Oct. 3rd.
hunting there was Mr. Heskaine, Mr. Syer &c: we found
noe Fox. We din'd at the Stand with my Lord Molineux,
Molin: of Mosburgh, Mr. Molin: of the Grange, &c.

I Bowled Hand to Fist at Crosby with Tho: Fleetwood. Oct. 5th.
I drank there with Parson Wairing, Mr. Whitley &c:

I saw my five Black Coach-Horses docked very Short. Oct. 10th.

James Marrow took a Cock in my Glead this morning, Oct. 27th.
'tis ye first I have taken this Season.

I had seaven Lads of this Town beaton at my Gate- Oct. 28th.
Hous with a Sterrop-Leather, some by their Fathers,
others by their Masters and some by other Persons for
Stealing my Apples and for other Peevish tricks.

I dined at Mr. Plumbs at Wever-Tree. Oct. 29th.

Prescot Post came with a Post-Letter to me wch was Nov. 7th.
rong directed.

Finsh a London Chimney-Sweeper swept some of my Nov. 9th.
Chimneys.

Cozen Butler sent his Servāt from Rock-Savage with Nov. 17th.
a Present of a Doe.

I went in my Coach to Th: Howerds where I found Nov. 19th.
Mr. Heskaine Mr. Jos. Poole Mr. Atherton the Wine-
merchant &c:

I Attended the Corps of Tho: Syer of the Ford from Nov. 24th.
his Hous to Sefton Church there was Parson Brooks,

1726.

Harrison and Wairing, Mr. Tho: Whitle &c. Mr. Green kept the Court at yᵉ Ailhous by Sefton Church.

Nov. 27th.

My Wife and Doughters made a Viset to Mrs. Syer of the Ford to condole the death of her Husband.

Dec. 1st.

Bryan Leas Son Richard being dead he was carried to Sefton on my Coach Carriage, I attended the Corps from the Hous into Ince Town.

Dec. 2nd.

I was at yᵉ Saile of goods at the Ford, the Sellors were Mr. Whittle and Tatlock the Dyar, there was Mr. Williamson of Litherland, Mr. Byron &c:

Dec. 5th.

Jos: Rigby brought Barnaby Hargrave to be my Butler but he is too Little.

Dec. 13th.

I began to lead yᵉ Chappell Chamber Stones from the side of yᵉ Terras and lay'd them in the Buriall Place.

Dec. 28th.

My Wife and Doughters went to yᵉ Funerall of Mr. Blundells Son Robert.

Dec. 29th.

I was at the Town Meeting at Ditton, there was Parson Langford of Haile, Atturney Halsold John Tarbolk, &c.

1727.
Jan. 5th.

I din'd at yᵉ Edg with Parson Acton young Williamson of Litherton and their Wives, Widdow Tatlock of yᵉ Bank &c: after diner I drank there with young Pluckington Parson Harrison &c.

Jan. 10th.

Tho: Marron's Corps was carried to Sefton Church on my Coach Bottom.

Jan. 16th.

Coz: Butler dined at yᵉ Grange with Mr. Rob: Fazak: Jemmy Singleton, Tom: Heskaine &c.

Jan. 18th.

Coz: Butler and I went to Bank-hall where we sat awhile with my Lord Darby, Mr. Standley of Cross Hall,

Mr. Wall from towards Preston, Mr. Eckleston of Eckles: and then we went to Lord Darbys Race Ground where a Gray Gelding of Mr. Gills bet a Bay one of Mr. Heskaines, there was upon the ground App: Lathom, Tom Whitley.

I went to Leverp: and made Major Broadnax a viset, Jan. 21st. he told me that in March next he will be 108 years of Aige, he has his Memory perfectly well, and talks extreamly strongly and heartally without any seeming decay of his Spirrits.

He died in the following January and was buried at St. Nicholas' Church.

I went part of the way with the Corps of Mr. Thomas Jan. 24th. towards Sefton, I was entertained upon yᵉ Funerall Account at Tho: Syors where there was Parson Wairing, Parson Harrison, Old Mr. Williamson late of Litherland, Mr. Sharrock of Formby, Mr. Byron &c.

Dined at Ince, there was at Dinner Alderman Tyrer Jan. 26th. Mr. James Tildesley, Henry Cottom, Mr. Heskaine and several others.

Hen: Swift went to Major Broadnax with a Swine wᶜʰ Feb. 4th. he had bought and killed for him.

Coz: Butler went to Wallosy Race where Sʳ Rich: Feb. 6th. Grannors Hors beat a Black Hors of my Lord Molineuxes. My Wife Doughters and I saw the Play called Loves Contrivance acted at Leverp: we Sup'd and Lodg'd at the Talbot.

Tho: Syer was here, we discoursed concerning Inclosing Feb. 12th. Crosby Marsh.

1727.

Feb. 14th.
Mr. Sherlock din'd here, he began to Improve my Doughters in their Dansing.

Feb. 17th.
Mr. Molineux of the Grange, Mr. Crisp and I marked out the Seperation between Grange Warant and mine.

Feb. 25th.
I tryed John Radcliff before Mr. Jos: Poole for Breaking Windows and fourcing open Ailes Davys Doar, he was order'd to be set in yᵉ Stocks.

Mar. 5th.
I found two Letters in a Clift stick (in the Great Courts) which I suppose were from W. Roo:.

Mar. 7th.
I bought some Wine of Captain Burch and took a Snap of a Dinner with him (at Liverpool).

Mar. 11th.
I made a Viset to my Coz: Eyre (at Preston). I went and wished Mr. Wᵐ Plumbe and his Wife Joy. I din'd at yᵉ Whit Bull with Coz: Gillibrond &c.

Mar. 16th.
Wᵐ Carefoot bought me a White-Hors Jack at Orms-church for a Thilar.

Mar. 20th.
Rob: Weedow, Tho: Marrow and Edward Pinington beged my Pardon for a Misdemaynor, I made them pay some Money which was yᵃ Day distributed to yᵉ Poore.

Mar. 25th.
I Order'd John Radcliff to be set in yᵉ Stocks in this Town according to Mr. Pooles Warant for breaking Windows &c: in yᵉ Night.

Mar. 26th.
I went to Leverpoole and saw Pat: Pinington distribute 256 Palms, then I went to Rock-savage where I Lodg'd, there was Briggadeer Moncall, Parson Hurt, Mr. Ross &c.

Mar. 27th.
Lord Barrymore went abroad upon Business. Old Sil: Richmond and his Doughter dined at Rocksavage.

I din'd at Mr. Actons with Parson Egerton, Parson Wairing, Robert Whittle &c:

I went to Crosby Greene there was Parson Brooks Parson Davys, Bannion of Ormschurch, Mr. Haymar, Doctor Bromfield &c: there were several Cocks brought from Leverp: and Ormsch: wch fought upon the Green, I saw three or four Battles.

A promising subject for the pencil of some local artist.

Mr. Williams not being at home Cap: Henry and his Sister Margarit came to prayers to Mr. Aldreds.

Mr. Houghton sent his Servant for some young Pigeons to Store his Dove-Coat, I gave him almost 3 dozen.

I went to Crosby Green but did not Bowl, there was Parson Jackson, Parson Kelsey, Mr. Tatlock the Draper &c: Mr. Cottom gave me my Gold Watch wch he has got mended at London.

Coz: Butler and I went to Crosby Green, I Bowled Hand to Fist wth Thom: Fleetwood there was Mr. John Trafford Junior Dr Bromfield, Will: Rollins &c:

I went to John Blansherds Reareing and drove a Pin, there was Mr. Molin: of ye Grange and I think Will: Blansherd and Nicho: Plumbe.

Cap: Hen: Bl: came to invate Coz: Butl: and me to com tomorrow to Ince to Solemnise Mr. Blun: birth, he being then 27 years old.

Pat: Walmesley the Monk din'd here.

My Doughters and I began our Journey towards York.

1727.

June 8th.   From Leeds we went to yᵉ Whit Hors in Todcaster where we dined Sister Midleton came to us in a Coach and took my Doughters with her to her Hous in York; I left my Horses at the Sighne of yᵉ Wind-Mill out of Midle-Gate.

June 9th.   We all went to Couz: Selbys to Prayers, he shewed my Doughters and me his fine Collecsion of English Coynes. Mr. Maior of Lartington made a Viset here.

The Maires of Lartington, which is in the neighbourhood of scenery commemorated in Rokeby, are now represented by the Rev. Thos. Witham.

June 10th.   I left my Doughters wᵗʰ their Aunt Midleton and came from York to Todcaster.

June 11th.   I was at Prayers at Mr. Tempests of Broughton Dʳ Traps was there.

June 15th.   Pat: Turner came to take leave of me he is going beyond the Seas.

June 16th.   I went to Wᵐ Tarletons Marlors and made them Shout.

June 26th.   Mr. Write of Cronton shew'd me his Proposall for geting an Act of Parleament for Enclosing the Commons of Ditton.

June 28th.   I put the Leaves of Whit Lillys into two Glass-Bottles, they are to make Oyl on for a Burn or Scald.

July 1st.   I fetched yᵉ old Hous-Clock from Ince, Coz: Blu: had given it to me.

July 5th.   I Bowled at Crosby Green wᵗʰ Parson Egerton, Wairing &c: it being Prescot race there was little Company, Parson Balden was there.

1727.

I sent to Wooton to see Mrs. Clifton who was lying in July 11th. of her first Child.

Mr. Rodger Diconson and Apothecary Gerard &c: were July 16th. at Prayers at Mr. Aldreds.

Going to Crosby Green I met Toping y² Parritor I July 19th. gave him something, I Bowl'd with Mr. Byron Rob: Bootle &c: there was Tatlock the Dior, Young Mr. Blase, Pat: Harper &c. Parson Acton was beging there for a Lame Son of Wᵐ Bushells.

Will Hull pay'd me some Money to be sent to Grav- July 21st. ling for his Sister Mary, he also gave half a Guiney for Mrs. Bridget Clifton from her Brother Cudbert.

My Maids went to y² Flowering of Ince Cross. July 24th.

I went to Leverp: and drank with Cap: Anderton and July 26th. Peter Wilkinson.

My Wife began her Journey towards York to fetch my July 31st. Doughters home, I went with her to Rufford where we baited at y² Spred Agle, thence to Preston where we Lodg'd at y² Whit-Bull.

I went in y² Evening to Crosby Green but did not Aug. 9th. bowl there was Mr. Danvers, Pemerton and Wilcock all from Leverp: as I suppose.

I went pritty late to Crosby Green, I Payed Mr. Aug. 16th. Egerton two Guineys wᶜʰ I had lost to him, he gave a Bowl of Punsh out of it, there was at y² drinking of it Parson Wairing, Mr. Th: Whittle, Tho Syer Mr. Brownsword y² Atturney &c: we were very Merry about Tho: Fleetwoods Wiggs.

1727.

Aug. 26th.

Nathaniall Buck came to see if I would subscribe to his Proposalls for Publishing the perspective vews of some old Abbies and Castles &c: in Lancash: Cheshire and Darby-Shire.

Aug. 30th.

I went to Crosby Green there was Alderman Goodin, Alderman Tyrer Parson Standley &c:·

Sept. 8th.

Pat Ald: not being well my Wife walked to yᵉ New-Hous to Prayers my Doughters and I went to Mr. Crisps to prayers.

Sept. 19th.

There was a Purs of thirty Pound run for on Crosby Marsh, 'twas won· by Miss Nusom a Bay-Mare of York-Shire, Lord Darbys Roger oCawverley, Roan and Pall ran against her.

Sept. 20th.

Three ran on Crosby Marsh for a Plate of £10 Maikings Mare wan it.

Sept. 21st.

Three ran on Crosby Marsh for a Plate of £5 one Hunts of Darby wan it.

Sept. 28th.

I sent a Present to Mrs. Trafford in Ormsch: of a Pigg and three Turkeys.

Oct. 1st.

Widow Molineux late of yᵉ Grange sent a How-do-You hither.

Oct. 2nd.

Being Lord Molin: Hounds ran a Fox past here which took over Alt I follow'd them to Formby but not finding eather the Gentlemen or yᵉ Hounds I came home again; Lord Molineux, Mr. Clifton, Mr. Pigeon &c: called here as they were going home from Hunting, they did not light, onely took a Glass at yᵉ Gates.

Oct. 6th.

Coz: Butler dined at yᵉ Stand with Lord Molin and went with him to Mr. Crisps to take a Glass.

1727.

Coz: Butler and I dined at Parson Wairings it being Oct. 16th.
Goosfeast Monday wth Parson Balden, Davis, Acton and
their Wives.

I was at ye Buriall of Mrs. Marge: Michelson and was Oct. 19th.
a Bearor with Mr. Blund: a son of Ewen Leas &c.

I went part of the way with the Corps of Tho: Bootle, Oct. 20th.
I was entertain'd at Henry Williamsons wth one Molineux
who Married a Doughter of Mr. Boltons of Eusom
(? Newsham) Robert Bootle, Parson Wairing &c:

Mary Wogden left her Service obruptly and without Nov. 9th
any Occasion and took no Leave.

Old Mr. Walmsley of Showley lodg'd here. Nov. 10th

Henry Williamson was here and insisted upon his Son Nov. 15th.
James his Coming to be my Servant.

I attended ye Corps of Parson Acton from his Hous to Dec. 2nd.
the Church there was Parson Balding, Harrison, Wairing,
Davis and Parson Mont, Mr. Moss, Ben: Branker &c.

My Wife sent to Condole Mrs. Acton for the Death Dec. 3rd.
of her Husband.

My Wife went to Mrs. Blundells Labouring she was Dec. 18th.
delivered of her Son Rowland.

1728.
James Williamson came to be my Groom and Jan. 2nd.
Husband-man.

Mr. Ald: not being at home my Wife I and Mally Jan. 14th.
went to Mr. Crisps and heard Mr. Curedon hold forth,
'tis the first time any of us heard him.

I attended ye Corps of Mr. Molin: of Mosburgh from Jan. 24th.
thence to Melling I was a Bearor so was Mr. Cubbon

1728.

Mr. Scarisbrick &c: as I went I called at Mr. Bowers at Aintry there being a Saile there.

Feb. 2nd.   Mr. Ald: not being well my Wife I and Doughters went to Ince to prayers. I sent James Williamson to Garswood to see Sr Wm Gerard and to Mosburgh to condole Coz: Molin: for ye Death of her Husband.

Feb. 10th.   I drank at Mr. Cottoms (at Liverpool) with Parson Brooks and his Brother &c: I drank at ye Wool-pack wth Mr. Hamer, Mr. Rigby of Sutton Hall, and Apoth: Livsey.

Feb. 23rd.   Mr. Ald: dyed. I helped to lay him out and took charg of his best things.

Feb. 24th.   Pat: Hardesty prayed for Mr. Al: in his Chappell, there was a pritty large Congregasion. I sent my Cart to Leverp: for Meat and Drink for Mr. Aldreds Funerall and went to his Hous to see part of it carefully taken care of.

Feb. 25th.   Mr. Ald: was Buried in the Harkerk there was at his Buriall or at least in the Hous the Famoly of Ince, Parson Wairing, Mr. Cottom, John Rose, Rob: Bootle, John Blansherd &c:

Mar. 5th.   My Servants went to John Johnsons at Night to turne their Pancaikes and be merry.

Mar. 13th.   Mr. Lockard came to supply in Mr. Aldreds place till an other came to stay; he lodged here.

Mar. 16th.   Mr. Lockard went hence to live at the West-Lain-Hous.

Mar. 23rd.   Mr. Chisleton Dr Ferniough &c: came to my Lodging (Golden Talbot in Chester) I advised with him about Mally's eyes and mine and about Fannys Laimnes. Coz: Butler and I made a Viset to Sr Hen: Bunbary, we drank there with Mr. Semor Chalmondeley &c:

I paid Mrs. Acton and the Sexton the Buriall Dues for Mr. Aldred.

Mr. Sadlor brought me a Silver Tobacco Box on wch he had engraived my Crest.

Fanny rode out behind me I enquired of Richard Renold &c: for Seed Oats. I set som Kidney Beanes in y^e Hot-Bed, in Order to rais them early.

This entry is given in full because it is the last, and with it the Diary abruptly closes.

GILBERT G. WALMSLEY, PRINTER, 50, LORD STREET, LIVERPOOL.

Printed in the United States
100181LV00003B/180/A

9 781432 545765